C000148168

Gender, Sexualities and Culture in Asia

Series editors
Stevi Jackson
Centre for Women's Studies
University of York
York, UK

Olivia Khoo
School of Media, Film and Journalism
Monash University
Melbourne, Australia

Denise Tse-Shang Tang
Department of Sociology
University of Hong Kong
Hong Kong

The Gender, Sexualities and Culture in Asia book series provides a welcome new forum for monographs and anthologies focusing on the intersections between gender, sexuality and culture across Asia. Titles in the series include multi- and interdisciplinary research by scholars within Asia as well as in North American, European and Australian academic contexts. It offers a distinctive space for the exploration of topics of growing academic concern, from non-normative cultures of sexuality in Asia, to studies of gendered identities cross the region, and expands the field of Asian genders and sexualities by applying a cultural lens to current debates, including rural lives, migration patterns, religion, transgender identities, sex industry and family.

More information about this series at
http://www.palgrave.com/gp/series/15191

Ting-Fang Chin

Everyday Gender at Work in Taiwan

palgrave
macmillan

Ting-Fang Chin
University of York
York, UK

Gender, Sexualities and Culture in Asia
ISBN 978-981-10-7364-9   ISBN 978-981-10-7365-6   (eBook)
https://doi.org/10.1007/978-981-10-7365-6

Library of Congress Control Number: 2017961547

© The Editor(s) (if applicable) and The Author(s) 2018
This work is subject to copyright. All rights are solely and exclusively licensed by the
Publisher, whether the whole or part of the material is concerned, specifically the rights of
translation, reprinting, reuse of illustrations, recitation, broadcasting, reproduction on
microfilms or in any other physical way, and transmission or information storage and retrieval,
electronic adaptation, computer software, or by similar or dissimilar methodology now
known or hereafter developed.
The use of general descriptive names, registered names, trademarks, service marks, etc. in this
publication does not imply, even in the absence of a specific statement, that such names are
exempt from the relevant protective laws and regulations and therefore free for general use.
The publisher, the authors and the editors are safe to assume that the advice and information
in this book are believed to be true and accurate at the date of publication. Neither the publisher nor the authors or the editors give a warranty, express or implied, with respect to the
material contained herein or for any errors or omissions that may have been made. The
publisher remains neutral with regard to jurisdictional claims in published maps and institutional affiliations.

Cover illustration: Malorny

Printed on acid-free paper

This Palgrave Macmillan imprint is published by Springer Nature
The registered company is Springer Nature Singapore Pte Ltd.
The registered company address is: 152 Beach Road, #21-01/04 Gateway East, Singapore
189721, Singapore

To Mie, Hok and Sze-Yi

PREFACE

WHY THIS BOOK?

This book is very much an unexpected but reasonable result of several personal, political and emotional experiences. These 'historical moments' in my life have had a significant influence on my academic interests and have thus contributed to my motivation to undertake the underlying research that led to this book. Therefore, before introducing the content of the book, I should like to briefly discuss those moments to explain why I turned my hand to investigating the everyday doing of gender in the workplace in Taiwan.

If I have to mark a start date for this intellectual journey, it would be 26 August 2002. I was standing in front of the UK immigration section at Birmingham Airport. An immigration officer was checking my passport and asking about my purpose for visiting. I explained that I was an international student and would soon start my post-graduate study in the UK. He then followed up with questions regarding my discipline. 'Women's and gender studies,' I replied. He asked, 'Why this subject?', with a smile on his face, which I am not sure how to interpret even now. I replied that it was based on my concerns about gender inequality and women's suffering. 'What about men?' he said. What about them? To be honest, I did not care much about men when I applied for the taught MA programme, nor was I fond of enquires that questioned my research interests, particularly those suggesting that I was neglecting the needs of men. I had never heard of someone studying ornithology, for example, being asked to justify her interest in birds but not crocodiles, or a post-graduate history student focusing on the Victorian era having to explain why he did not research the Edo period. I almost rolled my eyes but managed to suppress it, considering my delicate status as a foreign migrant. The best reply I could come up with was something like: 'After women's lives improve, then I will think about that.' I admit that it was not very politically correct, but I was fed up with enquiries about the discipline I had chosen. It was a little rebellious gesture of mine. This short conversation very much summarises my later intellectual quest. The more enquiries I receive, the more I feel the need to insist on devoting myself to knowledge production which positions 'women' at the centre.

After receiving my degree, I went back to Taiwan and spent a few years working for charitable and human rights organisations. In my job I had many opportunities to sit at the same table with representatives of other organisations and government to discuss issues that concerned civil society. I noticed that there seemed to be a pattern to our discussions. We would begin with representatives from civil society voicing their concerns. Next the government officials would express their sympathy but emphasise that their hands were tied because of legal regulations. Then we would have to have more meetings to discuss the related legal issues. This was the stage at which the law enforcement departments or the Ministry of Justice would become involved. They would bombard us with jargon and legal principles. The bottom line was often that the legal system is complicated and delicate; if we change one little thing, it could cause serious damage to the whole system. I had no problem with engaging in heated debates. I understood that different organisations and government sectors would have different perspectives and opinions. That was the whole purpose of having so many meetings: to negotiate and find a possible solution. However, most of the time I just sat there and thought the whole negotiation was perfunctory. We spent so much time and energy on holding meetings but achieved so little. I felt that I had been lured into the arena of law, which was not my home field. Finally, a perfect storm moment occurred in which my anger was triggered. A government legal adviser dismissed the opinions of civil society at a meeting by attacking the staff of organisations who had not received any academic training in legal studies. Attending the meeting as a representative of my organisation, I was furious. Rather than focusing on the issues on the table, the adviser was dismissing our suggestions because we had not acquired the 'proper' academic training. Indeed, what he said was true. None of the staff members in my organisation was a professionally trained legal specialist. My colleagues were experienced social workers and activists with academic backgrounds mostly in sociology and social work. I could not tolerate the fact that our academic background was being used as an excuse to ignore our concerns. It was not the first time our opinions had been dismissed by disqualifying our professions, but his sarcastic and contemptuous tone just struck a raw nerve. I made up my mind to do a second MA in legal studies. Some people engage in impulse shopping; I do that too, and I also engage in impulse studying. As a result, my battlefield shifted from meeting room to seminar room.

The year was probably 2008. The location was still Taipei, Taiwan. I was debating with a post-graduate student over the 2007 Civil Code Amendment. I was a 'mature student' studying law. It was a taught programme specifically designed for individuals who had no relevant academic background but were interested in the discipline. Most of my colleagues were successful professionals in other areas, such as medical science or construction. They had chosen to expand their knowledge and abilities into law for a practical reason: to deal with the legal issues they had encountered and would possibly face in the future in their career. As for me, as I have explained, my motivation was pure anger. From the day I stepped into the legal world, my anger was not extinguished but rather kept blazing. I was attending a seminar session. Most attendees were 'ordinary' law students with a BA in legal studies. I was arguing with one of them about the latest legal regulation of surnames. One important change implemented by the 2007 Civil Code Amendment was to abolish the legal regulation that children should have their fathers' surnames.[1] The new law states that children can have either the paternal or the maternal name as their surname. A post-graduate argued that this amendment caused damage to the existing social and moral order. He claimed that there would be consanguineous marriages and intermarriages without people knowing that they are actually marrying their relatives since the surname system would be 'chaotic' after the amendment. I found his argument absurd and very difficult to follow. I said to him that if he really believed that the purpose of having a surname is to prevent intermarriages or consanguineous marriages, the previous legal regulation would fail in that purpose too. The old system only kept records of fathers' surnames. The record of mothers' surnames had been neglected ever since the day we accepted Civil Code. After a few exchanges, he accused me of delivering 'a surprise judgement'; I had no idea what he meant, and he emphasised that what he had said was also the legal opinion of a prestigious professor specialising in Civil Code.

A deep sense of frustration welled up from the bottom of my heart. It was not because of his accusation but rather because I could not believe that I still had to argue against this kind of statement, which was obviously full of patriarchal bias. I thought we were already past this. I thought we should have entered an era in which gender equality was regarded as an essential legal principle. Since the late 1990s, after decades of struggle, the women's movement in Taiwan has reached tremendous landmarks in legal reform. By the 2000s, we already had the Sexual Assault Crime Prevention Act (1997), the Domestic Violence Prevention Act (1998), the Gender Equality in Employment Act (2002), the Gender Equity in Education Act (2004), the Sexual Harassment Prevention Act (2005) and several major Amendments in Civil Law (1998, 2002, 2007) to secure women's rights. Yet there I was, debating against the taken-for-granted patriarchal ideology that passing on the paternal name would bring prosperity to society.

Then came the year 2009. An industrial action inspired me to ponder the situation of employed women in Taiwan. I was browsing news articles online and a public statement caught my eye. On 8 July 2009, an open letter entitled 'We Would Rather Be Nice and Sweet' [如果可以,我們寧願永遠甜美] was posted on the website of Coolloud [苦勞網], an independent online news agency. It was written by the members of the Self-Help Group of Outsourced Employees in the National Taiwan Museum of Fine Arts. In the statement, the outsourcing company was accused of gender discrimination for demanding that female employees provide a pregnancy test report. Although it was not listed as a condition of employment, it was obvious that the outsourcing company was discriminating against pregnant employees. It was a case that involved a violation of the Gender Equality in Employment Act. However, what caught my eye was not only the accusation, but also the personal struggles revealed in this statement. It was expressed in the following words:

> This is a really tough decision. We have struggled not only with the oppression of the outsourcing company but also with ourselves. Can we fight? Can we roar with anger? Can we show to our husbands, children, and parents that we are not as obedient and tender as they have known?
>
> As women, it is difficult to fight, even in imagination. But we decided to stand up and fight [...] (National Federation of Independent Trade Unions, 2009)[2]

For these female employees, the decision to 'stand up and fight' was not an easy one, even though there was a law to legitimate their claim. They were fighting against both the discriminatory management practice and society's expectations of women. Their concerns about gendered perceptions clearly challenged the conventional idea of the legal subject, which is the autonomous, linear-thinking and rational male. Their story involves more than the legal case of damage compensation that a legal professional would probably perceive. This incident drew my attention to the experiences of women who have confronted gender discrimination at work and the gendered social conditions that might prevent them from filing a formal complaint.

For me, and also for some of my feminist friends, 2011 was a tough year. I was working on my dissertation about analysing courts' verdicts of sexual assault. While my study of law was coming to an end, I realised that, with my interest in feminism, I had probably been an outcast in the academia of jurisprudence all along. Yes, we did have modules about feminist legal theories. Yes, we did have (a few) professors and lecturers trying to bring gender into every seminar discussion. However, apart from those specific sessions, women's experiences and gender were seldom the focus. The institution of law always occupied the central seat. My feeling of discontent was growing. I was sick and tired of studying everything through the lens of law.

While I was struggling with academic law, my feminist friends were fighting their own battles at work. I was accumulating written words, and they were accumulating experiences in coming across the dark side of the workplace. During our regular gatherings, I learnt that even the organisations which claimed a reputation for being female-friendly might have serious management problems in relation to gender equality. Then, a friend was unfairly and wrongfully dismissed by her employer. She was brave enough to file a formal complaint and go through the official dispute mediation and arbitration process. In the end, she received severance pay but nothing more. All the blackmail and character assassination carried out by her employer, as well as the real cause of her dismissal, were ignored during the mediation and arbitration. Moreover, according to the settlement, the details of this case had to remain confidential. She was gagged. After this incident, whenever I read the documents of a legal case, I could not help wondering how much information had already been filtered out. Was there something the plaintiff wanted to say that could not be included because it was considered 'irrelevant' to the law? And what about those who did not have the social resources, capital or support to go through the legal process? Driven by my dissatisfaction with the legal knowledge approach I was taking, and also my deepening concern about female employees' situation in the workplace, I felt the urge to undertake another intellectual adventure. I wrote a PhD research proposal on investigating gender discrimination at work with a focus on the experiences of female employees who had not filed a formal complaint. I believed their voices should not be silenced merely because they chose not to go through the adjudication process. Instead, their stories might provide more detailed information about the social and cultural context of gender inequality at work.

On 28 September 2012, my flight landed at Manchester Airport. It was my second visit to the UK, with the same purpose as the previous one. I was about to start my PhD in Women's Studies. This time, the immigration officer was more interested in my marital status and my future plans than my research interests. 'Are you planning to marry in the near future? 'Will you stay in the UK after your studies?' 'No' was my answer to both questions. The first was expressed with certitude; the second was more like 'No, maybe, I'm not sure'. After all, who could know where my study impulse might lead me? For instance, I failed to foresee that I would soon overturn and rewrite my research plan.

In autumn 2013, with the fieldwork data in my hands, it became clear that I had to adjust my research objectives. It was the beginning of the second year of my PhD and I had just spent a summer in Taiwan to conduct the fieldwork. The first year of training had been challenging and inspiring. I had received intellectual stimulation and encouragement to critically examine the assumptions in my original research questions. My attention was gradually drawn to the theoretical framework of doing gender. This seemed to provide an approach which would enable me to liberate my viewpoint from the limitations of the law. Before I entered the research field, I decided to revise my research proposal and came up with a fieldwork design which was flexible enough to include my participants' everyday experiences of gender at work. When I came back to my accommodation in York and started to sort out the initial data analysis, I realised that my focus had shifted to the everyday doing of gender in the workplace. Doing research is an organic process and this study is no exception. Of course, the actual twists and turns that occurred during my research process were more complicated than the description I have offered in this paragraph. I fill in the details in the following chapters.

OUTLINE OF THE BOOK

There are six chapters in this book. Chapter 1 is a literature review which focuses on existing literature that helped me to set up the research context for my own exploration of gender, work and Taiwanese society. It is organised as a three-part discussion. I first draw attention to research that depicts the economic and social background in relation to women's employment in Taiwan. I then move on to scholarship that offers a critical perspective on recontextualising East Asian and Taiwanese society. Finally, the focus shifts to the theories that have influenced my conceptualisation of women's labour and gender. After the literature review, I present a chapter concerning the methodology and research process of this project. Chapter 2 provides a reflexive examination of my research design, as well as the research process employed during this study. I explain how the envisaged relationship between the researcher and the participants from a feminist perspective served as the starting point for my ethical concerns and therefore influenced the research structure and findings. I also describe the unexpected aspects of this study and how I managed to adapt to them.

I then use three chapters to discuss the research findings. In Chap. 3, by presenting and analysing my participants' accounts, I draw attention to the practices of organisational management. With the help of feminist theories on gender and heterosexuality, I argue that organisational management is gendered and heteronormative in that it categorises female employees as naturally marriage- and family-oriented. Women are expected to work in certain industries and are confined to these, holding certain positions and doing certain jobs because of their gender. These practices therefore result in gender segregation in employment. In Chap. 4 I move on to the general interactions in my participants' day-to-day working lives. The analysis primarily focuses on my participants' accounts of everyday social practices, such as appellations, casual conversation and body language. I argue that, while everyday practices at work are happening in a gendered and heteronormative cultural context, they are also intertwined with the hierarchical social order. Extending the discussion about negotiating gender at work, in Chap. 5 I examine my participants' accounts with an enquiry into the mobilisation of agency and the construction of the social self. The examination is presented in two parts. I start with a discussion of my approach to theorising the social self. Through a reflexive reading of the work of George Herbert Mead, my own understanding of 'the self' as a conceptual tool in the context of Taiwan is proposed. In the second half of the chapter, the focus is on the construction of the social self in the process of negotiating gender. I examine the emerging social self in some of my participants' accounts and argue that, while their adopted strategies may vary, there is one common element in their narratives: a constructed misfit self. I point out that the realisation and the

construction of this misfit self may play an important part in the mobilisation of agency and may, therefore, make negotiation possible.

In Chap. 6 I provide a summary of my research findings as well as a discussion of the limitations of this study. I acknowledge that my feminist
stance and personal social network had a significant influence on the recruitment and sampling; therefore, I am aware that this study cannot offer a full
picture of employed women's experiences in Taiwan. When it comes to the
issue of representativeness, this monograph can probably only manage to
contribute a small fraction to the whole picture. However, I argue that this
limitation is also a virtue of my exploration. In addition I propose enquiries
that may lead to future research based on my observations of the most
recent changes in Taiwanese society and thoughts inspired by communications with my participants after I completed my fieldwork. Moreover, I
explain my intention to use this study as an academic attempt to participate
in the production of the sociology of everyday life and propose a contextu-
alised approach to exploring women's experiences in Taiwan.

Before presenting the content of the book, I would like to put forward
a note on names and romanisation. When the full name of a Taiwanese
participant or author is used, the Taiwanese convention of presenting the
surname first and the personal name second is followed. The same rule is
applied to names which share this cultural feature. Except in cases where
other common transliterations are available, two romanisation systems are
adopted to transliterate Mandarin terms: the Wade–Giles system for individuals' names and Tongyong Pinyin for other words. A methodological
discussion on romanisation can be found in Chap. 2.

York, UK   Ting-Fang Chin

Notes

1. Civil Code Article 1059 is a legal regulation regarding children's surnames.
   Prior to the 2007 Amendment, the regulation stated that a child should
   adopt the father's surname. Only in a few exceptional circumstances could
   the mother's surname be adopted, such as when the mother had no male
   siblings, or the father had married into the mother's family [入贅; *rujhuei*].
   In other words, the practice of passing on patronymics was the norm and
   was maintained through the institution of law. The 2007 Amendment
   changed the regulations, so that now a couple can decide whether their

child will adopt the mother's or the father's surname. This amendment is regarded as a challenge to the conventional patriarchal ideology in law and, moreover, a significant landmark for the women's movement in Taiwan.

2. The open letter is written in Taiwanese Mandarin. Please see National Federation of Independent Trade Unions [全國自主勞工聯盟]. (2009). 如果可以, 我們寧願永遠甜美—國立台灣美術館派遣工自救會給社會大眾 的一封信 [We Would Rather Be Nice and Sweet: An Open Letter from the Self-Help Group of Outsourced Employees in the National Taiwan Museum of Fine Arts]. *苦勞網* [*Coolloud*], [online] 8 July. Retrieved September 24, 2016, from http://www.coolloud.org.tw/node/43079

ACKNOWLEDGEMENTS

This book would not have come to fruition without the help of many people. Most of all, I owe an enormous debt of gratitude to my participants, who kindly granted me their trust and offered their inspiring experiences to serve as the foundation of this work. I want to thank Professor Stevi Jackson for her generous encouragement and guidance. I am also indebted to Dr Clare Jackson, Professor Susie Scott, Professor Paul Johnson and Dr Linda Perriton. Their comments helped me to shape my perspective in this study. I would like to express special thanks to all the members of the Centre for Women's Studies at the University of York for the intellectual discussions as well as the feminist laughter we shared.

The warmest thanks of all go to my 'misfit' family and friends. Thank you for being who you are and being there for me.

CONTENTS

LIST OF FIGURES

LIST OF TABLES

CHAPTER 1

Setting the Coordinates for an Intellectual Map of Gender, Work and Taiwan

INTRODUCTION

In Taiwan, the metaphor 'knowledge is an ocean' was a fairly common trope when I was a schoolgirl. Tutors would advise their students that studying hard is the only way to survive and reach one's destination. While school education at that time (and perhaps even now) was organised around compulsory memorising and exam-taking activities, this well-intentioned advice sounded intimidating rather than encouraging. It implied that studying is a matter of life or death, as if one were struggling alone and helplessly in the open water. My peers joked that, since the ocean is so difficult to cross, the best way to survive is to turn back rather than to move forward.

I recalled this metaphor at an early stage of this study on gender at work in Taiwanese society, not because I felt intimidated during the process (although I did have a few difficult moments), but because knowledge has presented itself like a boundless ocean in front of me. Next, the imagery of travelling from one location to another came to my aid. In a way, the thought that I was undertaking a journey was useful in helping me to make sense of the critical context of this study. If knowledge is the sea, then the main task for me as a researcher is not to investigate every drop of it but to discover where I am and, therefore, which direction I should be heading. As long as I have made proper preparations, I can travel in this ocean of knowledge. It will carry me rather than devour me.

© The Author(s) 2018
T.-F. Chin, *Everyday Gender at Work in Taiwan*,
Gender, Sexualities and Culture in Asia,
https://doi.org/10.1007/978-981-10-7365-6_1

This chapter is about the preparations I made in order to take this journey of knowledge. I introduce previous studies that constituted the academic context of my own exploration. I identify gender, work and Taiwan as the main coordinates on my knowledge map in this quest. I depend on them to confirm and reflect my own location during this intellectual exploration. I deliberately give empirical studies on Taiwanese society the central position in this literature review. I am certainly aware of the existence of 'Western' findings, but this is not the intellectual route I have chosen to take and they are of limited relevance to Taiwan. I begin by reviewing research that depicts the economic and social background in relation to women's employment in Taiwan. Second, I introduce studies that have helped me to re-contextualise East Asian and therefore Taiwanese society. My focus then shifts to the theories that have influenced my conceptualisation of women's labour and gender.

PICTURING EMPLOYED WOMEN IN TAIWAN

The rapid and 'successful' transformation of the Taiwanese economy and its distinct gender patterns in employment have brought the country some sociological attention in the global knowledge market. The former has drawn researchers to investigate women's roles in this transformation and how their social status has been influenced by the economic shifts. The latter poses puzzles for sociological examination of the relationship between women's labour-market participation and the social conditions of gender inequality.

Like other East Asian countries, such as Japan and South Korea, Taiwan is among the latecomers to industrialisation that have demonstrated impressive achievements. During the 1960s, with aid from the United States, the Kuomintang (KMT) regime drove Taiwan onto a path of labour-intensive and export-led economic development. While male officials and politicians often took the credit for the 'economic miracle' and occupied the spotlight, it was actually a fruitful result gained primarily at the expense of women's sweat and even blood, such as in the case of RCA (see Arrigo 1985; Chen 2011b). For example, the primary members of the labour force that supported production in the Free Trade Zones (FTZs) were women. The working life of female factory workers in Taiwan during that era has been well documented in previous studies (e.g. Kung 1978; Diamond 1979; Hsiung 1996). This research has shown that the booming economic development in Taiwan has actually been accomplished by relying heavily on gendered social institutions and arrangements.

With the continuing transformation of the economy within the context of international markets, social changes have occurred in Taiwan and, therefore, the focus of academic investigations into women's employment has shifted. Since the mid-1990s, Taiwan's economy has become 'much more diversified, and industries have been upgraded and become more capital intensive' (Lee 2004: 75). The industrial structure has been redirected away from low-skilled toward high-skilled manufacturing, and the economy has become service-oriented. Meanwhile, accompanying its repositioning in the system of global capitalism, Taiwan has become a site for examining local and migrant women's employment and how the lives of these two groups have intersected (see Lan 2003b, 2006). It has been shown that, during the second half of the twentieth century, Taiwan experienced rapid economic transformation, which was accompanied by massive social changes. Within just a few decades, the economic structure shifted from agriculture-oriented to industrialised and then post-industrialised. This very much fits the character of what Chang (1999, 2010) conceptualises as 'compressed modernity'.

In the context of the continuous transformation of the economy, there is one distinct and sustained characteristic of women's employment that has attracted researchers' attention. Compared with other rapidly developing economies in East Asia, statistics have shown that Taiwan has a consistently high and steady rate of women's labour-force participation. This persistent pattern has been manifested not only in women's labour as a whole over the years but also in terms of individual women's life trajectories. Women in Taiwan tend to stay in their jobs even after marrying and having children. Brinton et al. (1995) use statistics on married women's employment in Korea and Taiwan in the 1980s to examine explanatory models of women's labour-force participation. They identify three major differences in these two societies. First, in the 25–34 year-old age group, the so-called proper childbearing age, while many Korean women tended to stay out of the labour market, women's labour participation in Taiwan remained steady. Second, married women in Taiwan largely acquired formal jobs at any age, while their Korean counterparts were mostly in informal ones. The last salient difference is the relationship between education and women's employment. In Taiwan, a woman's level of education has a positive influence on the probability of her employment. In the case of

South Korea, it is the opposite. A similar pattern also emerges in the comparison between Taiwan and Japan. It has been suggested in later studies that the comparatively steady employment trajectory of women in Taiwan has survived the societal changes driven by economic transformation (see Yu 2009; Sechiyama 2013).

However, this steady employment pattern cannot be regarded as an absolute answer to the enquiry about gender equality in the workplace. The fact that women tend to stay in the workplace does not mean they have been treated equally with their male counterparts. One obvious gender inequality at work is the gender pay gap. Examining the gender patterns of quantitative data about employment in Taiwan, Zveglich and Meulen Rogers (2004) aim to provide an explanation for the persistent and even increasing gender pay gaps. They find that, while equal opportunities for women to access education and experience have increased, they are nevertheless paid considerably less than men. The authors suggest that 'substantial within-occupations pay gaps between men and women are the main source of Taiwan's overall gender wage gap' (ibid.: 867). Moreover, they point out that within-occupation pay gaps actually 'grew over time and contributed to a substantial decline in women's relative wages after controlling for their gains in education and experience' (ibid.: 867). In other words, women in Taiwan do not receive equal pay for equal work. These findings suggest that there is a persistent inequality in payment across the spectrum of occupations. Later studies have suggested that a less visible gender segregation might be occurring in employment in Taiwan. In their quantitative data-based study, Chang and England (2011) use data from 2006 to look at the pay gaps in South Korea, Japan and Taiwan. Their study finds that Taiwan has a smaller gender gap in earnings, but the variables they examined could not fully explain the reasons for the gap. They suspect that the pay gap in Taiwan might be partially due to discriminatory practices in hiring or 'supply-side preferences' which could not be examined through employment statistics (ibid.: 13). Moreover, 'the remaining unexplained portion of the gap may reflect discriminatory wage differences between men and women in the same occupation' (ibid.: 13).

Research also reveals that the high labour-force participation of women does not necessarily mean they are free from gendered labour in the domestic sphere. In her work on married women's lives in Taiwan and Japan, Yu (2001) aims to provide an explanation for the seeming disparity between married women's attitudes towards conventional ideas about gender and their consistent employment in Taiwan. She proposes that the reasons for this inconsistency could be revealed by investigating 'structural conditions'. By examining the differences in 'cultural and socioeconomic context' in Taiwan and Japan, she identifies several factors relating to the demands on financial resources and requirements for childcare and homemaking. She concludes that 'the fact that many married women in Taiwan play a role in supporting the household economy does not seem to actually shake their belief that a wife should be the primary caregiver in the household' (ibid.: 94). Furthermore, providing financial support for the family is commonly viewed as a way to take care of family members, especially children. Yu's research demonstrates the different social norms relating to motherhood in Taiwanese and Japanese society. In Taiwan, being a mother does not mean that a woman can escape the responsibility of contributing financially to the family. On the other hand, having a full-time job does not excuse her from caring labour in the household. Yu's interview data shows that women are still the main caregivers in their families, just as much as their Japanese counterparts. Married women in Taiwan are usually carrying a double burden as a result of their dual roles in the workplace and at home. This, then, raises questions about women's everyday practices and the management of this dual burden of labour.

In later research, Yu (2009) provides explanations for the socioeconomic conditions that enable married Taiwanese women to manage their family responsibilities without withdrawing from the labour market. Unlike Japan, which has an economic structure based on large enterprises and capital-oriented industries, Taiwan's economy is more labour-intensive, with small and medium-sized businesses serving as its backbone. Different state policies have shaped different labour-market conditions and employers' attitudes and management practices. Taiwan has experienced 'frequent labour shortage[s]' and therefore 'incorporating married women into the workplace' becomes a reasonable strategy for employers to manage labour demands (ibid.: 179). Moreover, the loose structure and management of small and medium-sized businesses that build up 'informal work climates' and 'workplace practices' enable married female employees to manage the balance between work and family (ibid.: 179).

Putting forward the hypothesis that there is a correlation between changes in childcare practices and changes in gender roles, Ochiai et al. (2008) have conducted comparative research on East and South East Asian societies. They focus on women's employment patterns over the course of their lives and the contextual factors behind the pattern in each society. While there are societies that share similar patterns, they find that the socio-economic conditions which enable these patterns to emerge are quite different. Societies such as Korea and Japan show an M-curve pattern in women's employment, because women tend to leave the labour market upon marriage, first pregnancy or childbirth. On the other hand, according to the data, which covers the time period from the 1980s to 2004, Taiwan shows a suggestive tendency from a M-shaped curve to an inverse U-curve. Moreover, they point out that there is a divergence within this pattern that is related to women's educational levels. In Taiwan, 'the employment rates of married women vary significantly by educational background' (ibid.: 45). While it is not uncommon for less educated women to withdraw from the labour force in order to perform childcare, highly educated women show a preference for remaining in work after marriage and childbirth. This divergence may show different patterns correlated with educational level, but the difference in education does not by itself provide a sufficient explanation for it. Highly educated women receive informal childcare support from relatives, particularly parents and siblings, and also babysitters and maids who are mostly migrant female workers from South East Asia (see also Wang et al. 2013; Loveband 2004; Lindio-McGovem 2004; Lan 2003a; Lan 2003b).

While several studies have provided insightful analysis that helps us to understand women's employment in Taiwan, there are still questions that remain unanswered. More academic research is required to provide further inclusive and thorough investigation into women's working lives. Firstly, alternative and diverse perspectives are essential to obtain a better understanding of women's experiences. The distinct pattern of married women's employment seems to direct most of the academic attention towards married women's experiences and leaves unmarried women's working lives largely neglected.

Moreover, in the light of the social changes occurring in the twenty-first century, I argue that it is essential to continue the enquiry into women's experiences of work in Taiwan. The conditions that previously enabled women to maintain stable career trajectories are now being contested. For example, Yu (2009) suggests that the dramatic change in education policy and the continuing transformation of the economy might have a negative impact on women's employment. Beginning in the late 1990s, the government initiated a project of educational expansion, including in university enrolment. The number of highly educated men is increasing. In addition, the development of Taiwan's economy is being channelled in the direction of capital- and skill-intensive work. The thriving high-technology industry demonstrates this economic change. The market demands more professional and skilled employees in the technology industries. Yu suggests that the increasing availability of labour offered by highly educated men might decrease career opportunities for women. This concern should be understood in the context of national educational policy. Since the education system in Taiwan helps to produce a division of labour, this demand for labour is hardly a gender-neutral one. The expansion of education has indeed increased access to higher education; however, gender segregation among disciplines persists. There is still an obvious gender gap between the so-called 'female disciplines' and the 'male disciplines'. According to the latest statistics provided by the Ministry of Education, university departments are categorised into 23 faculties. During the academic year 2015, women constituted the majority of students in the Humanities while men were clearly dominant in Engineering. In the Humanities, there were 77,755 female students and 32,945 male students. In Engineering, there were only 35,111 female students compared with 227,333 male students (see Fig. 1.1 and Table 1.1). The gender gap among disciplines is not only a consequence of cultural factors, such as gendered presumptions about aptitudes, but also government policies in the areas of economics and education. For example, Hsaieh and Yang's (2014) study indicates that groupings within the high school curriculum and the College Entrance Examination play an influential part in constructing and sustaining this

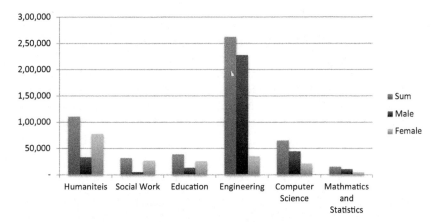

Fig. 1.1 Five disciplines with obvious gender disparities

Table 1.1 Numbers of female and male students in disciplines with obvious gender disparities

	Humanities	Social Work	Education	Engineering	Computer Science	Mathematics & Statistics
Female	77,755	26,687	25,654	35,111	21,004	4819
Male	32,948	4925	12,946	227,333	44,018	10,070
Total	110,703	31,612	38,600	262,444	65,022	14,889

gender gap. In the 1950s, the Taiwanese government established the grouping system of the College Entrance Examination. Disciplines were generally categorised into groups and there was an individual scheme for marking and exam subjects for each group.[1] This policy then resulted in the grouping of the high school curriculum. Since education is an important factor in forging professional skills and human capital, the gender gap in education then contributes to the gender gap in employment. In other words, gender segregation has shadowed women's career development from school education to occupational choices. Along with the economic transformation, there are more opportunities for both college admission and jobs for men since the technology industries are developed under the guardianship of government policy.

On the other hand, the enactment of the new law on gender equality has also brought potential changes in labour conditions for women. Since the 1990s, there has been a legal reform movement in Taiwan to promote women's rights and gender equality. For instance, the Domestic Violence Prevention Act was passed and enacted in 1998, the Gender Equality in Employment Act in 2002, and the Gender Equity in Education Act in 2004. The reform has introduced new regulations and reasoning in legal doctrines, law enforcement and government administrative practices. The provisions of these new laws have also contributed to social changes that impact on women's lives. Therefore, I would argue that all these newly emergent factors mean that enquiries into women's employment remain timely.

(RE)CONTEXTUALISING 'EAST ASIA'

The quantitative data on women's employment has prompted diverse and sometimes even contradictory interpretations of the cultural context of gender in Taiwan. On the one hand, Taiwan is identified as a society that shares similarities with others in East Asia. On the other hand, there are also studies indicating that Taiwan is entirely different from these other societies in terms of patriarchal values.

There seems to be an academic common assumption to assuming similarities in culture between Taiwan, Japan, Korea and China. In the realm of East Asia, Taiwan shares its historical and cultural heritage with other countries in the area, such as Japan and Korea. In their examination of the value-based explanation model, Brinton et al. (1995) rule out the possibility of patriarchal values being a meaningful factor that contributes to distinct differences in women's employment in Korea and Taiwan. Although they acknowledge that there 'may be some distinctions between Taiwan and South Korea in sex-role values', they find these to be insufficient in terms of providing 'detailed evidence on systematic, subtle differences' (ibid.: 1107). Therefore, they generally assume that both societies share 'similarities in patriarchal values' (ibid.: 1106). However, other researchers have attempted to identify differences as well as similarities. Sechiyama's (2013) comparative study on patriarchy in East Asia is one example. Drawing upon quantitative data, he identifies the characteristics of Taiwanese patriarchy and its cultural and social bases. He argues that women's participation in the labour force seems comparatively more stable across all ages, and regardless of marital status, than in Japan or South Korea. The results of surveys on women's attitudes towards working also indicate that it is considered acceptable for married women in Taiwan to stay in the workplace. In other words, married women who have children in Taiwan tend to continue working. Sechiyama then proposes two interpretations of Taiwanese patriarchy based on a review of related statistics and surveys. One is that 'Taiwanese patriarchy does not have any strong taboo against women being in the labour force', and the second is 'the lack of any great strain associated with the role of the mother' (ibid.: 197). I generally agree with his findings that, compared with other societies under the influence of Confucian thinking, Taiwan exhibits a distinctiveness on the issue of gender and employment. However, I hesitate to fully agree with his interpretations of this distinctiveness. It seems too simple to jump to the conclusion that 'a form of patriarchy has emerged in Taiwan that does not place particular emphasis on the role of the mother' (ibid.: 200). Other studies have shown that, while women in Taiwan have the liberty to work, this does not mean that their 'responsibility' for the domestic sphere is lessened. Instead of claiming that there is no 'particular emphasis on the role of the mother', I would argue that there are different kinds of social norms about the role of mother in Taiwan. It is constructed within a specific social and cultural context. As I will elaborate later, other studies have indicated that the domestic labour accompanying women's family roles, such as mother, wife and daughter, probably requires more sophisticated analysis than Sechiyama has proposed (see e.g. Yu 2009; Liu and Osawa 2013; Wang et al. 2013). I would argue that both interpretations might have overlooked the complexity of the context of East Asia and the heterogeneity among the societies in the area.

Confucianism, which spread throughout East Asia and China, is often identified as the foundation of cultural similarity in East Asia. Yet this does not necessarily mean that the Confucian values of these societies are identical. Moreover, in some countries, this cultural heritage is not 'purely cultural' but is very much a political one. By studying the differences in the endorsement of traditional Confucian values among college students in China, South Korea, Japan and Taiwan, Zhang et al. (2005) aim to challenge assumptions about cultural similarities in the region. They propose that researchers 'should resist the temptation of generalization and be sensitive to the "localized" Confucianism and its spheres of influence' (ibid.: 114). Zhang et al.'s proposition of a localised viewpoint offers an alternative standpoint from which to approach Confucianism in any individual society. While being sympathetic to their argument, I would like to further elaborate upon the idea of localisation. I argue that to acknowledge localisation means to see that there could be more than one version of Confucianism in the East Asian context. Instead of viewing the Confucianism in each society as a copy of the 'original' and 'true' prototype, I suggest regarding each version as a specific fabrication that has emerged within a particular historical context. Moreover, this fabrication should be examined in the light of various dimensions of practices. Other than the level of endorsement and implementation, the aspects of negotiation and resistance should also be acknowledged. In locations such as Hong Kong and Taiwan, where Confucianism is deliberately promoted and maintained through social institutions and government policies, the political background and context are especially indispensable for understanding this cultural component of society (see e.g. Leung 2014). In other words, the culture of a society is not merely cultural. In the case of Taiwan, the specific historical and political background has offered a critical social context within which to ponder the oppressive and suppressive influence of Confucianism. While it is an ideology that is promoted and institutionalised by the KMT government to justify and sustain its governance, it has been pointed to as a supporting factor in autocratic and hierarchical social control. For instance, Chen Fang-Ming (2002, 2011a), a Taiwanese literature scholar, identifies the period of martial law (1949–1987) under the KMT regime as the recolonial phase. In his view, during this period Taiwanese society was forged by the ideologies of Han-centralism, male supremacy and Confucianism. These three operated together to suppress and oppress any attempts to express alternative political or cultural ideas.[2]

Studies have shown that, although the concept of East Asia is useful as a socio-geographical division, it should not be used to narrow the sociological view or to make generalisations about all the societies in the region. It is important to indicate that I consider Taiwan to be a society that is influenced by Confucian thinking, but one in which the practices and interpretations associated with it have their own specificity. Just as Japan and Korea have adapted their own versions of Confucianism, so too has Taiwan. Comparative studies on countries in the geographical region of East Asia have shown that the similarities in historical and cultural heritage do not justify a homogeneous view of these societies.

China, Japan, South Korea and Taiwan are commonly identified as natural members of the Confucian patriarchy club. They are described as societies sharing similarities which 'can be traced back to the common origin of the Confucian model of the family' (Raymo et al. 2015). It is indeed a recognised historical fact that Confucian thinking originated in China and has had an impact on various societies in Asia, for complex historical and political reasons. While acknowledging the significance of its influence, I would also argue that a universal view of Confucianism is an obstacle to a comprehensive understanding of each society in East Asia. In his intriguing work on deconstructing Chineseness, Chun (1996) challenges the idea of Chineseness as an absolute and homogeneous cultural entity, especially when it is understood in specific social, political and cultural contexts. I am not denying that Taiwanese society contains Chinese elements within it. The perspective that I would like to suggest is to be critical about the naturalisation of Chineseness in Taiwan.

The Chineseness of Taiwanese society is the post-war outcome of the political project of the Kuomintang regime. In deconstructing 'Chineseness', Chun (1996) begins with the ambiguity of language itself. While, in English, Chinese is a common term used to refer to 'Chineseness', within Chinese-speaking societies there are different terms that could be used to refer to 'Chineseness' by different Chinese communities and societies, each with a slightly different meaning, and each with its own specific cultural and historical connotations, such as *tang* [唐], *hwa* [華] and *han* [漢]. He argues that the understanding of 'China as an unambiguous political entity and Chineseness as a feature shared by ethnic Chinese on the basis of discrete traits and traditions' is underpinned by 'a homogeneous notion of culture that is essentially modern, if not national, in origin' (ibid.: 113). For example, in Taiwan, Confucian values were deliberately institutionalised and promoted by the Kuomintang to secure its own rule and its legitimate role as 'the' Chinese ruling party. In order to secure itself as the legitimate 'Chinese regime' against the China ruled by the Chinese Communist Party, the Kuomintang has 'depicted itself as the guardian of traditional Chinese culture' (ibid.: 116). Thus, while it is an undeniable fact that Taiwanese society is deeply influenced by Confucian thinking, it is not a cultural heritage that can be naturalised by its prevalence. Rather, it is a cultural reality very much generated by political conditions, and it has been critically debated.

The historical context has made the idea that Taiwan shares a cultural legacy with China a sensitive issue. Considering the political tension between these two states, it is always potentially problematic to claim that Taiwan is the land where the 'true traditional Chinese culture' has been preserved. The first point of contention emerges with the concept of 'tradition'. The conceptualisation of China as an individual and specific political and cultural entity is actually a modern one. The second concern regards authenticity: thinking that there is a true, authentic version of Chinese culture. I would argue that to see Taiwan as the land that preserves true Chineseness is actually to adopt a China-centred perspective. Ironically, the concept of a true and original Chinese culture is a political ideology promoted by both the Kuomintang regime and the People's Republic of China, which are supposed to be political rivals. The political discourse claiming that Taiwan is the representative of Chineseness ignores the organic process of cultural practices.

One crucial factor which has enabled Confucian thinking to survive the dramatic changes in various East Asian societies is that it has been constantly reshaped and reinvented. As Jackson et al. indicate, 'even when cultural precepts and practices have a very long documented history, they may be reinvented and their current form may be the product of successive revivals and revisions, as is the case with Confucianism in East Asia' (2013: 669). Departing from the critical conceptualisation of tradition and modernity, Jackson et al. (ibid.) seek an alternative framework to examine social change and social life. Instead of viewing tradition and modernity as oppositional concepts which cannot coexist, they advocate a framework that deconstructs the dichotomy between the two. By doing so, they seek to avoid an assumed cultural essentialism and argue that 'the persistence of traditional values and practices is mediated through socio-economic context' (ibid.: 689). That is, in their words, 'difference and shifts in the ordering of personal and family lives are not only the result of cultural diversity and change; much depends on the socio-economic and political context' (ibid.: 683). One common analytical approach to comparative study, whether of societies with similar or different cultural values, is to give culture the key role in making sense of social practices. Jackson et al.'s study indicates that cultural elements are not the only sources of variation. Socio-economic and political context is equally important.

While comparative studies are meaningful and indeed useful in addressing sociological enquiries, there is also a temptation to regard one society as the norm against which to evaluate the rest, both in the context of West–East comparison and in assessing East Asian societies, as well as to make generalisations about similarities between different societies that share a certain cultural heritage. Culture should not be used as a convenient answer to all sociological enquiries. If we treat the Western pattern as the norm, we might miss alternative and crucial explanations for understanding the lives of people in different 'non-Western' societies. For instance, on the issue of adulthood, the distinctly late age for young people to leave their homes in most Asian societies could easily be interpreted as an outcome of filiation, for it 'has been one of the cornerstones of East Asian societies for thousands of years, and it is still highly valued' (Yi et al. 1994: 77). However, it is equally important that other socio-economic aspects not be entirely dismissed by focusing on existing cultural norms. Studies of women's employment in East Asian societies have shown that there might be a gap between what people believe in terms of cultural values and what they can actually do in the context of specific conditions, such as the cost of living, housing and education as well as the accessibility of social welfare (Raymo et al. 2015).

Reflecting on the critical aspect of knowledge production, my role as a researcher from an Asian society doing research in a European society has led me to reflect upon my own research perspective. To write about Taiwan is to claim a critical position; my role as an Asian international student in a 'Western' country becomes one of the many conditions of my reflexivity.

It influences not only my everyday social life but also my role in knowledge production. In everyday conversation, I worry that I might be perceived as THE representative of Taiwanese society, or even of Asian society. As a researcher, I am alarmed by the risk of universalising Eurocentric knowledge to other social contexts. Jackson critically reflects upon the politics of knowledge production from the position of a 'Western' researcher. She writes that 'some caution is necessary in approaching any analysis of societies other than our own, in particular comparison between "The East" and "The West"' (2015: 3). This critical reminder is also meaningful for researchers with an 'Eastern' background or standpoint and researchers studying societies of which they acquire membership. In the case of this study, my identity as a member of Taiwanese society does not guarantee the innocence of my position in knowledge production.

The focus so far has been on previous findings about women's employment in Taiwan. I have discussed its distinct patterns and the specific historical, political, cultural and socio-economic conditions in which these patterns are embedded. It has been clearly demonstrated that women's career trajectories are influenced by social factors and not purely by labour-market demands. Moreover, I have revealed my approach to contextualising women's working lives in Taiwan. However, the scholarship on women's employment can only partially locate my position on the map of knowledge production. Since the enquiry proposed here is primarily about women's experiences of gender at work, I feel it is essential to pinpoint the conceptualisations of 'work' and 'gender' in this project. Therefore, in the second half of this chapter I deliberate upon the sociological and feminist studies that have shaped my approach to these concepts.

Reshaping the Knowledge Boundary of 'Work'

Mie, the very first married woman I knew in my life, used to say that a holiday was an extra working day for her. When the whole family is having a break and staying at home, that is the time when she has to do more household work. She describes the trickiness of the labour contribution of a housewife in the following words: 'if I do everything, nobody notices. But if I miss one thing, everyone notices.' Mie is my mother. From the first day of her marriage she has fulfilled the role of housewife, regardless of whether or not she had a 'proper' job. There was even one point in her life when she was working full time as a housewife, as a college student and also as an insurance salesperson. Having been nurtured by a woman such as Mie, it seems sensible to ponder the work that falls upon women's shoulders. (It is probably fair to say that home is the very first research field that I experienced.)

I think Mie's words on housework perfectly capture the dark secret of women's work: it is often 'invisible' when it is performed well. At first glance, this might seem contradictory. How can something so essential and important be so easily ignored? Unfortunately, when it comes to women's contribution, this is often the case. Women are usually the ones taking care of essential tasks to manage the household and keep the institution of family going. Their work is naturalised and therefore taken for granted. It is tricky indeed for women's work to be recognised. Moreover, this dark secret has a hidden place not only in the household but also in the so-called 'public domain'. When women 'step out' of the family domain and engage in activities in the labour market, their contributions still remain largely unseen, uncredited and under-appreciated.

Contemporary sociological and feminist studies have revealed this dark secret of women's work and have contested the social institutions of gendered labour. One of the fundamental achievements of this substantial academic endeavour has been to push back the knowledge boundary by reshaping the conceptualisation of work. There is a growing corpus of academic studies that contest conventional views of work and labour. Alternative conceptual tools, along with new theorisations, are proposed in order to frame alternative approaches, such as 'emotion work' (e.g. Hochschild 1979, 1983), 'sexual labour' (e.g. Adkins 1995), 'aesthetic labour' (e.g. Warhurst et al. 2000; Witz et al. 2003), 'body labour' (Kang 2003) and 'body work' (Wolkowitz 2002, 2006). In this section I offer a brief introduction to previous research which throws light on different approaches to examining work activities and their entangled gender implications. It would be overly ambitious to attempt to cover everything intensively, and this is therefore only a partial and general discussion, focusing primarily on research that has helped to shape and expand my view of women's work and women's labour.

Care Work and the Multiple Labour Burden Placed on Women

As I have discussed in the previous section, steady employment status does not necessarily ease the burden of labour in the private domain that falls on women's shoulders. Employed women in Taiwan still have to perform the 'work' of certain gendered roles, and this is true not only after they call it a day and leave the workplace. It is a duty (if not a burden) that they bear at all times. It would be an oversimplification to see the workplace as a space that is purely 'public' and the individuals in it as free from 'private' matters. The concept of public/private domains can offer a critical perspective on how social life is constructed, arranged and interpreted. However, it would be a distortion to view an individual's quotidian experience as divided into segments, some of which are completely 'private' while the rest are entirely 'public'. While my project is to investigate women's experiences of gender in the workplace, this does not mean that my investigation should or could be confined to an exploration of 'employment work' only. Care work is one form of gendered labour that transcends the boundary between public and private domains and therefore represents an indispensable dimension for studying women's experiences in gendered society.

It has been suggested that to simply use the term 'care work' might have critical implications in Taiwanese society, because the labour of caregivers is often overshadowed by social norms of gendered relationships, especially those among family members (see Yeandle et al. 2013). Care work is very personalised and primarily shared among family members. It is not only a social practice sustained by cultural norms but also a legal responsibility defined by Civil Code (ibid.). For example, a husband and wife share a mutual obligation to 'maintain' each other's lives. 'Maintain' is the official translation of the Chinese wording, *fuyang* [扶養], that is used in law, but this translation only partially captures the meaning of the original term. *Fuyang* also implies to bring up, to raise and to support. This mutual obligation between family members is about more than just providing one another with basic material necessities. It also involves other forms of support. To fulfil this legal obligation requires the complex practice of providing care for a spouse in need. Moreover, although the legal wording seems gender neutral, providing care tends to be a responsibility or obligation that is imposed on a certain gender. And it is usually women who perform those gendered tasks.

Studies have shown that women are the main caregivers in Taiwan and that the available support is mostly informal. In their comparative study of the system of care for older people in Japan and Taiwan, Wang et al. (2013) examine the situation of working carers. Women are the providers of unpaid labour in the care of older family members even when they are in full-time employment. Wang et al. point out that 'in practice, policies and societal norms that emphasize familial responsibility for the old often mean that women provide unpaid care' (ibid.: 90). Compared with Japan, Taiwan is far behind in terms of welfare provisions. State policy reinforces women's role as unpaid caregivers and there is limited formal support for them to fall back upon. When state policy and societal norms go hand in hand, the outcome is to reinforce the naturalisation of this unpaid labour performed by women. Their care work for elderly family members goes unrecognised and their role as carers remains unacknowledged. While care work is regarded as normalised socialised behaviour for maintaining functional familial relationships, a woman's role as carer is silenced. 'Because care responsibility is naturalized through family relations, carers tends to see themselves as mothers, daughters and/or daughters-in-law, and few think of themselves as "carers"'; therefore, 'to do so is a political move' (ibid.: 90). Formal support for carers is absent not only at the state level but also at an organisational level. 'Caring for an elderly family member tends to be seen as a "family matter" at work, rather than something an employer has the responsibility to share' (ibid.: 99–100). One previous study (see Yu 2009) shows that the 'informal working climate' is one of the factors that enables employed married women in Taiwan to balance their work and family life. However, it should be noted that this 'informal working climate' does not necessarily endorse systematic or organisational support for women working as carers. For example, an employer might be tolerant of an employee who leaves for a few minutes to breastfeed but reluctant to establish a policy or provide appropriate facilities for breastfeeding. In their study on non-family support for career women who practise breastfeeding in Taiwan, Chang et al. report that, although support from colleagues is available and negotiation with employers is possible, 'the workplaces were not family or breastfeeding friendly' (2014: 297). According to the study's participants, most organisations did not accommodate them with a secure and private space to express breastmilk until they requested one and initiated a negotiation with their employers. Moreover, while Chang et al.'s study indicates that colleagues were generally encouraging and supportive, I would argue that this 'friendly' attitude requires further analysis. This informal support in the workplace may have its roots in the gendered social norms about what a 'good mother' should be, as one of the participants reported that 'My colleagues said that if I stop breastfeeding, I will be teased by them... and they will blame me continuously' (ibid.: 297). Liu and Osawa's (2013) work on partner care in East Asia presents similar findings on gendered patterns in providing care in Taiwan. Firstly, while the law states that a couple has a mutual obligation to maintain and support each other, in practice they are expected to perform gendered roles. Similarly to other East Asian countries, women are mainly the ones providing care for their partners in Taiwan. Secondly, because the formal care service is strictly limited and does not extend to everyone who needs it, 'only the neediest are covered' (ibid.: 206). This results in a high level of dependence on informal support, especially by family members. This study further points out that workplaces are seldom care-friendly; for example, 'long working hours and leave provisions mean that workers have few ways of reconciling work and care' (ibid.: 213). All these findings illustrate a harsh situation for employed women who try to manage the 'dual burden' of providing care while remaining at work.

Through an examination of care work, the multiple labour burden of employed women is made visible. In conjunction with labour-market transformation, the social landscape of the gendered division of labour is far more complicated than simply women doing housework and men undertaking workplace activities. When employed women's life trajectories transcend the boundary between household/workplace and private/public, their involvement in formal employment does not necessarily spare them from labour responsibilities at home, while men in fact are largely spared. This situation was described by a participant in Hochschild and Machung's (2012) research on working parents as 'the second shift'. After calling it a day at the workplace, employed women must fulfil other labour demands in the household domain. Moreover, this gendered arrangement of labour occurs not only in the household but also in the workplace. There are particular forms of gendered labour in both social domains that are naturalised as 'women's work', which I will now describe.

Embodying Gender and Sexuality at Work

While studies on care labour reveal women's work that is generated beyond the scope of employment, the 'private' domain is not the only social sphere that should be scrutinised when investigating women's free labour. In the workplace, there also exist aspects of women's work that have been naturalised by gender norms and therefore go unrecognised. Such work remains unpaid even though it is commercialised to generate profit and bring benefits to the organisation. The scholarship on emotion work has provided a theoretical framework that reveals the commercialisation of gendered labour. Under the influence of gender norms, being caring is regarded as intrinsically female. Women in the workplace are expected to perform this caring activity for commercial value. The concept and theorisation of emotion work therefore offers a critical framework for investigating the 'invisible' labour that takes place as a part of employed work.

Reviewing the conventional theoretical frameworks of dramaturgy and psychoanalysis, Hochschild suggests an alternative research focus for social interactions. She proposes an 'emotion-management perspective' which brings social psychological enquiry to the relationships among 'the self, interaction, and structure' (1979: 51). As social beings, individuals adopt 'conventions of feeling' in their interactions. Instead of being something that happens naturally or instinctively, to have and express the proper feelings for a specific occasion or situation is the result of socialisation. Moreover, this socialisation is related to the social order in terms of class. Workers who have different class backgrounds acquire different forms of socialisation and therefore emotion work has a role in sustaining the social structure. Hochschild reveals that emotions and feelings are in part determined by socialisation. She further indicates that emotion work has a commercial aspect, because it not only happens during private, personal social exchanges but also in the commercial world. Hochschild promotes a further exploration of the emotion work that occurs in different occupations.

In her argument on the commercialisation of feeling, Hochschild compares middle-class work and working-class jobs and concludes that the former involves more emotion work. In her analysis she focuses primarily on the emotional display and exchange between the worker and the consumer. I would like to propose another perspective for viewing emotion work in the marketplace. The exchange of emotion and feelings in the marketplace could be happening within other relationships in the workplace, for instance, the exchange of emotion and feelings between colleagues or working partners. This exchange may also bring commercial value in a less direct way.

The perspective on emotion management is particularly critical when examining women's labour. Adopting Illich's (1980) concept of 'shadowwork', Hochschild (1983) argues that women's labour is often overlooked, labour such as housework, which is expected to be performed by women and is usually under-recognised and under-appreciated. Moreover, 'women are expected to do more of it' (ibid.: 168). There exists a social and cultural expectation that women will be nice. In other words, when women's labour is commodified on the market, it is often assumed that they should deliver service with a specific emotional touch. Women are not expected to do emotional labour but rather to naturalise it. When it comes to women's emotional labour, being becomes the way of doing. Thus, it is tricky in that the better women are at it, the less chance there is for them to earn credit for it. In Hochschild's words, 'the more her labour does not show as labour, the more successfully it is disguised as the absence of other, more prized qualities' (ibid.: 169). Hochschild's analysis reveals that there are gendered aspects to emotional labour. Women are expected to be nice, which means that being nice is their natural status, and so the management work that they perform on their emotions and feelings in order to present this desirable image is neglected. Therefore, when women engage in the workplace, they are faced with a double standard in terms of expressing feelings, particularly 'negative' ones, such as anger. While men are assumed to be rational and their feelings therefore are justified, women are regarded as irrational and emotional. Hochschild proposes the idea of a 'doctrine of feelings' as a framework for analysing women's disadvantaged status in terms of expressing feelings in the workplace. The biased rules governing women's expression of feelings and emotions are actually related to power relationships. She states that 'the lower our status the more our manner of seeing and feeling is subject to being discredited, and the less believable it becomes' (173). This double standard for expressing feelings also puts women in double jeopardy.

Hochschild's research on emotion work has served as a significant academic inspiration for later sociological scholarship. Some of her original ideas have been challenged, particularly the conceptualisation of emotional labour and emotion work, but her contributions remain influential (see e.g. Taylor 1998; Bolton and Boyd 2003; Witz et al. 2003; Bolton 2005; Wolkowitz 2006; Brook 2009). Her empirical investigation into the work experiences of flight attendants came to be seen as the pioneering sociological and feminist enquiry into service work. In subsequent studies in related empirical fields, gender became an important aspect in examining service labour. Taylor and Tyler's (2000) ethnographic research on the airline industry is among the academic endeavours that accord gender a key role in the analysis of employees' labour in service industries. They argue that 'emotional labour cannot be regarded as a "gender-neutral" phenomenon', that emotional labour is utilised by commercial organisations as a way to deliver 'quality service' and that it is expected that this labour will be delivered by female employees. This demand for quality service, which is often 'beyond managerial prescription', therefore mobilises gendered emotional labour and 'the production of sexual difference' through servicing activities (ibid.: 77, 91). Taylor and Tyler's study also explores 'surface acting' and 'deep acting' in the context of employee management. The research findings suggest that 'a surface commitment or act can conceal "deep" or "genuine" resentment and cynicism of quality improvement programmes in the service sector' (ibid.: 93). Quality management, which is accomplished by demanding emotional labour, therefore damages female employees' 'work autonomy'.

Following the investigation of the naturalisation and commercialisation of women's gendered shadow labour in the service industry, theories addressing the concept of sexual labour were developed to answer concerns about gendered sexualisation in the service sector. Focusing on the experience of employees in tourist organisations, Adkins' (1995) empirical work shows that, compared with their male colleagues, female employees' work and bodies are routinely sexualised and they are constantly located in a sexualised position within interactions in the tourist industry. Pondering the 'physical appropriation of women to men' in both sex work and other waged work, Adkins argues for a feminist perspective that foregrounds the gendered aspects of sexual labour in the workplace. She argues that 'the sexual servicing of men may not be specific to the "sex industry", but rather is a common feature of women's waged-work' (ibid.: 158). By highlighting that women's work is sexualised in both the sex industry and other 'common' employment, Adkins shows that sexuality provides a crucial perspective for comprehending gendered labour in employment. However, it should be highlighted that saying that women's labour is generally sexualised does not equate to promoting a homogeneous understanding of sexual labour in different industry sectors. Liu's research on the 'white-collar beauties' in provincial China has revealed a complex landscape of sexuality at work. By analysing professional women's employment experiences, Liu (2008) reveals that, while women's physical appearance is considered to be a commercial resource and business culture is very much sexualised, women also carry the moral burden of being 'too sexy'. Ironic and contradictory as it may seem, professional women are expected to be sexy in a desexualised way. The nuanced and arbitrary nature of sexuality management has located women in a vulnerable position from which to negotiate their way through sexual politics at work.

The research focus on women's shadow and naturalised labour in the service industry is challenged by studies that promote 'aesthetic labour' as an alternative theoretical foundation. The concept of aesthetic labour was coined by Warhurst et al. (2000) to investigate the emerging characteristics of the labour market in 'the new Glasgow'. Since the 1990s, Glasgow has striven to reinvent its local economy and to rid itself of the image of an industrial city. With its turn away from the path of manufacturing towards a service-oriented industrial structure, labour demand has reflected a different embodiment of labour. Warhurst et al. argue that aesthetic labour is one of the distinct but often overlooked skills that are required to contribute to this 'post-industrial rejuvenation' (ibid.: 1). Aesthetic labour is identified as 'a supply of "embodied capacities and attributes" possessed by workers at the point of entry into employment' (ibid.: 4). These capacities and attributes are then systematically reformed and managed through the processes of 'recruitment, selection and training' provided by the employers (ibid.: 4). They are mobilised, developed and commodified to produce a specific style of service representing and exemplifying the image that is favoured by the organisation. According to Warhurst et al., this service embodiment should be examined beyond the scope of 'physical appearance' (ibid.: 7). The aim of aesthetic labour is to provide the customer with a 'sensory experience' that touches and fulfils all the senses (ibid.: 7). While the theorisation of aesthetic labour brings forward analytic dimensions which broaden the discussion on service labour, such as the context of the organisation and the emphasis on embodiment proposed by Witz et al. (2003), gender seems to be rather blurred. Warhurst et al. (2000) argue that aesthetic labour is performed not only by women but also by men. As Wolkowitz points out, 'to say the work is not confined to either men or women is not to say it is not gendered, though, especially if sexual attractiveness is one of the attributes employers look for' (2006: 88). Although sympathetic to the proposed emphasis on embodied labour and how it is managed and transformed within organisational practices, I concur with Wolkowitz's critique that the theories on aesthetic labour might have a weakness in their gendered implications. I do regard gender as an indispensable lens when it comes to examining women's experience of work. This standpoint thus poses questions regarding my approach to gender, and I will discuss these next.

Conceptualising Gender in Everyday Interaction

It was a sunny afternoon. One of my colleagues and I were standing on a pavement in Taipei City having a short conversation. She was about to cross the road while I was explaining that I would go in another direction because I had to meet a friend of mine who lived nearby. 'Is your friend male or female?' my colleague asked me. I paused, because I did not know how to answer the question. I was processing many thoughts at once. I had never asked my friend the 'gender question'. I did not know which gender my friend identified with. However, that does not mean that I treat this friend as a gender-neutral person. I always assume that we have a similar gender identity. But still, how do I really know? Besides all these things, why does the answer to this question even matter? Why did my colleague need the gender information about my friend to have this conversation with me? So I replied with some hesitation: 'I'm not sure. Why?' My colleague looked surprised and then laughed. 'Nothing. Just asking.'

It was one of those very 'sociological' moments in everyday life that have inspired me to ponder gender as a social construction. Gender is one of the most important social categories in our daily lives. It is an essential indicator that people use to differentiate, distinguish and understand each other. From the moment of birth, or even before, a human being's gender is the subject of questions and concerns. It also affects how we act and interact with other people. Which toilet should a person go into? How should a person dress? What is their 'proper' degree subject, job, even lifestyle? To some extent, the answers to these questions all relate to gender. However, the definition of gender is not a straightforward one.

I am interested in women's experiences of gender inequality and discrimination at work. In order to turn this research interest into academic work, I first need to clarify my own understanding of gender. In other words, it is crucial to explain what gender means in the context of this study, why I define it in a certain way and how previous theoretical studies conducted by feminist scholars shed light on my conceptualisation of gender.

There are three parts to this section. First, I briefly introduce the ethnomethodological approach that serves as the foundation of this research. Second, I discuss the idea of 'doing gender' by reviewing some of the most important feminist works in this area. In the third part, adopting an interactionist perspective, I explain the concept of reflexivity as a crucial part of my understanding of gender in this research.

The Ethnomethodological Perspective

Regarding the contemporary research approach to gender inequality in Taiwan, I would like to encourage the study of gender from the perspective of everyday practices. I have concerns regarding the institution of law. Although it is important to discuss gender inequality from a legal perspective, the law should not be used as a filter to narrow our understanding of women's experiences. Furthermore, I believe that overemphasising the legal discourse might lead to a view of women who experience gender inequality as either active or passive legal actors. This dichotomous conceptualisation concerns me because it oversimplifies women's social situation and even reinforces the discourse of blaming the victim. I was looking for a theoretical framework that would allow me to analyse gender inequality in a situational context and prevent me from holding dichotomous assumptions about women's rationality. The ethnomethodological perspective was able to serve as a proper foundation on which to begin my research.

Garfinkel uses the term 'ethnomethodology' to refer to 'the investigation of the rational properties of indexical expressions and other practical actions as contingent ongoing accomplishments of organized artful practices of everyday life' (1967: 11). Criticising traditional sociology's limited research focus on 'extraordinary events', Garfinkel proposes a sociology that studies 'everyday affairs' (ibid.: 1, 9). This is a sociological approach that is interested not only in what people do in their daily lives but also how they do it. By exploring the 'how', Garfinkel suggests that there are 'methods' in everyday doing (ibid.: 30). That is, as a social being, a person's behaviour is always rational. It involves rational evaluation and discretion about certain rules, even though those rules may be taken for granted as 'common understanding' (ibid.: 30). For an ethnomethodological researcher, one of the primary tasks is revealing this 'common understanding' and examining the 'operation' of it or, in Garfinkel's words, 'making commonplace scenes visible' (ibid.: 36).

Inspired by the ethnomethodological framework, I am interested in studying women's experiences of gender inequality at work by focusing on the context of everyday social life. I am going to examine women's daily working experiences regardless of how 'mundane, ordinary, trivial' they might seem. In order to do so, I must first have a detailed discussion about the concept of gender. What is 'gender' according to an ethnomethodological perspective? What theoretical tools are available to help us reveal and challenge the common sense of gender in a given cultural context?

The Idea of 'Doing Gender'

The ethnomethodological perspective has contributed to the development of gender theories. It provides the foundation for considering gender as a social construction in everyday life. Kessler and McKenna (1985) are among those who adopt an ethnomethodological approach and reveal the social nature of gender in their work. They disclose the construction of gender in social practices conducted by individuals in everyday settings and conduct an in-depth analysis of 'gender attribution'. Reviewing some of the most important theoretical concepts relating to gender, Kessler and McKenna conclude that 'it becomes clear that no one piece of information about a component of gender is sufficient for making a gender attribution' (1985: 16). However, once a gender attribution is made, all other gender-based categories become settled. Kessler and McKenna use the term 'primacy of gender attribution' to identify this social phenomenon. They propose that gender attribution is neither guesswork nor probability. Rather, it is a 'complex, interactive process involving the person making the attribution and the person she/he is making the attribution about' (ibid.: 6). For Kessler and McKenna, gender is a social construction that happens in everyday interaction. We, as social actors, all contribute to it as well as being shaped by it.

While Kessler and McKenna direct their academic focus at how the gender of an individual is socially determined, West and Zimmerman's theorisation further expands the sociality of gender to the level of everyday interaction. Reviewing the conventional sociological theories of gender, West and Zimmerman (1987) set out to provide an alternative approach to understanding gender as something that a social being does rather than possesses or inherits. They propose conceptualising 'gender as a routine accomplishment embedded in everyday interaction' (ibid.: 125). Nevertheless, they point out that not only sex and gender but also sex category should be considered in order to form a concise theoretical view about the interactional work that a gendered being is constantly doing in society. As they explain and differentiate the definitions of sex, sex category and gender, West and Zimmerman demonstrate that regarding sex/gender as a binary opposition of biological/social is problematic. For them, the relationship between the biological and the social is complicated and the boundary between the two is rather blurred. They define sex as 'a determination made through the application of socially agreed upon biological criteria for classifying persons as females or males' and point out that these biological criteria may vary (ibid.: 127). Sex does not equate to sex category because the latter is constantly being accomplished in everyday life. In West and Zimmerman's words, 'a sex category is achieved through application of the sex criteria' (ibid.: 127). In everyday social contexts, an individual's sex is assured by her/his sex category. However, an absolute connection or relevancy between a person's sex and her/his sex category may be absent. Since the common biological features that are accepted as sex criteria in society are often hidden, people are usually looking for other visible characteristics which match 'our cultural perspective on the properties of natural, normally sexed persons' to categorise someone's sex during a social interaction (ibid.: 133). West and Zimmerman further suggest that gender should be viewed as 'the activity of managing situated conduct' according to the 'normative conceptions of attitudes and activities appropriate for one's sex category' (ibid.: 127). Furthermore, they emphasise the interactional and institutional aspects of the concept of doing gender. They argue that 'it is a situated doing, carried out in the virtual or real presence of others who are presumed to be oriented to its production' (ibid.: 126). They oppose the idea that gender is something a person possesses. For them, doing gender is not only a behaviour undertaken by a social being but also a complicated interactive process of 'situated conduct' (ibid.: 126). In other words, the 'doing' is an interactive activity.

West and Zimmerman's study makes it clear that doing gender is a social activity that cannot be performed without sex criteria and sex categorisation. There is an interdependent relationship between what is defined as biological/natural and what is seen as social/cultural. Moreover, it is not a process that can be fully accomplished by the individual but is rather a repeated, recurring activity that requires the interaction of all the participants in a given social context. When we interact with people in our daily lives, we are regarding them as gendered beings; therefore, we are all participants in the process of doing her or his gender. However, conceptualising gender as doing, that is, as a social practice in progress, does not mean that a person can do whatever she/he wants. As Rahman and Jackson clearly put it, 'doing gender is thus a continual process of action and interpretation' and 'we "do" gender as much by the interpretative processes by which we attribute gender to others as by our own actions' (2010: 162).

If gender is an ongoing interactive doing in everyday social life, then the process of this 'doing' requires further theoretical explanation. For instance, how should we regard the self in this process? How do we understand it in relation to social structures and social relationships? What kind of selfhood is emerging in this process? I will answer these questions by further discussing interactionist theory in the next section, focusing in particular on the concept of reflexivity.

Reflexivity, Self and Gender

Reflexivity has served as a crucial inspiration for feminists in their challenge to the conventional theorisation of gender. Critically reviewing the traditional theory of socialisation and gender roles, Stanley and Wise reveal the theoretical disadvantages that result from overlooking the reflexivity of selfhood. Comparing different studies on socialisation, Stanley and Wise (1993) identify the weak spot shared by the different models. They argue that the conventional socialisation model is 'psychologistic' and 'deterministic' because it assumes a 'pre-formed and almost autonomously unfolding ego which develops independently of the social' (ibid.: 101). Moreover, socialisation theory gives early childhood experience in the 'normal' heterosexual family a crucial and essential role in the process of constructing an individual's gender. They then outline a contradiction within the socialisation theory. While holding psychologistic and deterministic assumptions on the pre-social 'innate process', it also favours an 'over-socialized' explanation of a child's malleability (ibid.: 102). Stanley and Wise contest this socialised/non-socialised dichotomy, and point out that the socialisation model on gender construction is 'non-reflexive' (ibid.: 103). Stanley and Wise develop their argument further by examining the gender-role theory from a feminist perspective. In their words, the 'role-making' approach takes account of 'situation, personality and context in influencing events and behaviours', while the 'role-taking' approach 'describes a determinate reality in which absolute order exists and prediction is possible' (ibid.: 106–7). That is, if we see the gendered process as making roles, we must recognise the possibility and ability of an individual to make, to construct, to have a certain influence over the given situation. The role can only be fulfilled when one is in the situation. On the other hand, regarding gender construction as the process of taking a role is to assume a reality that determines the role that an individual is able to take; therefore, the role exists prior to the given situation. Challenging previous feminist studies which adopted the role-taking model, Stanley and Wise propose a more 'situational variable' approach that 'emphasize[s] the making and retrospective approach to "role"'; that is, they work from a theoretical foundation that does not overgeneralise women's life experiences or neglect various situated differences (ibid.: 110).

By clarifying the theoretical differences between role-making and role-taking, Stanley and Wise emphasise that gender is an ongoing social process that continuously happens in specific situations rather than something that is moulded during a pre-social life stage or during a certain limited period. Their theoretical reflection emphasises the situational aspect of doing gender. Moreover, their argument implies that a sufficient theory of doing gender should allow a researcher to see a gendered person's situated being rather than generalising it and neglecting the social details. They demonstrate that, in order to develop a practical social constructionist approach to gender, further conceptualising of selfhood with the concept of reflexivity is required to reconcile the contradictory dichotomy. A framework that enables a 'self' with agency to emerge without dismissing the significance of situational and relational conditions is needed.

Introducing Mead's thoughts on reflexivity to conceptualise the self-hood of a gendered being, Jackson proposes an alternative framework that moves beyond the social/non-social and social determinism/free choice dichotomy. According to Jackson (2011), Mead's conceptualisation of reflexivity considers social and relational parts of 'the self'. For Mead, reflexivity is 'the capacity to see ourselves as subject (I) and object (Me), which rests on the relationship between self and other' (Jackson 2011: 17). Jackson argues that reflexivity can only be understood within a social context. Because of reflexivity, the self is constantly being constructed through the process of reviewing its own being with an awareness of context. In Jackson's words, 'reflexive self-hood, then implies a degree of agency and active meaning-making, but it is always both produced within and bounded by its social context' (ibid.: 17). Jackson further argues that the concept of reflexive selfhood can shed light on gender theory, especially in understanding women's gendered daily lives. She suggests that 'reflexivity is not a quality opposed to sociality, but very much part of it' (ibid.: 18). Being fully aware of the social conditions of exercising reflexivity, Jackson points out that a reflexive being has the ability to 'imagine oneself from the other's perspective and anticipate the other's responses to oneself' (ibid.: 18). She also stresses that, all too often, this is a social capacity that the subordinate develops in order to survive the power relationship. Following Jackson's argument, due to gender inequality, women are highly reflexive social beings rather than passive and oppressed, or assimilated and ignorant, with false consciousness.

Gender is not something that a social being innately possesses. Rather, it is a doing that involves complicated processes. From an interactionist perspective, reflexivity is a crucial concept enabling us to gain an adequate understanding and explanation of an individual's being in a given social context. It provides an alternative framework that recognises a gendered being's agency without assuming total free will in doing. In other words, it can allow a researcher to see an individual's ability to negotiate without overlooking the structural limitations in different social contexts. That is, doing gender is neither compulsory nor entirely free, but a social construction involving reflexivity, interactions and relational practices.

Because I am conducting research aimed at studying gender inequality through women's experiences at work, I believe that the interactionist conceptualisation of gender, self and reflexivity can equip me with a rather flexible framework for investigating potential research data. But how exactly can the interactionist perspective potentially benefit this study? This is an important methodological question that will be addressed in later chapters.

NOTES

1. The four groups were: science and engineering, literature and arts, medicine and agriculture, and law and commerce (Hsieh and Yang 2014).
2. It should be noted that Chen's argument has sparked discussions and debates on historical interpretations of Taiwanese literature (see also Liou 2006; Chow et al. 2007).

REFERENCES

Adkins, L. (1995). *Gendered Work: Sexuality, Family and the Labour Market*. Bristol, PA: Open University Press.

Arrigo, L. G. (1985). Economic and Political Control of Women Workers in Multinational Electronics Factories in Taiwan: Martial Law Coercion and World Market Uncertainty. *Contemporary Marxism, 11*, 77–95.

Bolton, S. C. (2005). *Emotion Management in the Workplace*. Basingstoke: Palgrave.

Bolton, S. C., & Boyd, C. (2003). Trolley Dolly or Skilled Emotion Manager? Moving on from Hochschilds Managed Heart. *Work, Employment & Society, 17*(2), 289–308.

Brinton, M. C., Lee, Y. J., & Parish, W. L. (1995). Married Women's Employment in Rapidly Industrializing Societies: Examples from East Asia. *American Journal of Sociology, 100*(5), 1099–1130.

Brook, P. (2009). In Critical Defence of 'Emotional Labour' Refuting Bolton's Critique of Hochschild's Concept. *Work, Employment & Society, 23*(3), 531–548.

Chang, K. (1999). Compressed Modernity and its Discontents: South Korean Society in Transition. *Economy and Society, 28*(1), 30–55.

Chang, K. (2010). The Second Modern Condition? Compressed Modernity as Internalized Reflexive Cosmopolitization. *The British Journal of Sociology, 61*(3), 444–464.

Chang, C. F., & England, P. (2011). Gender Inequality in Earnings in Industrialized East Asia. *Social Science Research, 40*(1), 1–14.

Chang, S. M., Rowe, J., & Goopy, S. (2014). Non-family Support for Breastfeeding Maintenance Among Career Women in Taiwan: A Qualitative Study. *International Journal of Nursing Practice, 20*(3), 293–301.

Chen, F. [陳芳明]. (2002). 後殖民台灣:文學史及其周邊 [*Postcolonial Taiwan: Essays on Taiwanese Literary History and Beyond*]. 台北:麥田 [Taipei: Rye Field].

Chen, F. [陳芳明]. (2011a). 台灣新文學史 [*A History of Modern Taiwanese Literature*]. 台北:聯經 [Taipei: Linking].

Chen, H. H. (2011b). Field Report: Professionals, Students, and Activists in Taiwan Mobilize for an Unprecedented Collective-Action Lawsuit Against a Former Top American Electronics Company. *East Asian Science, Technology and Society, 5*(4), 555–565.

Chow, R., Harootunian, H., & Miyoshi, M. (2007). *Writing Taiwan: A New Literary History* (D. D. W. Wang & C. Rojas, Eds.). Durham and London: Duke University Press.

Chun, A. (1996). Fuck Chineseness: On the Ambiguities of Ethnicity as Culture as Identity. *Boundary 2, 23*(2), 111–138.

Diamond, N. (1979). Women and Industry in Taiwan. *Modern China, 5*(3), 317–340.

Garfinkel, H. (1967). *Studies in Ethnomethodology.* Cambridge: Polity Press.

Hochschild, A. R. (1979). Emotion Work, Feeling Rules, and Social Structure. *American Journal of Sociology, 85*, 551–575.

Hochschild, A. R. (1983). *The Managed Heart: Commercialization of Human Feeling.* London: University of California Press.

Hochschild, A., & Machung, A. (2012). *The Second Shift: Working Families and the Revolution at Home* (Rev. ed.). New York: Penguin Books.

Hsaieh, H. C., & Yang, C. L. (2014). Gender Implications in Curriculum and Entrance Exam Grouping: Institutional Factors and Their Effects. *Chinese Education and Society, 47*(4), 32–45.

Hsiung, P. (1996). *Living Rooms as Factories: Class, Gender, and the Satellite Factory System in Taiwan.* Philadelphia: Temple University Press.

Illich, I. (1980). Shadow-Work. *Philosophica, 26*, 7–46.

Jackson, S. (2011). Materialist Feminism, the Self and Global Late Modernity: Some Consequences for Intimacy and Sexuality. In A. G. Jónasdóttir, V. Bryson, & K. B. Jones (Eds.), *Sexuality, Gender and Power* (pp. 15–29). New York: Routledge.

Jackson, S. (2015). Modernity/Modernities and Personal Life: Reflections on Some Theoretical Lacunae. *Korean Journal of Sociology, 49*(3), 1–20.

Jackson, S., Ho, P. S. Y., & Na, J. N. (2013). Reshaping Tradition? Women Negotiating the Boundaries of Tradition and Modernity in Hong Kong and British Families. *The Sociological Review, 61*(4), 667–687.

Kang, M. (2003). The Managed Hand: The Commercialization of Bodies and Emotions in Korean Immigrant–Owned Nail Salons. *Gender & Society, 17*(6), 820–839.

Kessler, S. J., & McKenna, W. (1985). *Gender: An Ethnomethodological Approach.* Chicago: University of Chicago Press.

Kung, L. (1978). *Factory Women in Taiwan.* New York: Columbia University Press.

Lan, P. C. (2003a). Maid or Madam? Filipina Migrant Workers and the Continuity of Domestic Labor. *Gender & Society, 17*(2), 187–208.

Lan, P. C. (2003b). Negotiating Social Boundaries and Private Zones: The Micropolitics of Employing Migrant Domestic Workers. *Social Problems, 50*(4), 525–549.

Lan, P. C. (2006). *Global Cinderellas: Migrant Domestics and Newly Rich Employers in Taiwan.* London: Duke University Press.

Lee, A. (2004). *In the Name of Harmony and Prosperity: Labor and Gender Politics in Taiwan's Economic Restructuring.* Albany, NY: SUNY Press.

Leung, L. C. (2014). Confucian Welfare: A Barrier to the Gender Mainstreaming of Domestic Violence Policy in Hong Kong. In S. Sung & G. Pascall (Eds.), *Gender and Welfare States in East Asia* (pp. 114–136). Basingstoke: Palgrave Macmillan.

Lindio-McGovern, L. (2004). Alienation and Labor Export in the Context of Globalization: Filipino Migrant Domestic Workers in Taiwan and Hong Kong. *Critical Asian Studies, 36*(2), 217–238.

Liou, L. [劉亮雅]. (2006). 文化翻譯: 後現代, 後殖民與解嚴以來的台灣文學 [Cultural Translation: Postmodernism, Postcolonialism and Taiwanese Literature Since 1987]. 中外文學 [*Chung Wai Literary Quarterly*], *34*(10), 61–84.

Liu, J. (2008). Sexualized Labour? 'White-Collar Beauties' in Provincial China. In S. Jackson, J. Liu, & J. Woo (Eds.), *East Asian Sexualities* (pp. 85–103). London: Zed Books.

Liu, M. C., & Osawa, M. (2013). Partner-Care in the East Asian System: Combining Paid Work and Caring in Japan and Taiwan. In T. Kröger & S. Yeandle (Eds.), *Combining Paid Work and Family Care* (pp. 201–215). Bristol: Policy Press.

Loveband, A. (2004). Positioning the Product: Indonesian Migrant Women Workers in Taiwan. *Journal of Contemporary Asia, 34*(3), 336–348.

Ochiai, E., Yamane, M., Miyasaka, Y., Zhou, W., Onode, S., Kiwaki, N., Fujita, M., & Ook, H. S. (2008). Gender Roles and Childcare Networks in East and Southeast Asian Societies. In E. Ochiai & B. Molony (Eds.), *Asia's New Mothers* (pp. 31–70). Kent: Global Oriental.

Rahman, M., & Jackson, S. (2010). *Gender and Sexuality.* Oxford: Polity Press.

Raymo, J. M., Park, H., Xie, Y., & Yeung, W. J. J. (2015). Marriage and Family in East Asia: Continuity and Change. *Annual Review of Sociology, 41*, 471–492.

Sechiyama, K. (2013). *Patriarchy in East Asia: A Comparative Sociology of Gender.* Leiden: Brill.

Stanley, L., & Wise, S. (1993). *Breaking Out Again: Feminist Epistemology and Ontology.* London: Routledge.

Taylor, S. (1998). Emotional Labour and the New Workplace. In *Workplaces of the Future* (pp. 84–103). London: Macmillan Education UK.

Taylor, S., & Tyler, M. (2000). Emotional Labour and Sexual Difference in the Airline Industry. *Work, Employment & Society, 14*(1), 77–95.

Wang, F. T., Shimmei, M., Yamada, Y., & Osawa, M. (2013). Struggling for Recognition: Working Carers of Older People in Japan and Taiwan. In T. Kröger & S. Yeandle (Eds.), *Combining Paid Work and Family Care: Policies and Experiences in International Perspective* (pp. 89–106). Bristol: Policy Press.

Warhurst, C., Nickson, D., Witz, A., & Cullen, A. M. (2000). Aesthetic Labour in Interactive Service Work: Some Case Study Evidence from the 'New' Glasgow. *Service Industries Journal, 20*(3), 1–18.

West, C., & Zimmerman, D. H. (1987). Doing Gender. *Gender & Society, 1,* 125–151.

Witz, A., Warhurst, C., & Nickson, D. (2003). The Labour of Aesthetics and the Aesthetics of Organization. *Organization, 10*(1), 33–54.

Wolkowitz, C. (2002). The Social Relations of Body Work. *Work, Employment & Society, 16*(3), 497–510.

Wolkowitz, C. (2006). *Bodies at Work.* London: Sage.

Yeandle, S., Kröger, T., Cass, B., Chou, Y. C., Shimmei, M., & Szebehely, M. (2013). The Emergence of Policy Supporting Working Carers: Developments in Six Countries. In T. Kröger & S. Yeandle (Eds.), *Combining Paid Work and Family Care: Policies and Experiences in International Perspective* (pp. 23–52). Bristol: Policy Press.

Yi, Z., Coale, A., Choe, M. K., Liang, Z., & Li, L. (1994). Leaving the Parental Home: Census-Based Estimates for China, Japan, South Korea, United States, France, and Sweden. *Population Studies, 48*(1), 65–80.

Yu, W. (2009). *Gendered Trajectories: Women, Work and Social Change in Japan and Taiwan.* Stanford: Stanford University Press.

Yu, W. H. (2001). Family Demands, Gender Attitudes, and Married Women's Labor Force Participation: Comparing Japan and Taiwan. In M. C. Brinton (Ed.), *Women's Working Lives in East Asia* (pp. 70–95). Stanford: Stanford University Press.

Zhang, B., Lin, M., Nonaka, A., & Beom, K. (2005). Harmony, Hierarchy and Conservatism: A Cross-Cultural Comparison of Confucian Values in China, Korea, Japan and Taiwan. *Communication Research Reports, 22*(2), 107–115.

Zveglich, J. E., & Meulen Rogers, Y. (2004). Occupational Segregation and the Gender Wage Gap in a Dynamic East Asia Economy. *Southern Economic Journal, 70*(4), 850–875.

CHAPTER 2

Lost and Found in the Field: Methodology and the Research Process

INTRODUCTION

In Chap. 1 I introduced the metaphor of going on a journey. I used the imagery contained in this metaphor to help me build the meaning and purpose of a literature review: to explain where I am and where I intend to go intellectually. If I may continue to utilise such imagery, I would like to say that this methodology chapter contains the travel plans and the travel log of this research quest. It records what and how I planned in advance, the actual execution of this trip and what happened on the road. This chapter is composed of stories about the journey that I think are worth sharing from the perspective of a qualitative researcher. If the reader is expecting a methodology chapter which reveals 'the magic trick' behind the scenes, this chapter may be rather disappointing. Conventionally, in most academic writing, this section is tailored in a smooth and well-organised way, giving the impression that the researcher had a perfect plan before she or he went into the field. However, I will not and cannot present it as such, because that was not the case for my research experience.

Doing research is nothing like performing a magic trick. There is no foolproof pre-action design, but rather it is a process of constantly adapting, improvising and redesigning. Just as with any journey, unexpected things happen no matter how carefully one has planned. At least, that was the case in this research. As a scholar who adopted qualitative research methods, I was fully aware that, no matter how detailed and precise my

© The Author(s) 2018
T.-F. Chin, *Everyday Gender at Work in Taiwan*,
Gender, Sexualities and Culture in Asia,
https://doi.org/10.1007/978-981-10-7365-6_2

research design might be, something unpredictable could always happen in the field. And I believe, as a researcher, that it is precisely the unpredictability of qualitative research which should be valued. Rather than trying to control and minimise the unpredictable, I aimed to manage it in a reflexive way. This challenged me to rethink my methodology and even helped me to reveal and reconstruct it. Doing research is an 'organic' process rather than a mechanical one. I am not the one and only master of this research who has the total authority to determine its direction and results.

I would like to use this chapter as an opportunity not only to explain my research design but also to describe how it evolved as my research progressed. I start with how I envisaged the relationship between researcher and participants from a feminist perspective. This chapter is about the planned, the expected and also the surprising, unanticipated parts of my journey through the research field.

Designing It in a Feminist Way

Qualitative interviews will be used to gather information about women's experiences of sex/gender discrimination at work. Face-to-face interviews will be the main model to gather information. If an informant has doubts about a face-to-face interview, an interview via social networking platforms or telephone will be arranged.[1]

It is a somewhat painful experience to revisit and reread my original proposal for this research. It is vague, clearly not theoretically sophisticated enough and the wording implies that the writer's understanding of the researcher–participant relationship is oversimplified. Nevertheless, while many other embarrassing criticisms could be levelled against it, with some distance I recognise that the differences between the ideas implied in this premature proposal and those I now hold are evidence of improvement.

Some components have remained as they were in the original proposal. Most of these were general ideas about the designated research method. From the very beginning, the aim was to conduct qualitative research about women and work. I wanted to meet employed women in person and learn about their work experiences, particularly those relating to gender. Most of all, I wanted it to be a participant-friendly study. While these principal ideas remained at the core of the project, the actual implementation plan was modified considerably. This did not happen overnight but gradually during the research process with the help of feminist literature.

The changes were adopted in order to adjust the general objective of this research in response to realisations I had about the researcher–participant relationship and my conceptualisation of research ethics.

Revising the Objectives

I shifted my research focus from gender/sex discrimination to the experience of gender. This shift occurred for both theoretical and pragmatic reasons. In part it was the result of having developed a conceptualisation of gender with the help of the established literature on gender theories, which I presented in the theoretical discussion in Chap. 1. Along with the shift in my approach to gender, I also adopted a critical lens to examine the assumptions hidden in the original research subject. I found that the focus on gender discrimination reveals my own assumed projections of women's experiences in the workplace. Indeed, it was the news and stories about unequal and discriminatory treatment imposed on women at work that motivated me to conduct this research. However, I realised that I should not let my motivation narrow my vision when I went into the field. Clearly, my target participants were probably not the women in those news reports and stories. The recruitment of participants would be more exclusive if I used 'having experienced gender discrimination' as a required condition for participation. While gender discrimination is a theme that I wanted to discuss in this study, I thought that the actual generated data might go beyond it. Furthermore, I worried that the various possible interpretations of gender discrimination might be discouraging or confusing to potential participants. A more flexible and clear research question was needed to ensure that I remained open-minded about my participants' accounts as well as to prevent any misunderstanding. After filtering out the presumptuous hypothesis, shifting the research focus to women's experiences of gender at work seemed to be a much more appropriate and pragmatic approach.

Once the main research question was settled, I began to revise the objectives for the fieldwork accordingly. I set up the following sampling conditions: a woman who has or has had experience of full-time employment for at least one year. A white-collar job is preferred but it is not a necessary requirement. My decision to confine the research scope to office jobs is not purely a result of my research interest. It was also due to practical considerations around the accessibility of participants. The designed recruitment method was non-probability sampling. The beginning of the recruitment process would primarily depend on my social connections. Therefore, the limitations that my personal social and economic background might impose needed to be considered. In other words, based on the evaluation of my personal social networks, women who have office jobs seemed to be the most accessible group. This accessibility also implied that I might share similar social capital with the potential participants. Initial participants would be approached through my personal connections, including friends, relatives and acquaintances. Following this initial outreach, I would try to invite more participants through a snowball sampling technique. The prospective number of participants was 25 and I planned to interview each person at least once.

The face-to-face semi-structured interview was preferred as the main method. If a participant felt uncomfortable about an interview in person, alternative meeting methods would be arranged, such as an interview via social networking platforms or telephone. Interviews would begin with a general enquiry about daily life and then gradually turn to specific questions about her experiences of gender in the workplace. The interview questions were developed on the basis of seven themes, consisting of: work history, daily life routine, relationships with colleagues, work environment and atmosphere, troubles and disputes at work, gender inequality in the workplace, and personal experiences of gender discrimination. Although I had drafted an interview outline containing a list of specific questions, this was intended to serve as a memorandum for myself as an interviewer rather than a strict script that aimed to confine my participants' responses. The questions were generally open-ended in order to structure the interview in a flexible way and to encourage the participant to share any information that she found relevant.

Picturing the Researcher–Participant Relationship

Chih-Lu: She/he asked me, 'are you a feminist who puts feminism into practice?' And I said, 'eh? Of course, is there any other kind?' (laughs).[2]

Despite that feminism is generally perceived as a diverse body of knowledge, it is still very difficult for me to imagine how there could be a feminist who does not transform her knowledge into action. As Letherby argues, 'feminism is both "theory" and "practice"' (2003: 4). Therefore, when one participant, Chih-Lu, who identifies herself as a feminist, told me that she was once asked in a job interview whether she is 'a feminist who practises feminism', I could not help but share a good laugh with her. I totally understood her feelings and probably would have had the same reaction in that situation. As a feminist myself, I am inclined to regard knowing and doing as equally important and, most of the time, it is difficult to separate the two. To conduct feminist research means more than simply to 'produce useful knowledge that will make a difference to women's lives' (ibid.). It also means implementing that knowledge during the process in a reflective way. Doing research is itself a form of feminist action. As a feminist researcher, I had expected to do this research 'right' prior to doing it well. Once this principle was secured, questions concerning the detailed arrangements of the research design came to the surface. For instance, what should I do to acquire informed consent from a participant? How should I conduct the interview so that it showed respect for my participant's feelings and emotions? What if an interviewed participant decided to withdraw later? Should I keep in touch with her after the interview? If yes, how would I do so? The answers to all these questions led to the core issue of research design: the researcher–participant relationship. How I perceived and constructed the relationship would directly influence almost every aspect of my interaction with participants and, therefore, the research process.

The participant–researcher relationship is a crucial issue which has attracted the interest of many feminist researchers. Despite theoretical diversity, challenging the traditional methodology that treats participants 'as objects to be worked on' is a common standpoint among feminists (Abbott et al. 2005). Feminists are highly critical of the power relationship between a researcher and her participants; therefore, they approach the issue of research ethics with extra care and delicacy. Feminists have consistently reminded researchers never to become those who 'take, hit and run'. The researcher should not 'intrude into their subjects' privacy, disrupt their perceptions, utilize false pretenses, manipulate the relationships, and give little or nothing in return'; once she is satisfied, she should not then 'break off contact with the subjects' (Reinharz 1979: 95).

Since the moment I decided to undertake this project in a feminist way, Reinharz's words have been echoing in my ears. Doing it ethically and meeting a feminist standard have been my primary concerns. This is the core of my project. The first step toward easing the anxiety that arose from the thought that I might exploit my participants was to ponder what kind of researcher I would like to be and how I would perceive my participants

in relation to knowledge production. I did not do this by simply projecting my ideal scenario but rather sought guidance from the intellectual
achievements of experienced feminist researchers. Among them, Smith's
(1987) wise words concerning a sociology 'from the standpoint of women'
have had a particular influence on my understanding of the academic duty
of a researcher. Smith argues for a sociology that 'does not transpose
knowing into the objective forms in which the situated subject and her
actual experience and location are discarded' (ibid.: 153). Smith clearly
challenges the conventional idea of pursuing a transcendent level of knowledge as the main purpose of sociological research. Her approach to knowledge production emphasises that the actual social world that the subject is
experiencing should be a major concern for a feminist sociologist. A methodology that regards the individuals in the researched field as situated
subjects, therefore, conceptualises the subject and her social world as
inseparable. Smith's perspective sheds light on how I, as a researcher,
should perceive individuals in the researched field. I wanted to make sure
I treated my participants 'as subjects, as knowers', as women 'located in
their actual everyday worlds' (ibid.: 153).

    In order to perceive myself and my participants as situated beings in this
research, I began with something 'trivial'. I regarded using the term 'participant' as the first methodological step towards a feminist conceptualisation of researcher–participant relationships. I am fond of the idea that
naming is a powerful thing. As I have demonstrated in my writing, I prefer
to use the term 'participant' to describe an individual who is taking part in
this study. I chose not to use other common terms, such as 'interviewee'
or 'informant'. Indeed, I did interview my participants, but they are not
just interviewees. During the interview, it seems natural to see a participant as an interviewee and I, as the researcher, as the interviewer. However,
the actual interactions between us were often more than that. It was not
unusual for our interactions to begin long before the actual interview and
to continue afterwards. I became increasingly aware of this as I conducted
fieldwork. Therefore, I am hesitant to use the interviewer–interviewee
model to explain our relationship. Moreover, I am not convinced that
identifying the participant as an informant would suit the methodological
framework of this study. This relates to my view of and approach to the
research data. I regard research data as a creation that is cooperatively
produced by both the participants and the researcher. It is not a set of
packaged, well-kept records that are simply preserved and brought to the
interview by the participants, but material which is generated in a situated

and interactive context. Therefore, perceiving the women who took part as 'participants' has helped me to acknowledge not only their contribution to this research but also their subjectivity within it. Participants are individuals with agency with whom I interact in the field, and through our interaction the research data is generated.

Having noted that a participant is regarded as a contributor with agency, I am nevertheless very aware of the power relationship between a researcher and a participant. I do realise that a researcher has a certain influence over the fieldwork in a way that a participant does not. After all, the researcher is the one who initiates the interaction with a specific purpose and an agenda; moreover, the researcher is the one who holds the power to analyse and interpret the data. Before the fieldwork, my understanding of this power relationship was comparatively simple and straightforward. My focus was on the negative aspects of the power disparity between the researcher and the participant. I assumed that, as a researcher, my power position would consist of holding a clear high ground that would cause the participant to feel too intimidated or uncomfortable to share their thoughts with me. This view was seriously challenged once I actually stepped into the research field, as I discuss later in this chapter. Precisely because of my concern about the power that I as a researcher might exercise in the course of my research, my primary ethical concern was the possible exploitation that might be caused by my field practices. In an effort to avoid that outcome, I attempted to come up with a fieldwork plan that could help me and my participants interact in a less hierarchical way throughout the process.

Ethics Matter

A list of well-developed interview questions might initiate a meaningful conversation but will not necessarily make a participant feel comfortable about sharing her story. I am convinced that informed consent is the foundation of the basic practices of research ethics. There was no doubt about including the practice of informed consent in my fieldwork design. The question was how to do so. In order to prevent making informed consent nothing but a vague promise, it was necessary to transform this abstract concept into feasible practices. I found that visualising the interview step by step was a useful method to start with. During this visualisation process, I realised that its purpose was not simply to imagine the interview, but to engage in an envisaging activity that was based on my knowledge and experience of social interaction. Along with the ethical concerns, I also took into account my expectations of both my own behaviour and that of my participants.

At the beginning of each meeting, I would be the one who possessed information about the research. I wanted to remove any possible barriers caused by an information gap between a participant and me. Having stated that, however, I could not neglect the reality that 'there are limits to how adequately' a researcher can perform information disclosure to all participants (Mason 2002: 81). My solution to this problem was to deliver the basic information and then encourage my participants to ask any questions that had been raised in their minds. When formulating the interview procedure, I tried to make sure that my participants would have the best possible opportunity to understand the purpose of the research, the standard structure of the interview and anything else they wanted to know about my project before they agreed to take part.

I intended to use an information sheet and a consent form to help me achieve this. The information sheet provided general information about my research and an explanation of the basic procedure of the interview. Most importantly, it emphasised that the nature of the interview was voluntary rather than compulsory. A participant could decline the invitation or withdraw her participation even after the interview. I sent out the invitation together with the information sheet. At the beginning of each interview, I asked the participant whether she had already read it. Regardless of the answer, I would then go through the content of the information sheet to give the potential participant a verbal explanation. Next I would ask her if she had any questions. I tried to provide as much information as possible. I would not interview anyone who had not read the information sheet or had not understood the information on it. After all these steps, if the potential participant was still willing to join the project, I would bring out the consent form and obtain her signature.

Before I could go into the field and execute my research, there was an official procedure that I was required to complete. This was to obtain approval from the ethics committee of my university, which involved completing a ten-page ethics form. I admit that, at first glance, it all looked very 'bureaucratic' to me. However, during the process of completing it, this 'annoyingly bureaucratic document' inspired me to think about research ethics in a deeper way. It led me on a virtual tour of the research process, from research questions to data storage, and pinpointed practical issues. Previously, all my attention had been on how to acquire informed consent from participants. I had hardly thought about other ethical issues, especially those regarding the safety of the researcher. I had only thought about research ethics in terms of protecting my participants from abuse and exploitation by unethical conduct. I had failed to recognise that a researcher could be vulnerable in the field, too. The questions listed on the form reminded me to locate ethics within a two-way interactive relationship. Research ethics protect not only the rights of the participants but also those of the researcher. Of course, I am aware of the limitations of the 'regulatory model of research ethics' (Halse and Honey 2005: 2142). Obtaining approval from an ethics committee does not guarantee that research will be completely ethical. Research ethics is, after all, a matter of practices. The point I am trying to express here is that, if ethical practice indeed 'evolves from reflexivity', then the regulatory ethics form was useful material that served to trigger my reflexivity on the potential ethical issues raised by this study (ibid.: 2160).

Pilot Study

In addition to making plans, I decided to conduct a pilot study to prepare myself for fieldwork. The main purpose of this was to help me design and improve the interview questions. I undertook three pilot interviews in two stages. Two were conducted at a quite early stage, when I had only general ideas about the project. I conducted these two non-structured interviews without any specific questions in mind. Both pilot participants were my friends and the interviews were primarily conducted in Taiwanese Mandarin. These interviews were more like casual chats about work with a recording device by my side. Despite the fact that they seemed 'casual', 'non-academic' and not necessarily 'successful', these two interviews actually provided me with useful information from which to develop interview questions. For example, I experienced an awkward pause during one pilot interview while I struggled to formulate a specific and clear question. When I reviewed that interview, I realised that the difficult situation was caused by the insufficient design of the questions. I only had a number of bullet-point interview themes with me and had not developed concrete questions on each issue. For that reason, I failed to come up with suitable questions to encourage my participant to talk more in the interview. That 'failure' helped me to understand the importance of good interview questions. Having a list of gender-related issues was not good enough. I should have transformed them into concrete questions. Therefore, I started to design a draft of interview questions that echoed my research questions. I used this draft in my third pilot interview to practise and test it.

In addition to being more structured, the third interview was quite different from the previous two in terms of the linguistic aspect. My intention was to rehearse a formal interview in order to prepare myself for future fieldwork. It turned out to be a much more rewarding experience than I had anticipated. Originally, I developed all the interview questions in Taiwanese Mandarin. Due to the fact that the participant in the third pilot interview was an English speaker, I had to translate all the interview questions into English. The process of translation, surprisingly, became a useful strategy for me to examine the phrasing and logic of the questions. It triggered a reflexive mental activity that was more than just translating words. Choosing foreign words to substitute for the concepts I had expressed in my native language was like having a conversation with myself in which I criticised the vague and obscure aspects of my work. Translation became a crucial part of the research method, especially during the later stages of the research process, as I explain in the latter part of this chapter.

Although none of these interviews could be used as research data, the feedback from my pilot participants inspired me to tailor my interview questions in a more detailed way. Most of the questions that I designed focused on everyday work routines and office culture: What is your typical working day like? Do you usually have lunch with colleagues? Or do you prefer to eat alone? And why? What troubles you the most in the workplace? I organised the questions under different themes, such as overall work experience, daily routine, general management of the organisation, the official complaints procedure in the workplace and so on. I produced an interview outline detailing specific questions. When I conducted an interview, I would take it with me as a reminder for myself. It would not be a questionnaire for the participant. A participant could always refuse to answer any question that I proposed and she could say anything that she wanted to share. I intended to keep the interview structure flexible.

THE INCONVENIENT TRUTH ABOUT MY FIELDWORK

During the summer of 2013 I flew from an island nation in the Atlantic Ocean to another one situated in the Pacific Ocean. I spent two months in Taiwan, bathed in a perfect marine tropical climate. I was excited in general about what I considered to be my first complete fieldwork experience.

I had conducted interviews for research purposes before, but they had not been for my own project and my engagement was limited. Therefore, this research represented my first fieldwork journey as the main researcher, in which I was responsible for managing the entire project. There were both expected and unexpected occurrences. They came together to instigate a critical inspection of the original design and my perception of fieldwork. Writing about what happened in the field is therefore a dialogue with myself, a method to examine my own ideas and practices of feminist methodology.

Recruitment Is Bittersweet

Met with three potential participants. They showed interest in both interviews and focus group. I will do follow-up. (Fieldwork journal, 25 July 2013)

This is the first entry I wrote in my fieldwork journal. It recorded my earliest move in the field. It probably looks quite academic because of the wording. One thing I did not explain in this entry was that the three potential participants were actually my friends. I knew that my personal social network would be a valuable resource for recruiting participants, but I did not realise that the recruitment would intertwine so closely with my personal life. The sense of maintaining a clear boundary between research fieldwork and a researcher's personal life seemed to dissolve secretly without me noticing. The stage curtain of my fieldwork was pulled up quietly in a gathering with my friends. Whenever I went back to Taiwan, I always met up with friends for nice meals. My social routine then became a form of reaching out as part of the recruitment process. Since my friends cared about how I was doing in the UK, the progress of my research seemed like a natural topic to bring up. Our conversation then turned to a discussion of whether they could take part in this study. As previous research in East Asian societies has revealed, personal connections often play a significant role in qualitative interviews (Liu 2006; Park and Lunt 2015). My personal networking was a tremendous help during the recruitment process. In addition, the feminist bond that I shared with my friends was a particularly strong force that had a substantial effect.

I soon realised that the quality of my personal connections was serving as an influential positive factor in recruitment. I first reached out to friends whom I knew well. Our mutual understanding and shared living experience contributed to a certain sense of trust that is difficult to build through proper research conduct alone. This does not mean that I skipped the step of informed consent, but I did feel that the invitation process could be initiated in a more nuanced way than simply by a formal offer from the researcher. For example, some participants already knew that I was about to undertake fieldwork and expressed their willingness to participate even prior to my formal invitation. While good friendship offered a solid platform for the invitation, I did worry about the pressure and tension which could be caused by interpersonal relationships. I did not want to be perceived as an unscrupulous salesperson who exploits personal connections to gain every possible profit for her own interests. The 'real' and already existing social relationships in the field had raised my awareness of the implications of research ethics.

In my fieldwork, the recruitment and the interview were two different but overlapping stages. The latter accelerated the former. I did not start interviewing after I had finished all the recruitment work but managed to do both simultaneously. This is the pattern of my snowball sampling. Before I had enough participants, I ended every interview by asking the participant to recommend another potential participant if she were willing to do so. Therefore, conducting an interview was not only about collecting data but also about building extended connections. While I was interviewing a participant, she was probably gathering information about the research and evaluating the feasibility of inviting her friends to join. I would like to use an email as an example to explain the snowballing process. One participant, who is a friend of mine, wrote a wonderful invitation encouraging her friends to participate in my research. The original email is in Mandarin and I translated it as follows:

Dear you [the female you],[3]
No matter how long you have known me, I believe you know me as a grumpy person who cares about gender equality. Thank you for your tolerance of my 'nagging and complaining' [...] my friend, Chin Ting-Fang, is doing her PhD research in order to tackle gender inequality from an academic approach [...] If you are willing to share your work experience, please contact her. The interview is about 1 hr long and as for the venue, any place in Taiwan will do, as long as you feel fine about it. Chin will climb the mountain and swim the ocean to get there for you.
The attachments are the information sheet for the research and a list of interview questions I got from Chin. **If you are a little bit hesitant, I am willing to share my interview experience to help you evaluate the pros and cons of participation** [emphasis added].

Thank you for supporting women, no matter what approach and what perspective you are taking, even if it's just something small such as listening to my complaints.

Chih-Lu

This email was sent after I had conducted an interview with Chih-Lu. She also sent me a copy. It is a well-written invitation. To be honest, it is even better than the one that I wrote. I was touched. Moreover, it was rewarding to realise that she was willing to describe her own experience of the interview to help her friends understand more about the nature of participation.

Chih-Lu's email prompted me to think more deeply about the process of snowballing recruitment. It is not only about a participant introducing other potential participants through her personal network. I developed my own sense of how those I interviewed were participants in the research. I am now refer to the women I interviewed as 'participants' not merely because the classic feminist texts on methodology say that I should, but because I am truly convinced that this project is a collaboration between myself and my participants.

Once the first few interviews had been completed, the recruitment process began to accelerate. I felt that my social life had never been so complicated. Small things such as handling my diary became crucial in order to manage the fieldwork. On one occasion I did three interviews in a single day, which was exhausting. Reviewing my personal diary from that period, I can see that it was probably the peak of my social life. With such a busy schedule, management work became crucial. The first aspect was time management. At first, I thought I could manage to transcribe the recordings while the fieldwork was progressing, but I reluctantly realised that this was overly ambitious. My time was segmented due to interview appointments. Furthermore, making contacts and following up with them was more time-consuming and energy-intensive than I had anticipated. In order to minimise my own social anxiety, I used a spreadsheet to track the progress and development of my fieldwork, consisting of a list of my potential participants and a record of the transition through different contact stages. For instance, I would keep records on invitations, follow-up, interview date and setting, and after-interview contact. It was a record as much as a to-do list to keep my fieldwork on track. It also documented the recruitment and interaction process with my participants. The general process is presented in Fig. 2.1. The snowballing process and the connections between the researcher and the participants are illustrated in Fig. 2.2.

Fig. 2.1 Recruitment procedure

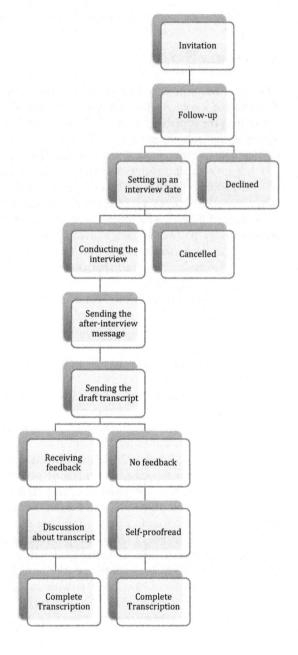

Fig. 2.2   Snowballing process

Alongside the diary and spreadsheet, I also included a research journal in my fieldwork toolkit. The idea of keeping a research journal was first suggested to me by my supervisor at the time. Its original purpose was to keep her updated about the progress of my work while I was far away from the academic institute with which I am affiliated. It turned out to be a strategic approach to both fieldwork management and data analysis. My record covers all the things that I found interesting in my fieldwork. I wrote down not only the recruitment process and the interview arrangements but also my thoughts about fieldwork. After each interview, I would summarise the highlights of the interview and quickly write down my initial thoughts about it. This journal then became a source of potential themes to develop. The notes I took during the process of transcribing also helped. I would mark the parts of an interview that were interesting and might relate to other interviews in one way or another, and provide short explanations. Later when I went through the finalised transcripts, I also wrote down notes in the margins. I chose five interviews that had more notes than the others as introductory cases to develop a draft of potential themes. After examining other transcripts, I then revised the draft.

In addition to the interviews, I also conducted two focus group sessions with some of my participants. I intended to use these sessions as an alternative way to generate data that probably could not be produced through interviews. I had never conducted a focus group and wanted to give it a try. The participants were acquainted with each other and held regular social gatherings. I took advantage of that and proposed that I conduct the focus group sessions at their regular social meetings. They agreed to this idea and we organised two sessions. All the participants in the focus group sessions had already been interviewed individually. The two group sessions were basically conducted with the same participants, apart from one who was unable to join the first session, so she only took part in the second.

Altogether, I successfully recruited 30 participants. The age range was approximately 24–48 years. The industries in which my participants work are quite diverse and some have experienced significant career changes. Most of my participants occupy basic positions in their organisations, while some have made it to the mid-managerial level. Overall, I conducted 32 interviews and two focus group sessions. The total length of the recorded data is approximately 68 hours. The average length of each interview/focus group session is more than two hours. However, due to my evolving concerns regarding the ethics of data preparation, I decided not to use the data generated through focus group sessions in the analysis. I still regard these as useful but decided not to present them in my writing, and particularly not to quote them directly.[4]

The general background information about my participants is shown in Table 2.1. It is obvious that the majority are single. This sampling result might reflect both the characteristics of my personal social networking and the demography in Taiwan. According to demographic statistics collected by the Ministry of the Interior, the total population of single women who have reached the legal marriage age is around 30 %. I did not include sexual orientation in the basic information about the participants. This is not because I did not see it as important information or because I did not know anything about it. It is deliberately excluded for ethical reasons. This research recruited participants with various sexual identities. I acquired that information based on our friendship prior to this study. There are participants whom I have known well for some time who simply did not bring up their sexual identities in the interviews. There are at least two possible reasons. The first possibility is that they did not think it was relevant to the interview. The other possibility is that they did not feel comfortable allowing that piece of information to be included in this research. It would not be ethical for me to force them to come out in this study, even under the protection of a pseudonym. Therefore, I would like to remind the reader to avoid making assumptions about the sexual identity of any participant simply because she did not disclose that information.

Every Interview Is Unique

There may seem to be no point in emphasising the uniqueness of every interview, since I adopted the semi-structured interview as my research method. This is a method that encourages a flexible agenda and is deemed to allow each interview to produce a fieldwork result that could be different from all the others. Although I would not have been surprised to hear about similar and common experiences from different participants, I did not expect them to provide homogeneous accounts. However, despite this initial assumption I was nevertheless amazed by the richness of the data generated by the interviews and the unique accounts given by each participant. In addition to emphasising that the interview data is more heterogeneous than I expected it to be, I would also like to point out that I developed different interview approaches, including the strategy of personalised preparation.

Table 2.1 Participant description

Name (Wade–Giles)	Age	Years of work experience	Industry (when interviewed)	Relationship status[5]	Education
Chi Chih-Lu	34	10	Banking	Single	MA
Lei Yu-Nung	50	30	Social work	Single	BA
Lin Hsi-Shu (Katja)	34	10	Telecommunications	Married	MA
Chao Hsiang-Yun	34	10	Banking	Single	BA
Yang Chieh-Ming	33	13	Social work	Single	BA
Tsao I-Chieh (Nora)	23	1	IT	Single	BA
Yu Liang-Wei (Zoe)	36	16	Insurance	Single	BA
Cheng Ya-Hsin	34	10	Government	Single, Divorced	MA
Chou Ying-Hua	34	11	Education	Single	BA
Sung Yu-Tai	32	7	Publishing	Single	MA
Chiang Shih-Ching	49	25	Media	Single	Diploma
Han Lu-Fan (Shirley)	32	10	IT	Single	BA
Tang Yu-An	39	15	Social work	Single	BA
Lu Chia-Chun (Kristin)	32	8	Insurance	Single	MA
Hsu Kai-I (Sabrina)	35	3	Publishing	Single	PhD
Feng Hsiao-Yin	34	4	Education	Single	MA
Fang Chih-Jui	34	9	Government	Married	BA
Chang Pei-Ching	33	10	Social work	Married	BA
Liao Yu-Hsuan	30	6	Banking	Married	MA
Wei Han-Ting (Jess)	28	4	Education	Single	MA
Hsiang Yu-Chen	30	8	IT	Single	BA
Tu Ying-Hsuan	22	5	Service	Single	Diploma
Liang Yueh-Chao	55	34	Government	Married	Diploma
Huang Hui-Li (Trixie)	35	13	IT	Married	BA
Wang Pin-Yen	36	11	Publishing	Single, Divorced	MA
Kao Chi-Lun	29	5	Social work	Single	BA
Hsieh Che-Yuan	26	4	Government	Single	MA
Tsai Tzu-Ling	55	34	Law	Married	BA
Ho Pei-Ju	39	16	Transport	Single	BA
Su Ko-Chi (Iona)	29	6	Education	Single	MA

Influenced by ethnomethodological and symbolic interactionist thinking, most of my interview questions focused on everyday work routines and office culture. These questions might have sounded 'gender neutral' to my participants and sometimes even made them wonder why I, as a researcher, was asking about such 'irrelevant stuff'. However, this 'irrelevancy' functioned as a potential breakthrough point for my participants to share things that were not covered by specific questions but were relevant to this research project. The method of the semi-structured interview also allowed me to collect data that I had not anticipated.

Therefore, many of my participants provided accounts that went beyond my initial research scope, and those accounts led me to cultivate unexpected but fascinating themes. For example, towards the end of each interview, I usually asked my participant whether she had any personal working rule or motto. One of them replied: 'always be myself'. She said that if the work environment or organisational culture makes her feel unable to be herself, then she will quit. Her answer inspired me to initiate a sociological enquiry into the meaning of being oneself in the workplace. Thus, after that interview, I added questions regarding 'the true self' to my interview outline.

Moreover, while preparing for the first interview, I realised it would be necessary to personalise the outline for each participant and also for myself. Prior to the fieldwork, the interview outline was designed for a faceless participant. She was a general figure and not anyone specific. Once recruitment began, this general figure was replaced by real women with vivid personas and characteristics. It felt wrong to use the 'prototype' interview design when a specific individual appeared in front of me. This was especially so in the case of participants whom I already knew. Strictly speaking, the truth is that, due to my recruitment method, I never interviewed a 'complete stranger'. As the graph of the recruitment shows, the snowballing process demonstrates an expansion of my social network. However, it should be noted that the recruitment process does not represent the actual social connections between my participants and myself. Having a participant introduced to this project by another participant does not necessarily mean that she was a stranger to me. Instead, she might be a common friend or someone I knew. Moreover, even if she was a stranger at first, after our interactions during the recruitment process, by the time we actually met for the interview, we would already have a certain amount of knowledge about each other. Experiencing the actual interactions during the recruitment process, I then realised that my original interview outline was too general and 'stiff' because my assumption had been that I would be interviewing complete strangers. If I had adopted this proto-outline to conduct all the interviews, it would probably have been perceived as socially awkward. Therefore, before each interview, I would revise the outline in order to personalise it for the specific participant.

Interview Interactions Are Complicated

Hsi-Shu: You know, how you let people think you're unmarried? It's actually quite easy. When the topics you're interested in are not about family, people will assume you're unmarried. Because a married woman, she would constantly mention 'my husband' and 'my children'. Or say 'my family' is blah blah blah. On the other hand, single people only talk about 'I'. 'I' went to see a movie yesterday; instead of 'we' went to see a movie. 'I went to see a movie.' 'My friends and I are going to', 'My friends and I have tried that restaurant before.' **My colleagues and I are going to a music event in August, ah, would you like to join us?** [emphasis added][6]

Hsi-Shu is not just a participant but also a friend whom I know well. For that reason, it is quite understandable that our interview is composed of conversations that cannot be identified as purely research-oriented. For example, in this quote, Hsi-Shu was at first sharing the experience of being misidentified as a single woman by her colleagues because of the way she speaks. Then it suddenly occurred to her that there was an event which she thought I might be interested in and therefore she turned the sharing into an invitation. I think this is a perfect example to demonstrate the complexity of researcher–participant interaction in my fieldwork. It shows how the conversation during an interview could shift seamlessly from a research-related topic to a private matter. It also clearly reveals that I was not the only one asking questions in the interview. Hsi-Shu is not the only participant who asked questions during the interview. Exchanges such as this were not rare in the course of my fieldwork. These 'not so formally research related' conversations have shed light on the complexity of researcher–participant interactions in the field.

I frequently interviewed acquaintances in the course of my fieldwork. This resulted in complex social interactions that led me to question the boundaries of researcher–participant relationships. It is fairly clear that the interview interactions between my participants and me cannot be fully explained by the conventional researcher–participant model. Before the interviews, we had developed certain patterns of interaction based on our pre-existing personal and social connections. It would have been awkward for me to just ignore these established connections and abandon the communication style with which we had become comfortable and familiar. I could not just put on the mask of a 'stranger researcher' and pretend that I knew nothing about them and they knew nothing about me. For me, fieldwork is not a game or a scripted role-play. It is a situated social event rather than an ahistorical and asocial performance. My participants and I are situated social actors. Our social beings and relationships should not be overshadowed by oversimplified ideas about researcher and participant. However, this does not mean that I treated my participants exactly the same as in our ordinary and private interactions. The major difference was the involvement of research ethics in our social exchanges. The pre-existing relationships not only diversified the fieldwork interactions but also sensitised me to the subtleness and nuances of ethical practice, which I further discuss later.

The questions that my participants raised were not just invitations to social events or general enquiries to clarify our discussions. They also proposed questions about the research, about me (as a researcher or acquaintance/friend or both), about institutions and the social world as a whole. These were not necessarily easy questions and I did not always know the answers. According to Oakley, the traditional model of interviewing is a one-way mechanical process of communication in which the interviewee is passive and managed and the interviewer is self-reservedly objective (1981: 36–7). Based on a review of methodology guidelines in textbooks, Oakley argues that this traditional approach suggests it is preferable to prevent an interviewee from asking questions in return. This is regarded as something that 'properly socialized respondents' would not do (ibid.: 35). Moreover, a correctly socialised interviewer should never share her own 'beliefs and values'. In discussing the issue of asking questions in return, Oakley challenges this traditional model and the methodology embedded within it. She argues that the textbook model is problematic, and she suggests alternative strategies. Although I have no idea whether it is proper to identify my participants as 'properly socialized', one thing I do know is that I do not perceive taking questions from the participant as a negative thing. While some research benefits from providing participants with very limited information (see Ali 2010), this study does not share that agenda.

In response to my participants' questions regarding my opinions, I strove to be honest. This was a general principle which I reminded myself to apply throughout the process of fieldwork. The consideration underlying this approach is related not only to ethics but also to productivity. The research questions that I had prepared did not require a method that involved hiding the researcher's intentions. I was convinced that the better my participants understood this project, the more useful and meaningful would be the data that I could collect. The fact that my participants did ask questions in order to acquire more information about the research meant there were inevitably different levels of information disclosure. For example, one participant asked me about my research motive the first time we met. By answering that question, I provided more information to this participant than to the others.

Above all, I was particularly conscious of my identity as a feminist. In fact, the participants probably discovered this during the early stages of recruitment. For example, I included the following message in the information sheet:

> This part of the research is intended to learn about women's experiences of employment in Taiwan, especially experiences relating to gender inequality at work. I hope the research will contribute to understanding how to better promote gender equality in Taiwanese workplaces.

This passage disclosed my general stance on gender and work to my participants. In terms of methodology, I see revealing my research intentions, my purpose and also my standpoint as a way to be objective. This does not mean that I intended to judge my participant and persuade her to agree with me. I would leave space in the conversation to encourage the participant to express her opinions first. If that failed, I would ask for her opinion after I had shared my thoughts. By revealing my own ideas, my intention was to motivate my participants to engage in a conversation with me. Thus, the interview sometimes turned into a discussion on certain issues. On the occasions when my participants said things that I disagreed with, I would restrain myself from turning the interview into a debate. After all, my purpose was to have an active conversation with the participant rather than to reach an agreement on any particular issue.

On the other hand, I am aware of the possible influence that revealing my own stance might have had on sampling and data generation. Presenting myself as a female researcher who considers gender equality in the workplace to be a serious issue could already stir up all kinds of images even without me waving the banner of 'feminism'. My gender politics were likely to attract participants who, if they did not agree with me, at least had an interest in my perspective. Since the participants were my partners in generating research data, the characteristics of the sampling would definitely influence the fieldwork results. Furthermore, it appeared that my disclosure of the purpose and subject of this study had influenced how my participants prepared themselves for the interviews. The following conversation occurred when I asked one participant, Che-Yuan, about her thoughts on the gendered glass ceiling.

Ting-Fang: Do you think men are more likely to be promoted to managerial positions?

Che-Yuan: Actually, before attending today's interview, I did think about this question.

Che-Yuan's reply implies that she had thought about what questions I would raise during the interview. Her ideas might thus have been shaped by the information about this study that I had provided during the recruitment process.

Another type of question that was commonly asked during interviews related to participants' concern about whether their accounts were helpful to my study. For example, Ying-Hua, a high-school teacher, phrased it thus:

Ying-Hua: I feel that most of the children are more afraid of their fathers than of their mothers. Is this information helpful?

My response to Ying-Hua's question was an immediate 'yes'. As a feminist, especially one who is interested in the theorisation of everyday life, I am always fascinated by my participants' thoughts and experiences about gender and women's lives. I sincerely felt that all my participants' accounts could inspire me in one way or another. There were also times when participants expressed doubts about their own opinions. In such cases, I would emphasise that there was no correct answer to any question that I posed. I would further explain that in my previous research experience, I had learnt that sometimes information that a researcher considered less relevant turned out to be the most important piece of research data.

Through this discussion of my participants' enquiries and my responses, I have shown that, while I did adopt the method of interviewing, the actual exchanges were more complicated than just 'the researcher asked a question and then the participant answered it'. The semi-structured interviews that I conducted were composed of complex verbal interactions. It was within this interactive process that the research data was generated.

No Universal Model of Ethics Practice

Ting-Fang: This red dot here shows that it's recording. Let me check if the time meter is running properly. Okay.[7]

Reviewing the recorded data, I found that most of the interviews begin with me saying something similar to this passage. I considered it necessary to mention my recorder at the beginning of each interview for ethical reasons. Once the participant informed me that she was ready, I would bring out my recording device, which was a digital voice recorder. I would turn it on and place it somewhere visible. Then, I would draw my participant's attention to the red dot on the device before I asked any questions. In doing so, I intended to ensure that the participant had noticed the existence and function of the recorder. I wanted to confirm that she was aware of the recording during the interview and make it clear that I would never record anything secretly. I deliberately explained how to tell whether the machine was running or not. This practice also functioned as a demarcation between informal casual chatting and the interview. Regardless of whether the participant was someone I already knew or a stranger, our meeting always began with casual social talk. The interview was just a part of our interactions during the meeting. Precisely for this reason, I felt the need to indicate when the 'shift' from casual chat to recorded interview occurred. This is one of the many actions that I considered to be ethical conduct but which I had not thought of before I went into the field. It is also a good example to demonstrate how the actual practices of ethical conduct could vary. Although I introduced the recording device in all the interviews, it did not always happen in the same way. My wording was slightly different in each interview. Thus, of course, my participants' responses also varied. This is one of many trails in the recorded data demonstrating that I developed different communication styles to practise research ethics. The interactive differences emerged to suit the situational conditions of each interview and the relationship I had with the participant. In other words, my practice of research ethics differed from one case to the next.

As I have indicated, by describing the interviewees as participants, my intention is to address their agency in this research; however, I have no intention of pretending that power relationships are not an issue in my fieldwork. As Letherby stresses, 'it is the researcher who has the ultimate control over the data collection and presentation' (2003: 125). I was aware of the power relationship in the field, and would not naively claim that I could just erase it by undertaking my research ethically and in a feminist way. The power relationship not only influences the practice of informed consent, but also plays an important role in the process of data collection. After all, 'how we identify ourselves and how we are identified by respondents affects not only relationships during the research process but also the data collected' (Letherby 2003: 123). The fact that the nature of my relationship with each participant was unique reminded me to approach each interview individually rather than to conduct them mechanically.

An obvious example would be my interview approach to a participant with whom I was acquainted. When I interviewed an acquaintance, I did not pretend that I knew nothing about her. That would have made the interview interaction odd and unnatural. However, I did deal carefully with the information that I had due to prior knowledge. I intended to draw a clear line around the limitations of data collection. I explained to my participants that only the material generated during the fieldwork would be used in later production. If a participant with whom I was already acquainted did not bring up certain information in the interview, I would not use it as research data even if I thought it was relevant. However, I did not avoid asking my participants questions based on prior knowledge, as long as they were willing to discuss it. I would remind each one that if the following question was too personal or if she was reluctant to answer for any other reason, then she could refuse. I would also stress the principle of anonymity. I would not disclose any information that I gathered in the interviews to anyone, including our common acquaintances.

In addition to the potentially privileged power of the researcher, I also acknowledge the possible disadvantages of my position in relation to my participants. Cotterill points out that the power relationship between a researcher and her participants is not an unchangeable condition, but may shift according to 'different interview situations' (1992: 593). In other words, a researcher may not always be in a privileged position in terms of power. For example, the hierarchical social order in Taiwan and the common everyday practice of using appellations to show respect to that social order is a social reality which I could not avoid when conducting the interviews. Although I would not use the word 'vulnerable' to describe my situation, it is undeniable that there were moments when I felt compelled to obey certain social norms in order to demonstrate my awareness of my own social status. This was most obvious in interviews with participants who were senior to me both in work experience and *beifen* [輩分], the social order of generation. I provide a further discussion of this in later chapters.

Another example of varying approaches to certain ethical conduct was the timing of acquiring the participant's signature on the consent form. In my original plan, I regarded it as an indispensable step to acquire the signature before conducting the interview. I believed that only 'unethical and evil' researchers would make the 'mistake' of not doing so. In that case, that term would have to be applied to me as well. I conducted one interview without first collecting the participant's signature. She did not refuse to sign but said she would prefer to do so later. There was an immediate cry of 'oh no' echoing in my head. For a few seconds before I replied, there were hundreds of thoughts crossing my mind. My first instinct was to convince her to sign before we began the interview, but then the situational information came forward. We were in a restaurant and she was having dinner. It was indeed probably not the best time to sign a document. I knew this participant well; if she said she would do it later, then she would do it later. In our prior interactions, I had provided basic information about this study and she had given me her verbal consent to join as a participant. What should I do if she ended up refusing to sign the form? Maybe I should just accept it, because it is definitely the participant's right to do so. It would be unethical to coerce her into being part of this research. Above all, informed consent is not just about having the signature on a document. The actual practice should involve more than this simple formality. After processing all this information as quickly as possible, I decided to put the consent form back into my folder and say 'okay'. In the end, this participant did sign the consent form after the interview was over. I am not sure if it was the perfect way to deal with the situation. This episode has remained a vivid memory from my fieldwork. It serves as a reminder that sticking to rigid formality does not necessarily qualify me as an ethical researcher.

Because I believe that informed consent involves more than just obtaining a signature on a consent form, I did not regard my participants' signatures as a free pass for me to use all the information they shared. During the interview, if I sensed that the participant was hesitant in any way about answering a question, I would emphasise that she could skip any disturbing questions. At the end of each interview, I would ask if any information required extra coding or exclusion. After I finished the written transcript of each interview, I would send it to the participant for verification. I welcomed any suggestions or recommendations, especially those concerning privacy and personal information. In any case, before including details shared in any form other than interviews, I would always ask for individual confirmation.

Although there was no absolute solution for every unexpected occurrence in the field, research ethics always served as a compass that helped me figure out my direction and complete the fieldwork. This was particularly the case during the recruitment process. At a late stage of my fieldwork, I realised that ethics had actually played a crucial role in the recruitment process. If I conducted an interview properly and ethically, the participant would be more comfortable about introducing new participants. Every interviewed participant had the potential to be the core of my recruitment snowball. Doing research ethically is the best strategy to recruit participants. The recruitment of acquainted participants illustrates this point. Several of my friends replied with an immediate 'yes' when I mentioned my fieldwork, even before I explained to them how the interview would be conducted. However, I did not take that immediate 'yes' as valid consent. I insisted that they read the information sheet first and then contact me later if they would still like to participate. At first, I thought that I had probably complicated things for myself, but it turned out that my participants gained a better understanding of how I would process my research work and how much I cared about their privacy and valued their consent. Practising ethics properly was therefore a way to show them how serious and sincere I was as a researcher. When I received the carbon copy of the lovely invitation by Chih-Lu, I then understood that my participants' interview experiences could have a crucial impact on snowballing recruitment.

Shit Happens

Pardon my vulgar language, but shitty things do happen during field research. My fieldwork was no exception and I have no intention of covering that up. It could be something small, such as a confusing meeting point which prevented my participant and me from finding each other. For example, I was supposed to meet a participant by a casual-wear chain store. I arrived earlier than scheduled, as I normally did. I do not recall who made the phone call, me or my participant, but we were on the phone with each other half an hour past the meeting time. She said she had arrived and I said I was at the meeting point too. But we just could not see each other. We then realised that there were at least two stores of the same brand in that area; we were waiting for each other in totally different places. My participant managed to find me and we ended up apologising to each other.

Certainly, the shitty thing could also be something serious. In one instance my recording device suddenly stopped working. The interview had been proceeding for more than an hour and I had no idea how much data was missing due to the incident. I seldom took notes during an interview because it would distract me from listening to the participant with full attention. This means that I was entirely dependent on the recorder to capture the interview data. The participant sensed my anxiety when I indicated that the device had malfunctioned. She was very understanding and sympathetic. We discussed possible measures to rectify the situation. She then agreed to arrange another meeting. On another occasion, I forgot that I had an appointment with a participant. I was already three hours late when I remembered. It felt like all the blood in my veins had frozen. I grabbed my phone and rang the participant to confess my mistake. This was during her working hours. When she answered the call, her tone was very 'business-like'. After I explained everything and apologised, there was an abrupt pause in our conversation. The participant did not say anything for a few seconds. The silent moment was killing me. It turned out to be a pause of astonishment, because she did not know what I was talking about. She replied nervously and apologetically that she had completely forgotten about it too. It was an overwhelming workday for her and her mind was completely occupied with details of a long meeting. Thanks to this unexpected and yet 'lucky' coincidence, we were both able to assuage our sense of guilt.

About one month after I returned from fieldwork, I had an opportunity to share my experiences at a workshop. One theme of my presentation was the aspect of the unexpected. Naturally, I was discussing the inconvenient truths about my fieldwork. After the session, a colleague approached me and expressed her appreciation of my honesty. She said that not many researchers would admit to the shitty part of their fieldwork, even though everyone knows that it does happen. I felt as though I had just shouted out a big 'you-know-what' kind of secret in public. Frankly, my intention had been to use those episodes of failure as comic relief in my presentation. I had not anticipated that it would earn me any praise. Although I am certainly not proud of those awkward and even disastrous incidents, my colleague's comments planted the thought that it might actually be worth discussing. If 'feminist research has a tradition of demanding that the unseen and the unacknowledged be made visible and heard', then revealing these shitty parts of my fieldwork is perhaps a reasonably feminist thing to do (Ryan-Flood and Gill 2010: 1).

Undertaking a study is indeed like going on a journey; the unexpected tends to stay in one's memory. Those first undesirable moments have functioned as clues to keep my days in the field vivid and colourful. They were helpful while I was writing this chapter and reviewing the research process. Each of them also marked a point at which I evolved and learnt from my own mistakes. The research field, after all, is not a universe that unfolds according to the researcher's will. No matter how thoroughly a researcher plans ahead, unforeseen events will always occur. Nevertheless, I am not promoting the abolition of fieldwork preparation. Rather, I argue that researchers should not avoid discussing the unexpected occurrences in fieldwork. Exactly because no one can anticipate every possible situation or walk into the research field with perfect contingency plans, sharing experiences of failure becomes meaningful. While we may have to work individually in the field, this does not necessarily mean that we have to struggle alone.

In addition, I argue that revealing 'the shitty part' of fieldwork is a practice that can help to approach reflexivity. Feminist methodology has valued reflexivity as a method of critical knowledge production. I am convinced that admitting and reflecting upon a piece of research's limits, advantages and shortcomings during fieldwork is part of exercising that reflexivity. It is therefore a critical method to challenge 'the research ideology of "hygienic research"' (Stanley and Wise 1993: 153).

SURVIVING DATA PREPARATION

Ting-Fang: Mm ... I will finish the transcript within three months.[8]

In the end, I could not keep this promise to the participant, Hsiang-Yun. I was overly ambitious and thought that transcribing would be a simple and easy task. (How naïve I was!) I knew it would take time but did not realise that it was such a delicate job, composed of manifold methodological decisions. In addition, I thought that transcribing would be the last step before I started to conduct data analysis. Preparation work was required in order to transform the audio data generated in the field into usable research data, and it turned out that transcribing was only part of that process. The actual preparation also included translation, romanisation and negotiation with my participants. The multilingual nature of the audio material and the international aspect of this study also posed difficult questions about data translation. Moreover, the practice of asking my participants for feedback on the transcripts increased the amount of labour required for data preparation. It was far more time-consuming, labour-intensive and challenging than I had anticipated.

Doing Transcription Is Not Just Listening and Typing

During the research design stage, I had decided to do the data transcribing myself. I made that decision for several reasons. Firstly, it would increase the sense of security and privacy that I could offer to my participants. I promised them that any sensitive or private information that they disclosed would only be accessed by me and would be omitted from the research data. I wanted to ensure that no third party could access the raw data in order to keep my participants anonymous. Therefore, I felt it was my responsibility to transcribe the recordings myself rather than hiring others to do it. Secondly, it would enable me to become more familiar with the data. Transcribing is a long process and, quite often, it requires the transcriber to listen to recorded clips several times in order to get it right. This back-and-forth process provides the opportunity to review the details of every interview. Thirdly, since I was the one conducting the fieldwork, I knew the background information about each interview, which could be essential for understanding the participant's account and transforming it into text. Moreover, I could add non-verbal information to the transcript. The data that is generated by an interview is not only about words but also includes emotions, facial expressions and other elements of communication. As the person who actually conducted the interview, I could provide details that a transcriber would not know.

When I started to draft this methodology chapter, I realised that doing the transcription myself had a significant influence on how I reviewed my research methods. It enabled me to be critical and reflexive about my practice of data preparation, including the realisation of how complicated the process of transcription is. By reviewing how I did the transcription, I became aware of the nuanced decisions I made during the whole process. Although interviewing is a widely adopted research method, transcription has not received the attention it deserves. As Lapadat and Lindsay (1999) point out, in most academic publications, the transcription process is generally described in a few words and is not deemed to require further explanation or exploration. In doing so, they argue, researchers assume and present transcription as a 'transparent' research process that does not require further theoretical or methodological examination (ibid.: 65). Having experienced it myself, I agree with them that transcription is not a 'transparent' practice at all, at least in my case. It is a fairly complicated decision-making process which requires theoretical and methodological engagement.

Not surprisingly, the first transcription I did was the most painful. Transcribing is demanding work, and it took me some time to muster the discipline it requires. I have never heard a researcher say that she/he enjoys transcribing. I will not lie: it is indeed a dreadful process. The excitement and satisfaction that I felt when reviewing the total length of the recorded interview dissipated the moment I started transcribing. And all the awkward pauses in the interviews, surprisingly, became precious little breaks that I cherished. The second point is that it was not until I started transcribing that I realised there are millions of things to think about and to decide in the case of data presentation. The first step is to decide what should be included in the transcript. At first, I had this idea that I should keep all the details of the recorded data and transform them into text, including, for instance, the background noises. I soon realised, however, that this would be an impossible task. No matter what kind of strategies I adopted in the end, I would inevitably lose some piece of fieldwork in the process of transcribing. Firstly, a recording itself is actually 'incomplete'. It only captures the audio record of an interview and this is always partial. One obvious fact is that the sensitivity of my recording device determined the limitations of the recorded data. Duranti (2006) suggests that a transcript should be viewed as an artefact and transcription as a cultural practice. He points out that, because the production of a transcript happens after the actual interview event, a researcher has to acknowledge the temporality of the transcript as well as of the interpretation and analysis of it. I became convinced by Duranti's argument during the process of transcribing.

Ochs was among the early pioneers in theorising transcription. Although her theoretical ideas on transcription were developed from the perspective of linguistic studies, they are also inspiring for non-linguistic research involving transcription. She argues that 'transcription is a selective process reflecting theoretical goals and definitions' (1979: 44). That is, transcription is not a mechanical step that transforms the recorded interview data into text. When we do transcribing, it is inevitable that we draw a line between the data we want to include and that which we want to exclude. For example, do we include the noise of the surrounding area in the transcript? Ochs also argues that 'a more useful transcript is a more selective one'. However, in my study, this was not necessarily the case. This is because of the theoretical standpoint that I have adopted. My research approach is influenced by the ethnomethodological perspective that mundane daily life is worth examining. From the planning stage onwards, I deliberately designed the interview to be as flexible as possible. That is, I was willing to include potential data that I had not anticipated. For this reason I chose to undertake semi-structured interviews. Thus, when I transcribed my participants' accounts I had not yet decided which parts should be included in the analysis. Therefore, I felt hesitant about producing a very selective transcript.

In their inspiring discussion on how transcription matters in qualitative research, Oliver et al. (2005) point out that failing to choose a suitable transcription style will prevent a researcher from accomplishing their research objectives and may even cause concerns about research ethics. They therefore 'advocate an intermediate step: a period of reflection that allows researchers to contemplate transcription choices and assess how these choices affect both participants and the goals of research' (Oliver et al. 2005: 1274). Unfortunately, I did not take this intermediate step at the time that Oliver et al. propose: before the stage of actually doing the transcribing. As a rookie in academic work, I have learnt most of my research skills during the process of actually doing my PhD research. Yes, I did have a research proposal and plan before I undertook the project. However, one of the most important things I have learnt in this study is that research is never a linear process. Or, even if it is, it never goes according to plan.

Oliver at el. propose that various transcription practices can be understood 'in terms of a continuum with two dominant modes': naturalism and denaturalism (2005: 1273). While a naturalised transcript keeps all the details of every utterance in the audio data, a denaturalised transcript removes personal features from the conversation. There are different theoretical considerations behind these methodological differences. A study that adopts a naturalist style of transcription tends to examine the actual spoken language. Therefore, all the features of real conversations matter. On the other hand, a denaturalised style is usually adopted for research that focuses on the information and meaning in the reported accounts.

The primary task of data preparation for research of this kind is to make it easier to read and make the meaning of the data more comprehensible. Therefore, behind the continuum of these two modes of transcription actually lies a continuum of methodological approaches to research data. Accompanying different research objectives, there are various transcription styles that fit into this methodological continuum.

My research is looking at women's experiences of gender at work in Taiwan. That is, the research questions that my study tries to answer are about what women's experiences are and how they make sense of these experiences. It would be fair to say that my research leans towards the mode of examining the information expressed in the speech. Although the questions that my research aims to answer are not about, for example, patterns in actual speech, I still find it useful to note the 'verbal and non-verbal signals that can change the tenor of conversations and meaning' (Oliver et al. 2005: 1276). For example, I did transcribe laughter, physical actions, stuttering and pauses.

Some features of the data are dismissed in the denaturalised process of translation, but they include meaningful information that could provide the reader with a more complete picture of the context of this research. Davidson (2009: 38) argues that 'all transcripts are selective in one way or another' for 'it is impossible to record all features of talk and interaction from recordings'. Rather than treating it as something trivial and not worth mentioning, it is critical and meaningful to acknowledge and explain this selectivity 'in relation to the goals of a study' (ibid.). Duranti also points out that 'the recognition of the inherently selective nature of recording first and transcribing later should alert us to the fact that the real must be approached, approximated, simulated, and even induced and seduced by means of multiple selective processes' (2006: 306). As a researcher, I acknowledge and value the 'imperfect' parts of the research process because that is the material that keeps me critical and reflexive about my methodology. Therefore, I am convinced by Duranti's argument and aware of the selectivity and manipulation inherent in data preparation.

I have included emotional signals and environmental information in the transcription. Emotional signals, such as laughter, are important clues to help me to interpret my participants' feelings about specific events. I believe these clues were helpful for my participants as well. In the data preparation process, I deliberately involved my participants. After I had finished each transcript, I sent it to the participant and asked for her approval. Although I did try my best to finish the transcripts as soon as possible, transcription takes time. The participant might receive the transcript six months or more after the interview. Therefore, environmental information is important in terms of helping each participant resituate herself in the interview and recall her own memories of the day. On the other hand, I did not include non-response tokens in the transcription, primarily because they did not influence the information being delivered and might also prevent a good understanding of the presented data.

Although my research topic does not address cross-cultural issues, they are certainly relevant to the production and presentation of this project. Most of all, certain cross-cultural issues emerged during the data preparation process that are not necessarily revealed within the data analysis. Rather than sweeping them under the carpet, I believe it is meaningful to discuss them. The issue of language differences is an obvious one. Due to both the academic convention of the institute where I was based and my intention to participate in the anglophone academic world, I aimed to publish this study in English. However, English is neither an official nor a common language in Taiwan. It would have been unreasonable to conduct the fieldwork in English. This, then, means that translation is necessary when it comes to data reporting. The final presentation of my data is assuredly 'not authentic' in terms of displaying it in the original words. My role as a researcher is actually three-fold: I am the interviewer, the transcriber and also the translator.

Deciding on Pseudonyms and Romanisation

I think the way you designed the pseudonym is very interesting. Instead of using alphabetical or numerical coding, you created names that are very different from the real names. It makes the reader feel that it is a real person but at the same time they can't identify who the participant is directly. Is that the reason why you chose to use names rather than codes as pseudonyms in your study? [...] I'm now conducting interviews for my own research. And I'm thinking about how blurry I should go for anonymity.[9]

Ya-Hsin provided these comments in her feedback on an early draft of the transcript. We then exchanged our ideas about pseudonyms and anonymity via email. As she pointed out, I indeed had my own strong ideas about what kind of pseudonyms should be created for my participants. However, it was after having the discussion with Ya-Hsin that I began to regard it as a significant methodological arrangement worthy of deliberation.

Trivial as it may seem, it actually took me some time to figure out the pseudonyms for this study. There were two essential issues. One was the design and the other was the format, particularly which romanisation system to use. In terms of the design, my primary concern was to ensure my participants' anonymity without sacrificing the personal nature of the data. I am convinced that naming has an influence on image projection. If I wanted to present my participants as individuals with characteristics of their own, I doubted that referring to them using numerical or alphabetic codes would be an effective method. Therefore, I decided to create pseudonyms which read and sound like 'real names'. The design was based on my impressions of the participant and her personal preferences. Choosing a proper pseudonym was one of the basic items in my discussion with participants regarding transcription revision. As Fig. 2.2 and Table 2.1 show, some participants have a second, more anglicised pseudonym. This is because some participants use English names in the workplace. It is part of the working culture in Taiwan, particularly in companies dealing with international business. I therefore created pseudonyms for those participants accordingly.

The original pseudonyms for my participants were in Traditional Chinese. Because this study is targeting anglophone readers, I had to decide on a romanisation system to transliterate the fictitious names. This was a tricky problem that I left unresolved until the last stage of my research. The main reason was the tangled socio-political background of romanisation in Taiwan.[10] In response to the 'chaotic situation' of transliteration in Mandarin romanisation, the Taiwanese government has been trying to designate a unified system since the 1990s.[11] However, the official policy of promoting a unified system of Mandarin romanisation has triggered heated debates. The controversy has been primarily centred around two romanisation systems, Tongyong Pinyin and Hanyu Pinyin. Hanyu Pinyin is the only legal and official romanisation system recognised by China and has been widely accepted as the phonetic scheme for teaching and learning Mandarin internationally.[12] It is often referred to as Pinyin. Tongyong Pinyin is a system designed by Taiwanese researchers at Academia Sinica. The main purpose of the project was to 'find the maximum transferability between the Hanyu Pinyin scheme and Taiwanese vernacular scheme' in considering the multilingual reality of Taiwan (Chiung 2001: 30).[13] These two systems attracted different supporters with different political ideologies in the policy debate. While the Taiwanese pro-independence party, the Democratic Progress Party

(DPP), supports the local system, Tongyong Pinyin, the pro-unification Nationalist Party or KMT campaigns for Hanyu Pinyin to 'avoid contribution to pro-Taiwanese Independence activities' (ibid.: 29). As a consequence, different governments have adopted different systems as the standard scheme. After winning the presidential election, the DPP government decided on Tongyong Pinyin as the official romanisation system in 2002. The policy then attracted serious protests and a boycott by KMT local officials; therefore, it was not fully effectuated. Then, in 2009, after the KMT came to lead the government, it abolished Tongyong Pinyin and designated Hanyu Pinyin as the standard scheme. This policy shift could not be immediately implemented, however, due to the lack of budget and the ongoing political debates. The policy on Mandarin romanisation remains a controversial issue in Taiwan and, in reality, there still is not a unified system.

Although Tongyong and Hanyu roman scripts are at the centre of the debate about Mandarin romanisation, when it comes to the transliteration of names, that is another matter. The conventional romanisation system for names in Taiwan has been the Wade–Giles system. This convention has survived the policy changes implemented by both the DPP and KMT cabinets. Generally speaking, a Taiwanese citizen acquires the official transliteration of her/his name when she/he applies for a passport issued by the Ministry of Foreign Affairs. Before the unified policy, the Wade–Giles system was generally used in the transliteration of official documents. Therefore, most citizens have their names transliterated based on the Wade–Giles system. According to the application guidelines issued by the Ministry of Foreign Affairs, the romanisation of the name of a passport holder should be consistent with the one on their previous passport. In addition, the transliteration of the surname should be identical to the one shared by other family members. The usage of the Wade–Giles system is therefore sustained by administrative regulations and practices.

All of these factors turned the decision on romanisation for this study into a tricky issue. Considering the linguistic, cultural and political implications, I chose to employ two systems for different purposes in my writing. In the case of pseudonyms, I have used the Wade–Giles system in order to recognise the convention and to keep my participants' pseudonyms consistent with other Taiwanese names, such as those of the referenced authors and my own. For other Mandarin words, I used Tongyong Pinyin as the transliteration scheme if no other transliteration was available. Mandarin is not a single, homogeneous language. There are many varieties used in different Chinese societies and communities. The Standard Mandarin used in Taiwan (Guoyu [國語]) has its own features, which need to be distinguished from those of the official language of China (Putonghua [普通話]). It is usually easy to distinguish between them in writing because the orthography in Taiwan is Traditional Chinese rather than Simplified Chinese. However, in the case of romanisation, the distinct linguistic features would be lost if I just used Hanyu Pinyin. While I acknowledge that Hanyu Pinyin is internationally accepted and popular, I have adopted a 'minority' Pinyin system that depicts local linguistic characteristics to indicate the heterogeneity of the Chinese language. Therefore, besides the implied political connotations, I argue that it is a reasonable solution to adopt Tongyong Pinyin for this study. I know this arrangement may cause problems for readers who have studied Mandarin and are comfortable with Hanyu Pinyin. However, it may serve as a way to treat the reader to a taste of the actual linguistic situation around romanisation in Taiwan: it is confusing and chaotic, and debates about it are ongoing.

Troubling Translation

Han-Ting: *Tai niao le* [太鳥了].[14] Ah, how to translate '*tai niao le*'?
Ting-Fang: No worries. I will figure that out later.[15]

Han-Ting was not the only participant who expressed concern about the issue of translation during the interview. While confidently reassuring my sympathetic participants that I could manage it, I was also aware that translation is a delicate task and that it plays a crucial role in producing critical data analysis.

As a researcher who often comes across and contests the knowledge frontiers and boundaries on the intellectual map, my mobility during this era of the internationalisation of higher education has required that I confront the challenge of disentangling the political, cultural and social implications emerging through language differences. Previous studies have indicated that the growing globalisation of academia has brought forward new questions and challenges for qualitative researchers, particularly concerning methodology and research methods (Vulliamy 2004; Hsiung 2012; Kim 2012; Park and Lunt 2015). Examining the development of qualitative research, Hsiung (2012) points out that the relationship between 'the peripheral' and 'the core' in the globalised setting of knowledge production has been changing and challenged. According to her observation, 'a collective professional identity' has emerged among the researchers who adopted a peripheral position to interrogate the dominance of 'the Anglo-American core' (ibid.: para. 3). She further calls for 'a globally-informed, locally-situated analytical framework' in order to develop a globalised qualitative research that challenges the persistent 'core–periphery divide' (ibid.: para. 4). Within this critical framework, the capacity to capture and transcend 'contextual nuance across disciplinary and/or geopolitical boundaries' and the ability to 'share knowledge and engage [*sic*] intellectual exchange across languages, discipline, and geopolitical regions' are identified as crucial (ibid.: para. 27). Reflecting on my own research experiences, I argue that the former is not necessarily a separate matter from the latter.

When it comes to academic writing, the issue of translation always haunts me. Before this study, most of the translation difficulties that I experienced were about finding proper Mandarin words to represent certain English concepts, for example sexuality. For my previous research, I employed this concept to analyse legal discourse in cases of sexual assault. The translation I used was *singyu tejhih* [性慾特質]. *Singyu* [性慾] means 'sexual desire' and *tejhih* means 'characteristic'. Therefore the literal meaning of the translation is actually 'characteristics of sexual desires'. I was not satisfied with it but I could not find a better translation. The translation failed to depict the concept with the implication of social structure. It made sexuality a personal thing that someone possesses. As Jackson et al. (2008) argue, the fact that the idea of sexuality is difficult to translate into any Asian language reveals its specific historical and cultural connotations. Therefore, the emerging 'problems' caused by translation may have a productive effect on research because there might be valuable nuances hidden in them.

The bilingual (or even multilingual) nature of this study has presented me with new translation challenges. As Kim indicates, with the growing mobility of both the researcher and the researched, 'we can no longer suppose the ethnically homogeneous circumstance that the researcher, the researched, and the audience are from the same ethnic background or live in the same country' (2012: 133). When I took my place as a member of this internationalised academic community, translation became an inevitable task with which I had to engage. This time, rather than finding Mandarin words to translate theoretical concepts from English, the primary task was to decide whether to translate or transliterate the research

data from Mandarin and Taiwanese vernaculars into English. My participants and I share similar socio-linguistic background and we spoke the
same language(s) during the interviews. There was no translation involved
during the fieldwork. However, due to the audience and the academic
requirements of my study, translation was conducted at a later stage of the
research process. Because my PhD research was undertaken at a British
academic institution, the thesis had to be written in British English, making translation a necessity in terms of data reporting. The final presentation of my data, then, is assuredly 'not authentic' in terms of displaying it
in the original words.

Like transcription, the discussion on translation issues in qualitative
research has, more often than not, been neglected. Through pondering
the translation dilemmas inherent in research on sign languages, Temple
and Young suggest that, when it comes to translation, 'there are methodological, epistemological and ontological consequences in choosing particular methods' (2004: 174). For example, the decisions on when and
how to translate may not only be a matter of available linguistic and fund-
ing resources but may also involve power and the researcher's position
(see also Venuti 1998; Kim 2012; Park and Lunt 2015). In the case of this
study, there are at least two issues involving translation that I would like to
bring forward. One is the timing of the translation; the other is what to
translate and what not to translate.

In order to retain the nuances of the data, I chose to transcribe the
interviews in their original spoken languages, which included Mandarin
and also Taiwanese vernaculars. I read and analysed the data in its original
languages first and then translated the quoted passages into English. If I
found a word or a concept difficult to translate, I chose to transliterate it
in order to keep the pronunciation of the original word in the translated
transcription and explain it later in my analysis. I have paid particular
attention to original accounts that cannot be translated without sacrificing
significant cultural implications. In other words, to translate or not to
translate is itself a methodological issue. Translating became a method of
reflection on cultural and social specificities. The distinct term *tongzhi*
[同志] is a good example. It is a term widely used in Taiwan to refer to
lesbian, gay, bisexual, transgender, queer (LGBTQ) communities and
appeared quite a few times in my data. Its literal meaning is 'comrade'.
The first part or character of the word comrade in Chinese means 'sameness', which is also the first character of the Chinese term for homosexuality. LGBTQ communities in Taiwan often quote a famous saying of Sun

Yat-Sen, the so-called founding father of the Republic of China in the Kuomintang's political mythology, who said 'the revolution is not yet successful, the comrades still need to strive for the future'. It suggests that even the founding father of the nation is on the side of LGBTQ communities. The term contains 'an ironic twist on communist and nationalist discourse' (Rahman and Jackson 2010: 195). If it is translated into English as gay or lesbian or queer, then the twist will be lost.

Cooperating and Negotiating with Participants

Yu-Tai: Hey, I'm reading the transcript. It's so interesting and funny. I just realised that I have such a good sense of humour. [...] I haven't finished reading it yet, but I can tell you already that it has brought me mixed feelings, particularly when I read the parts about my expectations and interpretations about work back then.[16]

The interview style that I adopted is formal but not serious. I wanted my participants to feel comfortable sharing information with me. However, this does not mean that I intended to lure them into saying things that they would later regret. I was aware of the possibility that a participant might be willing to share her experience with me but feel uncomfortable about having it published in an academic work. Therefore, as well as the standard procedure of informed consent, I have intentionally involved my participants in the process of data preparation. I offered to send each transcript to the participant and invite her to make suggestions for revision. This was not compulsory work that I assigned to my participants. A participant could refuse or ignore this offer. Therefore, not everyone wrote back to me, and in once case I lost contact with a participant after the interview. I tried to contact her more than once to ascertain whether she would like to change anything in the transcript but there was no response. However, I did receive feedback from the rest of the participants.

In my original design, I categorised the potential corrections into four types and set up a different strategy to deal with each of them. The first is the case of adding things. If a participant wanted to provide more information after the interview, I would add it to the transcript with a comment that it was added afterwards. The second is altering. If a participant told me one thing during the interview and then wanted to change it to something else, I would discuss it with her and try to discover the reason for this change. If it was due to privacy or other ethical concerns, I would respect my participant's decision. If that was not the case, I would tell her that my preference was to present both versions in the transcript. The third is correcting mistakes. I would check the recording and discuss it with the participant. If there was a mistake, then I would correct it. The last kind of correction is typography, and this I would just correct. Later in the process of negotiating with my participants, I realised that my original design did not necessarily fit in with my participants' needs. My planned strategies became general guidelines but the actual negotiation was undertaken on a case-by-case basis.

Throughout the negotiation process, I remained aware of how crucial it was to practise research ethics in the field, especially concerning the power relationship between researcher and participant. By performing the transcription myself, I generated opportunities to ponder more deeply the power of a researcher. My triple role as transcriber, translator and researcher in this study has made me extremely aware of the power relationship between the participants and me.

It was at this stage of my research that I made the decision not to include the focus group data. My primary concern was about gaining the consent of my participants for the transcripts. The interactions during a focus group session are more complicated than those in an interview. They involve multiple participants in one fieldwork encounter. The transcript of one focus group session would therefore require the approval of every single participant. While I was more than willing to respect my participants' suggestions and feedback, there could be potential conflicts between different participants' opinions on the same text. For instance, one participant might want to revise or elaborate on what she had shared. That revised update could make the subsequent exchanges seem out of context. Therefore, other participants would have to change their accounts or object to the revision. On the other hand, I did not feel comfortable about the idea of breaking the transcript into segments and discussing each part separately with the participants who had given specific accounts. This would also affect the contextualisation of the data. This is not to say that the focus group sessions were not useful or meaningful for this research. They provided further information about my participants' experiences and thoughts on gender and work; in addition, they deepened my reflections on research methods. Nevertheless, I have not resolved my own thoughts and concerns about data preparation. Those unfinished thoughts about focus groups have thus stayed with me and may contribute to other intellectual projects in the future.

Through the process of data preparation, reflexive dialogues developed between my participants and me as well as between me and myself. Rather than a research phase consisting of trivial chores, I consider data preparation to be a challenging process for a researcher and an opportunity to critically review her research assumptions and her epistemological stance on the status of the data. While pondering the practice of transcription led me to revisit the purpose of this study, the cooperation and negotiation work with my participants advanced my recognition of the interactive aspects of data generation. The data for this project is the result of the situated and interactive doing of my participants and me. I did not see research data as the objective possession of the participants. In my opinion, conducting fieldwork is nothing like mining. I do not view research data as deeply buried material that is waiting to be discovered by researchers, nor the participants as keepers of objective information. Research data in this study is regarded as an intellectual product generated during the research process, which involves the doing of and interactions between the participants and the researcher. With this idea in mind, I perceive my data as a historical and contextual product that can only offer subjective findings. I cannot, and also do not intend to, present my participants' accounts as universal truths about women's experiences. However, I do consider their narratives to be true in the sense of meaning making. I am convinced that my participants shared what they believed to be true in the given situation and, in addition, that they wanted me to perceive it as such.

ANALYSING THE UNEXPECTED

The fieldwork design, which encouraged participants to share accounts that diverged from my assumed hypothesis, did indeed produce data that was full of surprises. In listening to and interacting with my participants, I found that the assumptions hidden in my fieldwork plan were revealed and gradually stripped away. It seems that the only research question left standing was the most general one: What is women's experience of gender and work in Taiwan? As a result, I could not just screen and select data based on the original outline of the interview questions. A more flexible method was needed.

The idea of allowing the data to lead the way served as the first step in preparing myself to analyse the unexpected. Instead of sorting out the data according to the original research questions and interview schedule, I decided to read the transcripts with fresh eyes. It was as though I changed from a traveller who only looks for specific things during the journey to one who becomes spontaneous and then examines what has actually been seen, experienced and discovered on the road. I tried to free myself from the limitations of the designed plan. In other words, the development of the themes for analysis in this study was very much the result of my field-work and experience.

In terms of actual practice, conducting the analysis was a research phase that cannot be viewed as a separate process from my fieldwork. As I dis-cussed earlier, the fieldwork was basically an interactive and reflexive pro-cess. The structure and outline of each interview was different from all the others. New interview questions were constantly emerging as the field-work progressed. Consequently, my ideas for analysis were inevitably evolving the entire time. My thoughts and reflections on the fieldwork were the original material that I used to ponder the themes of the analysis. My fieldwork journal then served as a starting point for sorting out the considerable number of transcripts on my desk. The journal was organised by date. At the end of each day, I would take some time to record and reflect on my progress. The journal not only recorded the tasks I had accomplished in the research field but also my immediate impressions of every interview. Although the notes were not necessarily analytical, some-times just a quick entry that pointed out a particularly interesting experi-ence shared by the participant, they were handy reminders that enabled me to identify the accounts that had fascinated me the most in the research field. The journal then became a memo for developing initial ideas about potential themes.

As well as reviewing the fieldwork journal, the transcription notes were another useful source. When I transcribed, I kept notes to mark the parts of an interview that were obviously related to gender. In addition, I included short comments to record my initial ideas about the marked pas-sage. Through assessing and reorganising these notes, I started to identify potential themes for the analysis. I then selected the five interviews that contained the most notes as introductory cases. I developed a draft of emerging themes based on an analysis of these cases. After that, I read the rest of the transcripts closely in order to revise the themes I had drafted. This reading was not conducted in an orderly way. Sometimes I focused on just one and sometimes I did comparative reading. There were also occasions when I decided to reread a particular transcript. Reading and rereading transcripts was essential work in analysing the data. Not only are fieldwork and data analysis inseparable, but conducting data analysis is also mingled with the process of writing.

Although, from the description above, the practice of conducting analysis in this study may look linear and fairly direct, the actual process was rather tangled. The final version of the themes was completely different from the initial one. I was constantly revising the content and structure during the process of reading the data. In other words, almost all my assumptions about research findings were seriously challenged.

The final themes can be categorised into three groups. The first category includes themes relating to organisational management. Compared with the others, these themes were identified at an early stage of the data analysis. This was primarily because the situational information relating to organisational practices was easier to recognise in the data, such as the scenario of a job interview or meeting. The second category covers themes regarding general communications or social interactions in everyday practices. The analysis for this category developed gradually while I was reading the data. Although I did conceptualise gender as an essential and crucial part of everyday doing, it was not clear at first what specific social practices I should be investigating. Compared with the material fitting the first category, data that belongs to the second group was at first glance more nuanced and subtle. The third category mainly included themes that I felt to be uncategorisable but too interesting to let go. This is material that I did not anticipate my research would include. It only occurred to me at a later stage that the 'uncategorisability' of those themes was actually a potential similarity that I could use to develop my analysis. I then organised the data analysis into three parts accordingly. In the next chapter, I start by presenting the research findings and analysis of the themes fitting the first category.

Notes

1. This passage is quoted from the original research proposal of this study.
2. All the names of the participants are pseudonyms transliterated using the Wade–Giles system. The process of deciding which transliteration system to use will be explained in detail later in this chapter. This is a quote from the interview with participant Chih-Lu.

3. Standard Mandarin in Taiwan has a female pronoun for the second person singular. In Chih-Lu's original wording, she used this female pronoun to address the recipients.
4. Further discussion will be presented in later parts of this chapter.
5. The relationship status shown here is more about marital status. In the interviews, I only asked about my participants' marital status as one of the standard questions. I did not ask whether they had a current partner or were in a romantic relationship, although some of them did reveal this information during the interviews.
6. This is a quote from my interview with participant Hsi-Shu.
7. This is a quote from my interview with participant Lu-Fan.
8. This is a quote from the interview with participant Hsiang-Yun.
9. This quote is from the feedback from participant Ya-Hsin. Her feedback was sent via email. I have acquired her permission to include the quote as research data.
10. Taiwan is a multiethnic and multilingual society with a complicated history of colonisation and immigration. With this specific background, Mandarin romanisation is scarcely the only linguistic issue that has significant political implications in Taiwan. There are currently other heated debates over various linguistic issues, for instance, the national policy on language education, the standardisation of writing of other vernaculars such as Taiyu and Hakka, preserving the endangered aboriginal languages and restoring Austronesian names for indigenous Taiwanese (see Hsiao 1990; Hsiau 1997; Klöter 2004).
11. Generally speaking, most Taiwanese people are not familiar with Mandarin romanisation. Romanised schemes have not been included in the national education curriculum. Mandarin romanisation is not a commonly written script. Prior to the unified policy discussion, the Wade–Giles system, the Mandarin Phonetic Symbols II, Postal schemes, the English K.K. phonetic symbols were all available schemes and could be adopted as romanisation systems. These multiple schemes therefore resulted in a 'chaotic situation' (Chiung 2001: 27).
12. Han [漢] refers to 'the Han ethnicity'. Yu [語] means 'language'. Hanyu literally means the language of the Han ethnic group. Pinyin [拼音] means 'phonetic transcription'.
13. The literal meaning of Tongyong [通用] is 'in common use'.
14. This is an informal colloquial expression. It could be understood as 'it sucks' in English.
15. This conversation is quoted from my interview with participant Han-Ting.

16. This is a quote from the feedback I received from participant Yu-Tai. It was sent as a private message via a social networking platform. I have acquired permission from this participant to include it as research data.

REFERENCES

Abbott, P., Wallace, C., & Tyler, M. (2005). *An Introduction to Sociology: Feminist Perspectives* (3rd ed.). London: Routledge.

Ali, S. (2010). Slience and Secrets: Confidence in Research. In R. Ryan-Flood & R. Gill (Eds.), *Secrecy and Silence in the Research Process: Feminist Reflections* (pp. 245–256). Oxon: Routledge.

Chiung, W. V. T. (2001). Romanization and Language Planning in Taiwan. *The Linguistic Association of Korea Journal, 9*(1), 15–43.

Cotterill, P. (1992). Interviewing Women: Issues of Friendship, Vulnerability, and Power. *Women's Studies International Forum, 15*(5–6), 593–606.

Davidson, C. (2009). Transcription: Imperatives for Qualitative Research. *International Journal of Qualitative Methods, 8*(2), 35–52.

Duranti, A. (2006). Transcripts, Like Shadows on a Wall. *Mind, Culture, and Activity, 13*(4), 301–310.

Halse, C., & Honey, A. (2005). Unraveling Ethics: Illuminating the Moral Dilemmas of Research Ethics. *Signs, 30*(4), 2141–2162.

Hsiao, H. H. M. (1990). Emerging Social Movements and the Rise of a Demanding Civil Society in Taiwan. *The Australian Journal of Chinese Affairs, 24,* 163–180.

Hsiau, A. C. (1997). Language Ideology in Taiwan: The KMT's Language Policy, the Tai-yu Language Movement, and Ethnic Politics. *Journal of Multilingual and Multicultural Development, 18*(4), 302–315.

Hsiung, P. C. (2012). The Globalization of Qualitative Research: Challenging Anglo-American Domination and Local Hegemonic Discourse [27 paragraphs]. *Forum Qualitative Sozialforschung/Forum: Qualitative Social Research, 13*(1), Art. 21. http://nbn-resolving.de/urn:nbn:de:0114-fqs1201216

Jackson, S., Liu, J., & Woo, J. (2008). *East Asian Sexualities: Modernity, Gender and New Sexual Cultures.* London: Zed Books.

Kim, Y. (2012). Ethnographer Location and the Politics of Translation: Researching One's Own Group in a Host Country. *Qualitative Research, 12*(2), 131–146.

Klöter, H. (2004). Language Policy in the KMT and DPP Eras. *China Perspectives, 56,* 1–11.

Lapadat, J. C., & Lindsay, A. C. (1999). Transcription in Research and Practice: From Standardization of Technique to Interpretive Positionings. *Qualitative Inquiry, 5*(1), 64–86.

Letherby, G. (2003). *Feminist Research in Theory and Practice.* Maidenhead: Open University Press.

Liu, J. (2006). Researching Chinese Women's Lives: 'Insider' Research and Life History Interviewing. *Oral History, 34*(1), 43–52.

Mason, J. (2002). *Qualitative Researching.* Thousand Oaks, CA: Sage.

Oakley, A. (1981). Interviewing Women: A Contradiction in Terms. In H. Robers (Ed.), *Doing Feminist Research* (pp. 30–61). London: Routledge.

Ochs, E. (1979). Transcription as Theory. *Developmental Pragmatics, 10*(1), 43–72.

Oliver, D. G., Serovich, J. M., & Mason, T. L. (2005). Constraints and Opportunities with Interview Transcription: Towards Reflection in Qualitative Research. *Social Forces, 84*(2), 1273–1289.

Park, S., & Lunt, N. (2015). Confucianism and Qualitative Interviewing: Working Seoul to Soul. *Forum Qualitative Sozialforschung/Forum: Qualitative Social Research, 16*(2). Retrieved from http://www.qualitative-research.net/index.php/fqs/article/view/2166

Rahman, M., & Jackson, S. (2010). *Gender and Sexuality.* Cambridge: Polity.

Reinharz, S. (1979). *On Becoming a Social Scientist: From Survey Research and Participant Observation to Experiential Analysis.* San Francisco: Jossey-Bass Publishers.

Ryan-Flood, R., & Gill, R. (2010). Introduction. In R. Ryan-Flood & R. Gill (Eds.), *Secrecy and Silence in the Research Process: Feminist Reflections* (1st ed., pp. 1–12). London: Routledge.

Smith, D. E. (1987). *The Everyday World as Problematic: A Feminist Sociology.* Boston: Northeastern University Press.

Stanley, L., & Wise, S. (1993). *Breaking Out Again: Feminist Ontology and Epistemology.* London: Routledge.

Temple, B., & Young, A. (2004). Qualitative Research and Translation Dilemmas. *Qualitative Research, 4*(2), 161–178.

Venuti, L. (1998). *The Scandals of Translation: Towards an Ethics of Difference.* London: Routledge.

Vulliamy, G. (2004). The Impact of Globalisation on Qualitative Research in Comparative and International Education. *Compare: A Journal of Comparative and International Education, 34*(3), 261–284.

CHAPTER 3

Being Employed as a '*Nyusheng*': Gendered and Heteronormative Management in the Workplace

INTRODUCTION

In 2006 the Vice-President of the National Taiwan University of Science and Technology, Chen Chin-Lien, applied for the position of President of National Ilan University. She was the only woman on the shortlist. In the end, the position went to a male candidate. Chen later argued that the selection committee had shown gender bias against female candidates during the selection process. Chen brought the case to court. She won in the Taipei District Court but lost in the High Court. According to the plaintiff's arguments on the verdict, one of the selection panel members asked Chen, 'Where is your husband?' She replied that her husband works at the National Taiwan University and they live in Taipei. The committee then asked, 'If you get the job and come to Ilan, what will you do about your family then?' and even made a general comment about female applicants, saying 'female candidates are disadvantaged in fundraising'. In this case, the fact that Professor Chen is married was brought up in the interview as something of relevance to the selection. The underlying assumption is that a married woman naturally bears the responsibility for taking care of her family and that she should place it before her career. Then, Professor Chen's ability to fundraise was directly questioned. The committee cast doubt on her suitability as a candidate, based not on her past work experience or qualifications but entirely on her gender.

© The Author(s) 2018
T.-F. Chin, *Everyday Gender at Work in Taiwan*,
Gender, Sexualities and Culture in Asia,
https://doi.org/10.1007/978-981-10-7365-6_3

Later that year, Koo Kwang-Ming, a senior Democratic Progressive Party member and politician, expressed his opinions regarding the four DPP candidates running for president. When speaking of the only female candidate, Lu Hsiu-Lien (a.k.a. Annette Lu), who was Vice President at that time, Koo dismissed her by saying 'one can judge her capacity according to his own light but there is no place for a skirt-wearing person to be the Commander in Chief' (Yen and Wu 2006). Although he did not use any terms referring directly to women or females, the expression 'a skirt-wearing person' unambiguously implies a gendered connotation in Taiwan. Koo made it crystal clear that, in his opinion, Lu would not be a suitable leader of the army solely because she is a woman. While Professor Chen's ability to perform a certain task was questioned, Vice President Lu was cast as automatically disqualified for the position of highest political power.

Then we come to 2014. Ko Wen-Je, a doctor who previously worked for the National Taiwan Hospital, declared that he would run for Taipei City Mayor as an independent candidate. During a campaign event, Ko told the audience that he had not chosen to major in obstetrics and gynaecology because he did not want to make a living between women's legs (Tu and Kuo 2014). During yet another event he criticised a female candidate running for Chiayi City Mayor, saying that as a young and pretty woman, she would be suitable to work at a counter or to be a tourist ambassador but not to fill the shoes of a mayor (Yu 2014). Thus, Ko first described obstetrics as a dishonourable medical field for a man due to its connotations of sexual services for women, then judged a female politician's career based on her appearance. And then, in 2015, when Tsai Ing-Wen was running her presidential campaign, her single status was targeted by her male political opponents as a way of questioning and undermining her personality and professional abilities. Some claimed that Tsai would not understand the needs of people who have families. Others accused her of being a 'closet lesbian', and therefore not an honest politician (Hioe 2016).

These extremely inappropriate and sexist comments about women with highly professional careers all occurred after 2002, the year when the Gender Equality in Employment Act came into effect. They serve as vivid evidence that there is a huge gap between the legal regulations and reality. Despite being steady and active participants in the labour force, women still endure discriminatory and hostile encounters in which their skills, abilities and accomplishments are all discounted because of their gender.

In this chapter, I present an analysis of my participants' accounts which shows that sexism towards women with careers does not occur only in high-profile cases. Rather, it is part of the everyday reality for ordinary female employees in everyday workplaces. The focus of the discussion is on the practices of organisational management. While there is a substantial Western literature on gendered management practices, I draw mainly on empirical studies which focus on Taiwanese society to develop my argument. In addition, with the help of feminist theories on gender and heterosexuality, I argue that management practices at work are both gendered and heteronormative. Female employees tend to be categorised as a homogeneous group. They are assumed to be naturally marriage- and family-oriented. Women are expected to be confined within certain industries, holding certain positions and doing certain jobs because of their gender. Such practices result in gender segregation in employment.

GENDER SEGREGATION BETWEEN AND WITHIN INDUSTRIES

Taiwan has indeed come a long away on the issue of gender equality in the workplace. Things have changed and are still changing. We have been making tremendous progress. For example, according to the official report issued by the Ministry of Labour in 2014, since 2004 more women have entered so-called 'men's professions', such as in the information technology (IT) and engineering industries. At the same time, the number of female managers is also increasing. These trends are all evidence that the division of labour and the glass ceiling in the workplace have been challenged. However, it is too soon to say that every barrier of gender segregation at work has been completely torn down.

Compared with other East Asian economies, such as Japan and Korea, women in Taiwan have more consistent career trajectories. Most women retain their careers even after marrying or having children (see Yu 2009; Sechiyama 2013). Despite this significant characteristic in women's employment, previous studies also indicate that, along with neighbouring countries, Taiwan still has a long way to go in terms of gender equality at work (Brook 2006). One obvious fact is that women's high rate of labour participation does not guarantee that all industries and occupations in Taiwan have been generally friendly or supportive towards female employees. Some industries and organisations are still largely dominated by men. In such workplaces, male employees have enjoyed a privileged status, and not just because they are in the majority. As Faulkner suggests, 'the largest cultural group will tend to shape the workplace culture' (2009: 16). Male-dominated workplaces tend to create a work culture which treats male employees as the norm. In this section, I present my participants' experiences regarding gender segregation between and within industries. I also discuss how they make sense of those experiences and how their career orientation and work strategies have been influenced by them.

Choosing a 'Better' Industry

Yu-Hsuan is among those participants who used their own experiences to illustrate how being a woman has constrained their career opportunities. Yu-Hsuan is a public relations (PR) specialist with an academic background in radio and television production. Originally she was interested in pursuing a career in both production and public relations. However, after consulting with a male acquaintance with experience in a similar occupation, she became convinced that, compared with production, PR management would probably be a more women-friendly profession.

Yu-Hsuan: He told me that, in his opinion, it would be better for a *nyusheng* [女生][1] in Taiwan to choose a career path in PR. In other words, it would not be easy to go for production. And I think so, too. There were only few of the *nyusheng* in my class who went for a career relating to our academic background. And they are all ... I think it's quite difficult for them.

In our interview, Yu-Hsuan did not provide further details about whether the male acquaintance had explained why he thought it would be better for a woman to choose public relations over media production as her occupation. His assertive advice, however, clearly had an influence on Yu-Hsuan's career choice. For Yu-Hsuan, the advice actually reflects the reality revealed by her peers' employment experiences. Therefore, it would be difficult for her to challenge it as a stereotypical assertion. When observing the career development of her colleagues, she noticed that only very few of her female peers have successfully pursued a career path in media production. There is a salient gender disparity in the industry. The career obstacles for women are not just caused by the fact that female staff are outnumbered by male colleagues. Rather, it is more about the unfriendly work conventions that resist accepting female staff to join the team.

Yu-Hsuan later realised through the experiences of others that the radio and TV industry is indeed very unfriendly towards female employees. She told me a story about a friend who had shown talent and professional skills while they were still university students. According to Yu-Hsuan, this friend won a national documentary prize with her graduate production. With such an outstanding résumé, it was really a surprise to Yu-Hsuan that this friend still found it difficult to pursue a career in TV and film production.

Yu-Hsuan: She is the kind of person who will fight [for her rights]. She actually asked, 'Why don't you hire me? In what respect am I not good enough?' And they said, 'Uh, because you are a *nyusheng.*' Then she said, 'But I can carry heavy things and I can handle outdoor filming or anything. I can drive and I have a driver's licence. Is there anything that men can do and I can't?' But they would tell her that, 'Because all the members of our team are men. We don't know how to teach a *nyusheng* to do things.' When people say things like this, it's very difficult to argue. I know that when she finished the post-graduate programme and started job hunting she came across a lot of things like this. I thought it would be easy for her to get a job and a lot of people should have shown interest in working with her. But that was not the case.

In Yu-Hsuan's description, this female friend was a talented individual with an active and persevering personality. From Yu-Hsuan's point of view, this friend had tried her best to negotiate in job interviews that were full of sexist comments and assumptions. As a job applicant, she attempted to convince the male interviewers that she was a competent candidate with her professional skills and abilities. However, all they cared about was her gender.

The way in which Yu-Hsuan perceived her friend's struggle was that gender bias was the main factor preventing a talented and qualified female applicant from pursuing a career in TV and film production. Moreover, she suggested that this bias was justified and excused by the gendered work culture. The male interviewers stated that, because it is already a male-dominated industry, it would be difficult for a male-only team to hire a woman. It was as though they did not know how to interact with women professionally in the workplace. The existing and conventional male working style was used as a sufficient excuse to reject a female applicant. In other words, gender segregation is legitimised by this discourse of a gendered work culture. Moreover, women are categorised as distinctly different from men in the workplace. Gender prevails over all the other individual characteristics and qualities of an applicant. While a female applicant could argue articulately, with evidence of her ability and professional skills, as Yu-Hsuan's friend did, all her efforts seemed to be easily dismissed by the categorisation of gender. She is a woman, so naturally she would not fit into a workplace already occupied by men. It has nothing to do with professional abilities and skills. It is all determined by gender. This overt gender discrimination was identified by Yu-Hsuan as something that is difficult to fight against.

For Yu-Hsuan, the unfortunate interview experience of this female friend served to demonstrate that women are not welcome in the TV and film production industry. What intimidated Yu-Hsuan was not that she would have to work with a male team but the frankly discriminatory attitude and practices revealed at the very beginning of the recruitment process. The assumed and assured male-dominated work culture ensures that women will have disadvantaged prospects. Moreover, it seems that, to the recruitment interviewers, there is nothing wrong with this work culture. It is as though sustaining a workplace that is exclusively for male employees is unproblematic even when a competent female applicant shows interest in joining the team. While I do acknowledge that the majority group tends to hold the power to shape the culture in any workplace, I also think we should be critical of the assumed justification for this cultural institution. The existing gendered culture at work should not be accepted as a valid excuse for excluding female employees. Having men as the majority in the workplace is one thing; deliberately creating a working environment that is hostile to women is quite another. What makes a male-dominated industry hostile to women is not necessarily that there are more men there, but the fact that it has been shaped as a professional field for men only. Men are the norm and they have exercised the power to maintain that norm. The sexist ideology and practices that secure men as the privileged and preferred employees are more problematic. By adopting such practices, the industry is sustained as a domain that is hostile to women who want to enter.

Yu-Hsuan's narrative demonstrates how the workplace experiences of other social actors with whom a person is acquainted can influence an individual's reflexivity on gender at work, and therefore her career decisions. From the advice of her male acquaintance, to her observations of her colleagues' career development, to the rocky start of a female friend's career, everything played a part in Yu-Hsuan's consideration of which industry would be 'better'. For Yu-Hsuan, the key difference between the two industries was obviously the level of friendliness towards female employees. In tailoring her own understanding of women's situation and experiences of gender in the male-dominated workplace, Yu-Hsuan was doing gender while developing her own strategy for choosing a more promising career.

Working in a Male-Dominated Workplace

Other reports from my participants suggest that biased and sexist recruitment is not the only gendered management practice preventing women from fulfilling their career ambitions in male-dominated industries. Some of my participants had survived the recruitment process and were working in those industries. As women doing a 'man's job', they have experienced other 'long-lived structured practices that disadvantage women' (Cockburn 1991: 220).

IT is conventionally a male-dominated industry in Taiwan. It is an industry that perfectly represents both horizontal and vertical occupational segregation. Men are not only in the majority but also occupy most of the top positions (Cheng 2010). Having worked in this industry as a computer programmer for more than eight years, Yu-Chen has observed that working arrangements are often gendered.

Yu-Chen: The thing is that a *nyusheng* is usually assigned paperwork. [...] They would not say that it is because you are a *nyusheng* [so you should do it]. For instance, when I worked in my first company, I was the only *nyusheng* in that department and I was the one answering all the calls.

Previous research has indicated that, in the computing industry, administrative jobs are often assigned to women (Panteli et al. 2001). Administrative work is constructed as gendered labour. Women are assumed to be 'naturally' good at it. It seems that Yu-Chen's company had adopted this gendered work pattern in a nuanced way. Despite the fact that she was hired as a computer programmer, Yu-Chen was expected to deal with administrative tasks, such as answering all the incoming calls, while her male colleagues could focus on the tasks that related to their 'professional skills'. Those jobs were not assigned to her, but all of her male colleagues just assumed that she, as a female employee, should or would do them. In the case of incoming calls, they simply ignored them and continued their 'real and serious' work. By answering the office phone, Yu-Chen was actually doing work for all of her male colleagues. However, because of her gender, her labour was very unlikely to be recognised as a contribution to the team. As a female computer programmer, Yu-Chen was expected to cover extra work which was not identified as related to her professional skills. I argue that, compared with the male computer programmers in the organisation, her employment status was degraded and so was her labour contribution. From Yu-Chen's experience, we can see that female employees face gendered work arrangements even when they acquire the same job appointment as their male colleagues.

When it is anticipated that women will manage both their professional tasks and 'women's work', it is actually not surprising to hear that women have to work harder to prove themselves professionally in the male-dominated workplace.

Yu-Chen: So a *nyusheng* has to spend more time and make more effort to prove that you can do this job and be in this position.

Because of her phone-answering experience, Yu-Chen has had many opportunities to explore people's gendered assumptions about female employees in the IT industry. Although they know that she works in that industry, people appear to assume that, because she is a woman, Yu-Chen's job has nothing to do with specific IT skills. She told me that she constantly feels that the individuals she encounters in the workplace have general doubts about her programming skills or simply assume that she has none at all. She learnt this from the experience of answering calls for her department. On more than one occasion the caller insisted on talking to someone else in the department, even though Yu-Chen had stated clearly that she was a member of the computer engineering team.

Yu-Chen: I've answered some calls like, 'Hello? I want to speak to anyone in the engineering department.' I said, 'Yes. This is the engineering department.' 'May I speak to ...' Then I said, 'He's not in at the moment.' Didn't I just say that this is the engineering department?

Episodes such as this constitute unpleasant verbal encounters. Yu-Chen felt that her membership of the computer engineering team was denied in that telephone conversation. By asking to talk to someone else in the department, the individual who made the phone call implied that the woman who answered the phone could not respond to her or his professional enquiry. Yu-Chen was regarded as a receptionist whose role in the team had nothing to do with computer engineering. Examining the classification of the level of job skills in the UK, Phillips and Taylor argue that 'skill has become saturated with sex' (1980: 85). In other words, the worker's gender determines whether the job itself is skilled or not. It has nothing to do with the actual content of the work. In Yu-Chen's case, this 'men/skilled, women/unskilled' equation is utilised in another way (ibid.). For the caller, since Yu-Chen is a woman, she must be doing 'women's work', an unskilled job, in this male-dominated workplace. The misidentification of Yu-Chen as a receptionist did not occur as a result of her answering the phone, but because the caller recognised her as a woman.

Yu-Chen's account shows that gender segregation at work is practised not only among industries but also within industries. Moreover, it is institutionalised by gendered working arrangements. Women are expected to choose certain professions and to do certain work within an organisation. According to Yu-Chen's experience, if a woman breaks the barrier by being in a 'men's' industry and doing a 'man's' job, then it is very likely that her professional abilities and qualifications will be constantly suspected or ignored. The fact that there are women working in the IT industry does not seem to be a sufficient condition to dissolve the gender segregation.

Research on women's employment in the IT industry in Britain has revealed that gender segregation is 'being reinvented' rather than 'loosening' (Guerrier et al. 2009: 506). Guerrier et al. (2009) point out that women are mostly employed in positions with fewer technical requirements. By looking at gendered hybrid roles, Glover and Guerrier (2010: 91) find that 'men with "soft" skills may be located in the client-facing external hybrid roles, and women in the internal teamwork roles' in the IT industry. These studies reveal that the gendered construction of jobs is one of the cultural factors that result in limiting women's opportunities in this male-dominated industry. While Taiwan has a very different social context, this reinventing of gender segregation also seems to emerge in my participants' stories. They have revealed that gender segregation in the workplace is patrolled by gendered interpretations of jobs and daily interactions.

From another participant's work experience, it emerges that the constant denial of women's professional abilities through gendered working arrangements is not the only problematic practice hampering their careers in a male-dominated workplace. Pei-Ju is a mechanical engineer with 16 years of work experience. When I met her for an interview, she was working in the transportation industry. Pei-Ju told me that, from her early days as a university student, she had been aware that mechanical engineering is a 'men's profession' and, as a woman, she is the one who has to adapt to the situation. At her university, the main building of the department where she was studying did not have any women's toilets. It was an environment where men were the norm. Years have passed; the scenario has changed from university to workplace. One thing that does not change is that men are still the norm. When Pei-Ju started to work as a professional mechanical engineer, she had to face the same issues all over again. She shared her thoughts regarding the recruitment of a woman to a male-dominated workplace. According to her observations, there is a generally negative attitude towards hiring female mechanical engineers. One of the reasons given is that to have a woman joining a male team is considered troublesome. I then asked Pei-Ju what the trouble is exactly.

Pei-Ju: They have to adjust a lot of things. Originally it's a purely men's ... for example, the way they dress. They all feel comfortable about it. And suddenly you come as an unwelcome guest, then everyone has to adjust for you. [...] Including, they might keep porn on the computers in the office. They want to watch it after work. You [a woman] got hired and they have to delete it out of respect for you. But we [women who work as mechanical engineers] always act like we're looking but not seeing. You've had to learn to act like this ever since the educational process.

Pei-Ju described herself as 'an unwelcome guest' stepping into an all-male field. The implied relationship between the guest and the host clearly indicates who is in the privileged position to set the rules of the domain and furthermore to form the culture of the workplace. In Pei-Ju's narrative, the already existing heterosexual masculine culture was a major challenge for her to overcome. The example provided by Pei-Ju portrays a workspace which is only friendly towards individuals who fit into the culture of heterosexual masculinity; therefore, it is easier for men to stay in that environment. It is a space in which men can do whatever they like because they are in the majority and because it has been like that for many years. The example of watching porn in the office shows that working culture actually covers more than matters relating to work. While Yu-Chen said that a woman has to make more effort to prove herself in a male-dominated workplace, Pei-Ju's experience reveals that this also includes making an effort to adapt, which might be invisible to her male colleagues. She has to act as though it is nothing, and not being offended by the masculine work culture is a way to prove that she can handle it and work with the team. Researching the work experiences of Taiwan's female seafarers, Guo and Liang (2012) argue that women who enter this masculine workplace might be able to 'reshape' it. I have no doubt that women who choose a so-called 'men's career' can contribute to breaking down gender segregation in the workplace. Nevertheless, I think it is important to acknowledge the personal struggles of women in the context of gendered power relationships and how women might also be 'reshaped', socialised or disciplined by the masculine work environment. When the organisation as a whole is not friendly to female employees, women are disadvantaged in the workplace. For those who have been breaking through the glass ceiling and the segregation barrier, it is not an easy thing just to be there, just working. To expect masculine practices in the workplace to be reshaped simply by enrolling women seems to burden an already marginalised and underprivileged minority. Gender equality at work is not merely about having diversity in the gender of staff. Diversity in culture also matters. Recruiting women will not automatically transform the workplace into an inclusive one.

When Women Are the Majority

Gender segregation exists not only in male-dominated industries but also in those industries in which the majority of employees are women. Ying-Hsuan, a marketing specialist working for a tourist agency, described her observations of gender disparity in different departments within her company.

Ying-Hsuan: In the case of the travel industry, women employees usually outnumber men but there are differences among different departments. [...] In the sales department, there are always more men than women. But in the ticketing department, I mean those relating to airline tickets, there are seldom any men.

In Taiwan, the business activity of sales is conventionally considered an 'outdoor' job because it involves business activities such as visiting clients or negotiating deals on social occasions. Influenced by the gendered dichotomy of outdoor/indoor labour, sales activity is thus interpreted as a job for men and a sales department is often male-dominated compared with other indoor desk jobs. This example illustrates that gender segregation at work is sustained through management practices which are underpinned by the ideology of gendered labour. When the assumed work culture supports this ideology, whether women are outnumbered by male colleagues or not, gender segregation will be sustained.

Social work is another profession in which women form the majority but still encounter gender segregation in work assignments. According to official statistics from the Ministry of Health and Welfare from 2014, more than 80 % of social work professionals are women.[2] Social work, along with professions such as nursing, is regularly perceived as an occupation for women, and indeed more women than men are drawn to it (see e.g. Evans 1997). It is a profession that welcomes women because they are considered to have the appropriate feminine qualities to accomplish the tasks. However, gendered work arrangements are still present. From my interview data, it appears that female and male social workers tend to be assigned different tasks even when they work in the same unit. Chi-Lun is a senior social worker. Social work has been her profession for five years. She told me about her work experience in an organisation providing labour welfare support and described how tasks are assigned to employees differently based on their gender.

Chi-Lun: *Nansheng* [男生][3] were usually assigned tasks that require more labour or involve complicated clients. In my previous unit, men were responsible for foreign workers. [...] Their jobs were more complicated. We [female employees] were taking care of standard services for the general public.

According to Chi-Lun, female social workers are assigned cases that are less challenging in terms of physical strength and professional skills. They are expected to deal with cases that can be managed by providing 'standard services' that can be applied to 'the general public'. On the other hand, her male colleagues are given opportunities to work on complicated cases which may require more time, energy and professional skills. There are at least two issues in this work arrangement. In the matter of physical strength, female employees are considered at a disadvantage compared with men by nature. This is no doubt a gender stereotype that reflects essentialism. Women and men are generalised as two distinct biological groups with undeniable differences in physical strength, without any evaluation of the specific requirements of the task or the abilities of each individual employee. The other issue is the gendered expectations of professional skills. It seems that female social workers are expected to provide routine services while their male colleagues are considered more capable of managing cases that may require advanced skills and the ability to deal with all possible contingencies. In addition, female social workers are advised to adopt different strategies from their male colleagues. This is manifested in Chi-Lun's account of the practice of home-visiting services.

Chi-Lun: I think, when a female social worker goes visiting, if, for example, the client is a violent offender, or from the reporting info sheet, it is known that he has problems such as substance abuse, if you as a woman wanted to do it alone, people would ask, 'do you need somebody to go with you? Do you need somebody, such as a volunteer, to keep you company?' or 'we can ask two social workers to do it together. Considering the safety issue.' Yep, this part, it looks as though, because I'm a woman and if my client is a specific case. It [my gender] would make a difference.

Ting-Fang: How about a male social worker? It's all right for him to visit on his own?

Chi-Lun: Yes.

Chi-Lun has noticed that only when the social worker is a woman is the issue of personal safety raised in her organisation. It is assumed that a female employee will need extra protection in a situation with the potential for exposure to violence. Therefore, female social workers are identified as employees who have special needs in undertaking their work routine. On the other hand, male social workers are just regular employees who are capable of managing their jobs on their own. Thus, the male is perceived as the norm. In addition, in Chi-Lun's organisation, this extra protection would be provided in an informal way. It is not a safety issue being managed through institutional protocol. Considering the occupational hazards of social work, a more reasonable solution to this issue would be to set up a system that allows every social worker to draw upon the personnel or related professional support they need. I have no doubt that gender is an issue when it comes to violent crimes, but it would be an oversimplification to assume that female social workers need extra protection while their male counterparts do not require it at all. By failing to recognise personal safety as an occupational issue which needs to be addressed and managed through institutional practices, Chi-Lun's organisation is actually constructing a gendered work pattern through the dereliction of its duty in work management.

Through an examination of the accounts of my participants, I have discussed gender segregation at work in Taiwan. Gender segregation has occurred both horizontally and vertically in terms of industry structure. Gendered management has prevented women from developing careers in certain industries as well as in certain occupations within a specific industry. Moreover, differential gendered treatments are implemented even among those who work in the same department or have acquired the same level of seniority. These management practices sustain gender segregation at work and situate women in a disadvantaged position compared with male applicants and employees. I want to emphasise that gendered management is not only manifest in male-dominated workplaces but also in those where female employees form the majority. My participants' accounts also reveal that gender segregation at work is legitimised by the ideology of gender. It has structured the dichotomy of gendered social and organisational roles. I investigate this issue further in the next section.

HOUSEWIFE AND BREADWINNER AT WORK

'*Nan jhu wai, nyu jhu nei* [男主外、女主內]' is an old-fashioned Mandarin saying in Taiwan. It means that men should take care of the outdoor business while women should take care of the indoor. The boundary that distinguishes the indoor from the outdoor is usually identified as the household. While the indoor space seems to be defined within precise limits, the outdoor can encompass various social fields. This saying is conventionally interpreted to mean that women should be housewives and stay at home while men should be breadwinners who pursue their careers in various professions. What underpins this interpretation is the norm of a gendered division of labour that builds on the base of the heterosexual family. It presupposes a social order sustained by gendered labour arrangements and segregated social domains. Of course, this is just one explanation of the saying. It could be argued that an alternative interpretation of the literal meaning of the saying is possible. That is, women are regarded as the authority figures in the domestic area and once men step into the household, they are in territory that is managed by women. While this is a possible interpretation, it is also one that neglects social, cultural and material reality. In a capitalist society such as Taiwan, those who have the opportunity to pursue careers will be more likely to have an advantaged social and economic status than those who do not. The status gap would therefore very likely create an unequal power relationship and result in the housewife being in a disadvantaged situation. In addition, it would be naïve to examine the meaning of the saying without putting it in a gendered context. 'Housewife' is a gendered identity. The constructed social meaning of this identity cannot be fully examined without acknowledging its gendered counterpart, the 'breadwinning' husband. Therefore, I suppose it would be fair to say that in a capitalist society that embraces heterosexual relationships as the norm, this saying actually promotes the idea of a gendered division of labour that is sustained by 'the continuing interaction of two interlocking systems, capitalism and patriarchy' (Hartmann 1976: 139).

It should be highlighted that, despite often being labelled a 'traditional' gendered identity, 'housewife' is actually a modern creation. Mies (1998) develops the concept of 'housewifization' to describe the gendered division of labour that arose in response to the demand for labour of the capitalist economy. A housewife is therefore a specific gendered labour provider in the modern economy. Ochiai further identifies 'housewifization' as a significant factor in the process of modernisation in the West and in Japan (2008: 3). Ochiai argues that 'modernization led to the gender division of labour between the "breadwinning" husband who labored in the public sphere and the housewife who specialized in housekeeping and childrearing in the domestic sphere' (ibid.: 4). When a society transforms its economy to the post-modern and post-industrial stage, the shift in the demand for labour results in 'de-housewifization'. As Ochiai proposes, 'economic development first "housewives" women, then "de-housewives" them' (ibid.: 5). As I have discussed in Chap. 1, different societies follow different patterns of modernisation and economic development that do not necessarily fit the 'Western' model. Research also indicates that in Taiwan, as in many other contemporary Asian societies, there is no real evidence to show that housewifisation has occurred (Ochiai et al. 2008).

Although, in reality, being a full-time housewife is not a popular choice for women, there are social practices which normalise the ideology of a gendered division of labour. The saying, *nan jhu wai, nyu jhu nei*, is just one example. According to my participants, some management practices repeat and reinforce this ideology in the workplace as well. In this section, I utilise interview data to demonstrate how female employees are perceived as housewives or housewives-to-be by their employers and colleagues.

The Invisible Female Breadwinner

Gender segregation at work takes several different forms. It could be barriers between industries. Or it could be differential job arrangements within a certain industry. It could also be a gendered hierarchy within an organisation. Data gathered in 2005 indicates that only 16.58 % of managers were women in Taiwan, and they earned almost 16 % less than male managers (Chou et al. 2009). Improvements have been made since then, but power in the workplace is generally still held by men. According to an official report from the Ministry of Labour (2015), in 2014, 25.38 % of managers were women. As for the average hourly wage, women earned 15 % less than men. I would argue that this unequal distribution of promotion opportunities is related to the ideology of gender. Although women are active in the workplace, men are still identified as the breadwinners for their families. Tzu-Ling, a senior legal specialist who has a managerial position in the company where she works, shared her observations with me.

Tzu-Ling: In my department, all the staff are women. If we compare the manager with one who works in a department that has both men and women, and take a look at the salary, it would be like this, very obvious [using body language to indicate that the manager who supervises men receives higher pay] [...] But the reason is that men have to feed their family. This is what has been considered by those in higher positions. Men have to be the breadwinners. [...] So whenever we have a salary adjustment, they will take that into consideration.

Tzu-Ling's account indicates gender bias in the salary structure. In her firm, although women are promoted to higher positions just as men are, this does not bring them an equal opportunity to earn as much as men. On the ladder of promotion, women may seem to have shattered the glass ceiling and stepped up to acquire higher positions in the organisation. However, when it comes to their salaries, they are allocated on a different track from their male counterparts. They are paid less. This shows that their professional skills and managerial abilities are devalued and not properly appreciated. Tzu-Ling's observation also indicates that the gender bias in payment is justified by the ideology of gendered roles in a heterosexual relationship. Male employees are identified as breadwinners while women are not. Considering that women's labour market participation is not uncommon in Taiwan, the assumption that men are the breadwinners who provide financial stability for their families is obviously a myth. Take Tzu-Ling, for example; she is married with children and has proved her ability in the workplace. There is no obvious reason to deny her role as a financial supporter of her family. However, she is not regarded as a breadwinner by her employer. In the case of Tzu-Ling, we can see that the ideology of gendered social roles has effects that are revealed in the workplace. Married female employees are assumed to be dependent on their husbands, who are seen as the breadwinners for their families. Therefore, a woman's income is considered to be a 'secondary income' (Cockburn 1991: 23). In this way, the ideology of the gendered division of labour has shadowed individual female employees from the domestic domain into the public sphere. While the stereotype of gender roles has its roots in cultural norms, it does indeed have a material effect, resulting in female employees' unequal status in the workplace.

Marital Status as an Issue

The assumption that women should take certain social roles not only determines the salary they can earn at work but also the jobs for which they can apply. Hsi-Shu shared an unpleasant job interview experience with me. Hsi-Shu is in her mid-thirties and already has nine years of work experience in marketing. She started sharing her observations on gender inequality at work by talking about the personal information check during the recruitment process.

Hsi-Shu: First, the unfairness for women in the workplace. I think, in other countries, you can choose not to disclose your marital status and even your age on the CV. But in Taiwan, these are required information. Examining the marital status and age of the applicant is an essential part of the recruitment evaluation. I think, at some level, they [interviewers] start the selection process in the recruitment interview. They will identify what kind of person suits the specific job. For example, if a married woman applies for a job which requires the applicant to go on business trips in the future, she will not be considered suitable.

The practice of a job applicant informing a potential employer of her or his marital status is regarded as common sense. Since it is assessed as essential information, it is assumed to have a certain value in candidate selection. Hsi-Shu noted that a married woman would not be viewed as a competent candidate for a position which includes business trips in the job description. That is to say, the marital status of a female applicant would determine what kind of job she could obtain. Hsi-Shu is not the only participant who feels that her personal information, such as marital status, is a target of scrutiny in the recruitment interview. Han-Ting, who works as an administrator at a university, told me about one of her most unforgettable interview experiences. She was stunned by the interviewer's questions regarding her personal relationships.

Han-Ting: She/he then asked 'do you ... do you have a boyfriend?' I said 'no'. She/he then continued by asking 'what if you have a boyfriend and he has a job in Taipei, will you follow him and return to Taipei? And what if after you get married, he works in Taipei. Will you follow him? Will you still stay here?' But I think, how should I answer that? Because I had no boyfriend and no husband at that moment, how would I know that? If I do have, so what? How can I anticipate what will happen in the future?[4]

As a job applicant, these interview questions confused Han-Ting. She did not know how to answer them. Firstly, they are questions about her personal life. She could not understand why the interviewer would assume there to be a connection between her personal life and her competence for the job. Secondly, they are hypothetical questions. Although she was reluctant to do so, Han-Ting did inform the interviewer that she was single. However, that did not stop the interviewer from prying into her personal choices regarding her role in a relationship. For Han-Ting, it seemed nonsensical to ask such questions. She was single at that moment, and she might or might not be in the future. Her decisions in the future should not be used to judge her work ability at the recruitment stage. Thirdly, they are questions with stereotypical gender implications. It is probably not surprising to find that the questions refer to heterosexual relationships only. The interviewer even implied a concern that a female employee would leave her job in order to 'follow' her male partner. This personal information about relationships and marital status seems to be used to categorise what kind of employee this applicant would be, or, to put it more specifically, what kind of female employee she would be. Women are not only categorised by their gender but they are also sub-categorised as suitable or unsuitable women, and the underlying presumption is made based on the status of their heterosexual relationships.

In Han-Ting's case, we can see how a single female employee's personal life choices are of concern for an interview panel; Hsi-Shu's experience, on the other hand, describes the experience of a married female applicant. Hsi-Shu used her interview experience to illustrate how a woman's marital status will influence her employment opportunities.

Hsi-Shu: If you're married then they'll ask 'in three years, will you …' 'Do you have kids? Do you plan to have children in three years?' Do you know what this means? This means that [they are thinking] how much it would cost to hire you. A married person, an unmarried person … if you're unmarried, they'll ask 'do you have a boyfriend?' It's the same. You might apply for [marital, parental] leave and you might have children.

Hsi-Shu's account suggests that when a female applicant comes in front of the recruitment interviewers, she is examined and evaluated as a negative asset. The possibility that a woman may marry and have children are viewed as potential personnel costs to the company. Moreover, there is an assumed pattern or script about the career development of a female employee. This script follows the norms of heterosexuality: she will eventually be in a relationship with a man and then marry him to create a family with children. The interview panel might appear to be concerned about her career plans but actually it is all about her family plans. And somehow all of this is regarded as relevant information when making recruitment evaluations. Hsi-Shu interprets this investigation of personal lives at the recruitment stage as unequal treatment of female employees. This interpretation was reinforced by her personal experience of job applications. She was once rejected precisely because she was a married woman.

Hsi-Shu: Then, about the job that requires going on business trips, they would ask ... they wouldn't ask if you're willing or not. They would say 'but this job may not be suitable for you. It's because we would probably move the office to ...' blah blah blah. 'Your ability is good but ...' I was once rejected that way because the interviewer thought the job required going on business trips or being allocated to an office abroad. 'You have a family so how could you go?' What do you mean by how? Just go by myself. By walking, by taking a flight, by whatever it takes.

As these generalised ideas about women's role in the family prevail, an individual woman's inclinations and career ambitions are dismissed. Through the feedback she received from the members of the interview panel, Hsi-Shu sensed that she was not considered the right candidate for the job. While praising her ability, they revealed their doubts about her suitability because she was a married woman and hence had to 'stay' to take care of her family. I could sense Hsi-Shu's annoyance in her description of the exchange. She was not particularly impressed with the assumptions behind the question expressing concerns about her being away from her 'family'. As a married woman, she was expected to stay with 'her family' and therefore would not fit the job. It is assumed that married female employees are highly family-oriented. Moreover, the concept of family is here linked with marriage. That is, marrying is regarded as the only way to establish a family. In other words, unmarried women are not considered to be people with families.

I could not help but compare Han-Ting's and Hsi-Shu's accounts with an old-fashioned Mandarin proverb on marriage advice for women. The literal translation may sound a bit bizarre. It says that if you marry a dog, then just follow the dog's way. My interpretation of the meaning of this proverb is two-fold. Firstly, it suggests that a woman should be content with the man she has married and hence must endure all the difficulties he creates in the marriage. Secondly, it conveys the supposed power hierarchy between a husband and his wife. A husband's role in the family is to lead, and the wife's is to follow. This proverb is seldom heard nowadays and the referenced advice would be considered out of date if not discriminatory, especially by younger generations. Nevertheless, I could still perceive the residue of the cultural foundations that support the proposed ideology of this proverb in both Han-Ting's and Hsi-Shu's unpleasant interview experiences. Women are supposed to follow their male partners even if it means sacrificing their careers. When a recruitment panel asks a female applicant questions such as 'will you follow your boyfriend?' or 'how could a married woman go on a business trip?', the panellists are adopting cultural assumptions about gendered social roles and making biased and gendered management decisions accordingly.

Besides the cultural implications, these inappropriate interview questions also demonstrate the failure of the implementation of legal regulations on equal access to employment in Taiwan. In other countries, such as the UK, which have established specific guidelines to enforce the Equality Act in the workplace, the uncomfortable and unnerving questions reported by my participants would be considered illegal and would never be asked in a job interview. However, it is clear that in Taiwan, legal regulations concerning gender equality at work have not yet been transformed into specific guidelines for actual organisational practices. Article Seven of the Gender Equality in Employment Act 2002 clearly states that 'employers shall not discriminate against applicants or employees because of their gender or sexual orientation in the course of recruitment, screening test, hiring, placement, assignment, evaluation and promotion'.[5] When my participants were asked about their marital status, personal relationships and future 'family' plans, the interviewers were projecting their gendered assumptions about women. In other words, they saw gender in female candidates and would deliver recruitment decisions based on those biased assumptions.

The Abnormal Single and the Stable Married

By examining my participants' personal experiences of job interviews, I have shown that, when a woman presents herself as a job applicant, her suitability for a specific job is judged according to cultural norms about gendered family roles. There are also accounts further suggesting that those cultural norms will be adopted as criteria to evaluate a female applicant's characteristics. Hsi-Shu once overheard an interview panel's discussion about a job applicant. She noticed their unfriendly attitude and negative comments about the applicant because she was single.

Hsi-Shu: The interviewee probably knows nothing about it, because we won't discuss it in front of her. I might be the one who is much closer to the supervisor, so I can hear his/her true opinions. For example, my supervisor would say, 'but I think she's a bit weird'. [...] She/he would say, 'she's already 37 or 38 years old and still single. It seems no good' ... blah blah blah ... all sorts of things. [...] How many employers think that way? I say almost 80 %. When they see a woman at the proper age for marriage, 30-something, they will judge her normality by her marital status and relationship status. Thinking about where she should be in terms of job position and not thinking about her ability.

In Hsi-Shu's opinion, her supervisor was using the fact that the applicant was single to form a negative opinion about her personality. This implies that the idea that women are 'naturally' family-oriented is the baseline for assessing a woman's normality. Because it is her nature, a woman will marry a man at the so-called 'proper' age. Any woman who strays from that life design is a reasonable target for stigmatising labels.

It seems that women in the workplace face a dilemma. If they are married or family-oriented, they are regarded as a negative asset. If they are not, they are labelled as abnormal, not 'normal' women. Either way, such perceptions could have a negative impact on a woman's career opportunities. This binary interpretation is a trap that constrains women from pursuing careers in the public domain. A woman's marital and relationship status is treated as something essentially negative in terms of an organisation's management. In this way, the institution of gendered social roles is sustained, or even reinforced, by management practices.

On the other hand, married men are regarded as reliable employees who can offer stable labour for the organisation. This is shown in Hsi-Shu's account of the gendered perceptions of married women and men in the workplace. Hsi-Shu feels that, in her organisation, the married status of a female employee is evaluated differently from that of a male employee in terms of human resource management.

Hsi-Shu: I think a married man at work will be evaluated as a stable employee, a trustworthy employee who has specific goals. He will be regarded as emotionally stable and someone who will not quit his job easily. A married woman only gets the last bit.

Hsi-Shu identifies three positive comments a married man might receive in relation to his job performance. The first concerns his career ambitions. The second is about emotional stability. The third is related to employment retention.

Although a woman cannot be denied the right to have a job in Taiwan, published equal rights in legal documents do not necessarily bring equal support or equal treatment within organisations. According to Hsi-Shu's observation, this seems particularly obvious when it comes to the issue of employees' marital status. At the level, female employees are perceived as less valuable than male employees. This presumption is entangled with the ideology of gendered labour arrangements in . It influences a woman's career from the very beginning of the recruitment process. However, men are treated differently. If a man gets married, he will be appreciated by his organisation as a useful asset. He will be thought of as a stable employee who will be likely to stay in his job longer. This unfair assessment of married female and male employees reveals assumptions about gendered responsibility for the family. A married man is assumed to be the main financial supporter of the family and therefore should be ambitious at work. On the other hand, a married woman is expected to place her husband's career ahead of her own. Even though she may also have a full-time job, her primary responsibility is supposed to be taking care of everything in the household in order to enable her husband to give his full attention to his career. Therefore, married men are identified as stable employees for two reasons. Firstly, they are regarded as being devoted to their jobs in order to earn a steady income for the family. Secondly, they have their wives to take care of household matters. These gendered assumptions are derived from the ideology of the division of labour.

By examining Hsi-Shu's accounts, I have shown that organisational management is dependent on the institutional establishment of marriage. Married employees are perceived not as individuals, but as half of a couple. As Jackson and Scott indicate, the feminist critique of monogamy 'was never concerned only with sexual exclusivity, but with the institutionalization of coupledom and the presumed "ownership" of another individual' (2004: 152). Marriage is therefore an institutionalisation of gendered relationships which excludes alternative options. The ideology of coupledom therefore serves as a foundation for the construction of marriage. A married couple are assumed to be exclusively available to each other in a variety of areas, such as sexuality, emotions and feelings, and sociality.

Hsi-Shu's account reveals how this 'coupledom and the presumed "ownership" of another individual' are manifested in economic activities (ibid.). Married employees are assumed to work as a couple in their daily life. Even when a married woman is present as an individual employee in the workplace, she still cannot rid herself of her membership of a heterosexual married couple.

However, it is not only women who are negatively judged in terms of this binary gender categorisation in the workplace. While women are perceived as 'naturally' family-oriented and marriage-oriented, men are expected to be career-oriented. Those men who have chosen so-called 'women's jobs' are also marginalised and identified as not sufficiently career-oriented; therefore, they are labelled as not masculine enough or are disqualified as breadwinners.

Han-Ting: [...] It's just paperwork. And men who worked in universities would be regarded as a little bit sissy. [...] an administrative job, for example, requires carefulness and being scrupulous about every detail. It's kind of a girl's job. A man doing it, it would be regarded as a bit weird.

In Han-Ting's narration, indoor administrative tasks are considered jobs for women and girls and convey a negative meaning. A man doing a job that is usually for women is one thing. A man doing a job that is degrading and supposed to be done by women is another. Jobs are not only gendered but also sorted into a hierarchical order. Women's jobs are less valued than men's. Yu-An provides another example about men who choose to work in a 'women's' industry.

Yu-An: If a man chooses social work as his career ... generally speaking, here's the thing. The earnings of a social worker aren't enough to support a whole family.

In Taiwan, social work is mostly dominated by women. As in other occupations labelled as women's professions, a social worker's salary is comparatively low. Therefore, if a man is a social worker, he will generally be judged as a disqualified breadwinner.

By examining the gender categorisation during recruitment processes, I have shown that the division of labour is not only arranged along the binary setting of private/public domains but also by the gendered arrangements of the workplace. In the eyes of recruitment personnel, female applicants are often categorised as distinct from men and are assigned jobs differently. Women are perceived as naturally marriage- and family-oriented; therefore, it is seen as better to assign them jobs that will not prevent them from 'enjoying family life'. This categorisation is not only gendered but also implies a heteronormative ideology. That is, the concept of 'family' that is utilised in management practices is usually a heterosexual one.

THE HETERONORMATIVE WORK–LIFE BALANCE

In this section, I continue the discussion on the heteronormative management of work by focusing on the organisational practices that are used to help employees achieve a work–life balance. I first introduce the long-hours culture in Taiwan in order to illustrate the 'imbalanced' context within which female employees are situated. I then present an analysis of organisational practices. I argue that organisational support is generally designed for married female employees only, if there is any. In other words, the conceptualisation of the 'life' in work–life balance is primarily about family life. Furthermore, it is specifically limited to the model of a married heterosexual family. Rather than being female-friendly, these practices are actually both constructing and reinforcing this heteronormative institution.

The Long-Hours Culture

In 2013, the Ministry of Labour revealed the results of a labour report on working hours. According to this report, the average number of hours worked annually per person in employment in Taiwan is 2140.8. In comparison with most Organisation for Co-operation and Development (OECD) countries, an employee in Taiwan works much longer hours. In the United Kingdom, for example, the average annual working time per person is 1654 hours, around three-quarters of the amount in Taiwan. More surprisingly, Taiwan's working hours also exceed those of most advanced developed economies in Asia, such as Japan. More information is shown in Table 3.1.

The statistics show that it is not uncommon to spend long hours in the workplace in Taiwan, but the reason for this is not made explicit. Research has been conducted on the issue of working hours, but mostly with a focus on legal issues (e.g. Hou 2013; Wang 2012; Cheng et al. 2011). The issue of work–life balance has drawn the attention of Western scholars

Table 3.1   The average annual working hours per person in six countries

Year	Taiwan	S. Korea	Japan	Singapore	Hong Kong	UK	USA
2002	2176.8	2464.0	1798.0	2392.0	2438.8	1684.0	1810.0
2003	2175.6	2424.0	1799.0	2392.0	2423.2	1674.0	1800.0
2004	2202.0	2392.0	1787.0	2407.6	2449.2	1674.0	1802.0
2005	2182.8	2351.0	1775.0	2418.0	2438.8	1673.0	1799.0
2006	2170.8	2346.0	1784.0	2402.4	2407.6	1669.0	1800.0
2007	2166.0	2306.0	1785.0	2407.6	2423.2	1677.0	1798.0
2008	2156.4	2246.0	1771.0	2407.6	2371.2	1659.0	1792.0
2009	2121.6	2232.0	1714.0	2392.0	2340.0	1651.0	1767.0
2010	2174.4	2187.0	1733.0	2402.4	2392.0	1652.0	1778.0
2011	2144.4	2090.0	1728.0	2402.4	–	1625.0	1787.0
2012	2140.8	–	1745.2	2402.4	–	1654.0	1789.9

(e.g. Smithson and Stokoe 2005; Crompton and Lyonette 2006; Watts 2009; Bacik and Drew 2006); however, in Taiwan it is a comparatively new and under-researched issue (Lu et al. 2006).

Due to this long-hours culture, it is not surprising to learn that working overtime is a common experience shared among many of my participants in different industries. Ying-Hsuan, for example, works in the travel industry and talked about working overtime as something that routinely happens in her annual work schedule.

Ying-Hsuan: If it's the busy season then I have to work overtime. For example, we have three travel fairs annually. And the one in October every year is the biggest. Then from two months prior to the fair, we get busier. During that period, I work overtime almost every day. When it gets closer to the fair, the hours are longer. Because there are just so many things to be done and we couldn't finish them [in normal hours].

Yu-Chen, an IT engineer, provides another example. She told me it had been common practice to work overtime in her previous job, and that that the exhaustion caused by working overtime drove her to leave the job.

Yu-Chen: The reason why I decided to quit is not because I felt that there was no chance for me to be promoted but because I felt so tired. I was exhausted and my health got worse because I had to work overtime a lot.

Ting-Fang: How many hours did you work a day back then?
Yu-Chen: From 9 a.m. to 4 a.m.. [...] I had worked like that for at
              least two years. So I spent a lot of time sleeping at weekends
              and during holidays. If I didn't work overtime on those
              days, I must have slept a lot. My boyfriend back then quar-
              relled with me for that. I needed sleep and he needed break-
              fast. He wanted us to breakfast together.

From Yu-Chen's experience, it is obvious that the overwhelming
demands of work were occupying most of her time and damaging her
health. In other words, at that time she did not come anywhere near to
attaining a work–life balance. Moreover, based on observing her colleagues' career trajectories, she thinks that women's attempts to have a job
and maintain a relationship have been hampered by routinely working
extra hours.

Yu-Chen: I think a lot of women quit their jobs for their boyfriends.
              [...] Because ... um ... like my first job, my company
              required employees to work overtime quite often. They got
              into fights with their boyfriends because of that. And then
              one came in tears and told me that her boyfriend had told
              her that he was going to break up with her, so she must quit.

Like Ying-Hsuan and Yu-Chen, Yu-Hsuan, a PR specialist, observed
that working late on weekdays and working extra hours at weekends is
quite common among PR professionals. She also pointed out that it pre-
vents women in this industry from having steady relationships.

Yu-Hsuan: [...] Most of the employees in my work field are women and
              most of them stay unmarried. And even get ... um also stay
              single, no boyfriends. Those who have boyfriends end up
              breaking up. It's difficult to keep a relationship [with a job
              like that].
Ting-Fang: Um, do you think it's because of the work?
Yu-Hsuan: I think work ... I think it's very difficult to keep a romantic
              relationship if you've got a busy job. [...] Because you ...
              we have to work extra hours at weekends for PR events. On
              a normal working day, to get off work before 8 p.m. would
              be considered early. In most cases, the usual time to leave
              work is between 8 p.m. and 9 or 10 p.m.

There is no doubt that working overtime is one of the major challenges for career women attempting to achieve a work–life balance, but the reasons for the overtime are not obvious. A quick and reasonable answer would be the excessive workload that they are taking on. However, my participants provided more information beyond that quick answer. According to their experience, there might be significant cultural factors contributing to this phenomenon of long working hours. For example, Yu-Chen reveals that the attitude of those in managerial roles plays a significant role in the amount of overtime their subordinates work.

Yu-Chen: Then the attitude of the boss is that, I pay you, therefore, I am your BOSS. You have to do exactly what I've told you. I told you to work overtime so you have to do overtime. [...] And also, his standard [of evaluating performance] is kind of weird. It's not about whether your performance is good or not. It's about whether you work overtime a lot. [...] It's a myth. I don't do overtime. Why not say that I'm much more efficient?

Working long hours seems to be a useful indicator for her boss to evaluate an employee's performance. It is more about the time an employee spends in the office than the results or outcomes. In these circumstances, an employee who wants to show that she/he is valuable and indispensable to the organisation has to get used to the practice of working overtime. If this is considered together with the hierarchical culture in the workplace, it is probably more about showing obedience to one's superior than loyalty to the organisation.[6]

When I talked with Ko-Chi, an administrator at a university, about her experience of unspoken rules in her workplace, she brought up the practice of being a team player by not leaving the office before her colleagues.

Ko-Chi: I am a more *renfen* kind of person.[7] So I will observe. I like watching people, paying attention to trivial things. When I was a rookie, I didn't think about it [as an unspoken rule]. I just feel, um, most of my colleagues are still working, so if I leave work first, even though I've finished my work, it still seems wrong to leave first. So I will actively ask [if my colleagues need a hand or not] and do my best to help [them do their job].

Yu-Chen's story reveals that working overtime is regarded by her boss as evidence of dedication and devotion to work. In her boss's mind, he is the one hiring people and paying their salaries; therefore, the staff must do what he wants. As for Ko-Chi, her rationale for working extra hours to help her colleagues illustrates that it is a way to demonstrate your caring and team spirit to your team. She puts herself in the role of a good team player. Both sense the organisational hierarchy and the power relationship within it.

I am not suggesting that this is a universal fact within every work organisation in Taiwan, but rather, I would like to use these as examples to illustrate that certain factors relating to Taiwanese work culture play an important role and contribute to the result of long working hours. By addressing the issue of working overtime, I intend to use it as an example to show how work influences women's lives and how a work–life balance has become an almost unattainable goal for any employee in Taiwan.

Gendered and Heteronormative Organisational Support

Because the idea that women are naturally family-oriented and marriage-oriented still lingers in the workplace, the work–life balance support offered by organisations is largely underpinned by ideas about wifehood and motherhood rather than an actual individual's needs. I-Chieh, who worked for an international company, described a lecture event organised by her company to support female employees.

I-Chieh: Ah, I remember there was this lecture event for women employees. One theme was work–life balance. [...] It's kind of like having coffee together and female colleagues would share their experiences of family life and work. [...] Then, I think most of them were talking about children. At that moment, I felt, um, it was kind of difficult to participate. [smile] People were talking about how to raise children and then ... I forget the details. It was about things related to raising children.

According to I-Chieh, the event was about work–life balance, but most of the active participants were married women with children. As an unmarried non-mother, she felt distant from the topics of conversation and found it difficult to participate.

Yu-Nung, an experienced marketing and fundraising specialist, shared the uneasiness she had felt at a book club session organised at her workplace. She was told that the topic would be gender and she went with the expectation of having a discussion about issues of gender and work. However, it turned into a session that triggered intense sharing of family problems among the married women. It was quite a shock to her, as a woman with no personal experience of having a husband or raising children.

Ting-Fang: So did you feel shocked that they were talking about personal stuff at a work meeting? Do you think ...

Yu-Nung: For me, it's not that you can't talk about it [any personal problem] but you do have to have a certain foundation and instructions. It should not be like you go into a [meeting] ... and then pop! [using body language to express the feeling of being exposed] It really feels like, you organise a ... come, now we have a meeting and then suddenly everybody ...

Ting-Fang: Being nude?

Yu-Nung: A nudist-camp style meeting. But you don't do that kind of thing on a daily basis.

I have no doubt that married career women with children are marginalised and face tremendous challenges and pressure when it comes to the issue of work–life balance. My intention in presenting I-Chieh's and Yu-Nung's thoughts on these events is to indicate that the life part of the work–life balance equation is usually limited to heterosexual married life. Furthermore, the support provided to married female employees is often offered not by institutional management but through other female colleagues' sacrifice. Ko-Chi's story about unequal workload arrangements and unfair performance evaluation by her supervisor is a suitable example to demonstrate this.

Ting-Fang: Couldn't you bring this issue up at a meeting?

Ko-Chi: Nobody dares.

Ting-Fang: Why not?

Ko-Chi: It would be like we ... we're fussing about trivial things. Because the chief is more ... biased? I don't know how to put this. I don't know how to describe it. She's [the supervisor] more tolerant towards her [a married colleague]. She thinks that because she has a family and children to take care of, so ... um, not so much work should be assigned to her. And when she sometimes does overtime, my supervisor would think, um, even the one who has a family to take care of is staying. It really shows her dedication. So sometimes we feel that it's kind of unfair. We feel like, so do we, unmarried or single people, have no family? It shouldn't be seen like that. And then, we've got a male colleague in our office. He thinks that we're fussing about trivial things and being childish. Why are we fussing about this kind of thing?

Ting-Fang: Is that so?

Ko-Chi: Yep, [he thinks that] she has family, or what you ...

Ting-Fang: Is it taken for granted?

Ko-Chi: Yes. He keeps wondering why are you [unmarried women] picking on her? He said, 'when you get pregnant and get married then you'll know'.

It seems to be an extremely tricky task for feminists to raise issues about non-mothers without running the potential risk of revealing tensions between mothers and non-mothers. Similarly, Ko-Chi found it very difficult to discuss a potential management problem involving the way in which her supervisor treats married female employees differently from the others. Ko-Chi, as an unmarried woman, was accused by her male colleague of picking on a married woman. However, what she was trying to do was to point out the unequal workload arrangements among her colleagues.

Ko-Chi: He would say, 'why are you fussing so much about it?' But there are some among us who have already married and had children. None of us like her [the married colleague]. We've got the same work attitude. What needs to be done needs to be done. We wouldn't become someone like her.

Ting-Fang: So she's not the only one who is married and has children, there are also ...

Ko-Chi: Yes, gradually ...

Ting-Fang: But their workload?

Ko-Chi: Never less.

Giddings (1998) argues that while all women are marginalised, mothers are marginalised even further. Reflecting on Giddings' argument, Ramsay and Letherby (2006) suggest a new framework for studying non-mothers at work in their research on non-mothers' work experience in higher education. They argue that the model of adopting the 'division between mothers and others' is insufficient (ibid.: 27). Rather than dividing women and comparing them with one another, they argue that 'both mothers and non-mothers were affected by the dominant discourse and the ideology of motherhood that pervades our society' (ibid.: 28).

I think my participants' experiences have shown another approach to conceptualising women's marginalisation in the workplace. The marginalised status of a woman is contextual. I argue that the acknowledgement of plural forms of marginalisation is crucial for understanding women's situations. A woman's marginalised status is not universally the same in different situations. In addition, it is difficult to quantify. That is, one woman's specific marginalisation in a given situation is difficult to compare with another's. A mother is not always more marginalised than a non-mother in the workplace or vice versa.

Previous studies have suggested that the informal working climates and flexible management style that emerged with the economic structure based on small and medium-sized businesses in Taiwan is one of the factors enabling married women to manage their double burden of home and workplace (Yu 2009). However, what remains unclear is how these informal practices are actually stipulated in the workplace. Ko-Chi's experience indicates that the informal support given to married female employees might actually be at the expense of single female employees, who are expected to provide free labour and put in more overtime.

While gender equality in the workplace is improving, it is important to be aware of women's different experiences and backgrounds. As in the case of work–life balance, a career woman's life is not only about family and family life is not only about marriage. There is more to it than that. The concept of family should be broadened, along with the concept of work–life balance. Chih-Lu, a participant who works in the banking industry, shared her thoughts and experiences as an unmarried woman in a team with a head who emphasises 'work–life' balance.

Chih-Lu: Then she said, 'and she has been married for five years'. And then I said, 'um, yes, I remember that. I was at her wedding banquet.' I don't know why she brought that up. But my supervisor, she really, really cared that she could offer a so-called 'work–life balance' environment. But her definition of life seems to be only about family, nuclear family, relating to family only.

Ting-Fang: And it's a heterosexual nuclear family.

Chih-Lu: Yep, yep, yep. Then, therefore, she keeps telling everybody that if you get married, don't worry, all of us will back you up. Don't worry about having a baby, because all of us will back you up. I think, probably for some women, this is a very friendly environment. But the problem is, for me, what if I don't want to marry and I don't want children, how would she back me up?

Ting-Fang: Does it also come to your mind, what if I'm single, will you back me up?

Chih-Lu: Or if I'm single, will you particularly not back me up? Because I have to back up others.

Chih-Lu is aware that, for her supervisor, there is probably only one version of life that a female employee is supposed to have: a heterosexual family life with a husband and children. In such circumstances, women who choose to live a life that involves something other than building a family with a husband are disadvantaged in the workplace by the unequal distribution of supportive resources. By emphasising the support system the company could offer, the supervisor was actually reinforcing a heteronormative structure with managerial measures.

These management practices may be cast as female-friendly or indeed performed with the intention of reducing the stress experienced by those who bear the double burden of both paid work and domestic work. However, the underlying heteronormative assumptions deliver alarming messages about reinforcing the heterosexual ideology of motherhood and differentiating women according to their marital status. In her study investigating men's responses to the equal opportunity strategies of organisations, Cockburn argues that the policies which support the so-called 'mothers' privileges' are actually confirming women 'as the domestic sex' (1991: 217).

WOMEN WHO GO BEYOND THE GLASS CEILING

In previous sections of this chapter, my intention has been to reveal that gendered and heteronormative management practices have resulted in the limitation of women's career development. Women are often expected to work in certain industries, professions and positions, and are indeed confined to them. Women are not welcome in industries that are generally male-dominated. They are identified as naturally family-oriented and are often assigned jobs that allow them to have more time to take care of their family duties. These jobs often attract lower earnings than those occupied by their male peers. When it comes to promotion, women are less well supported than men. However, there are career women who have broken through the glass ceiling and are trying to make a difference.

In this section, I discuss the experiences of women who have broken the glass ceiling. The discussion presented here is developed from examining two types of interview statements provided by my participants. The first includes accounts from participants who have attained managerial or senior managerial positions. In other words, it is first-hand information from women who have broken through the glass ceiling. The second includes interview statements by participants who have worked with female supervisors. While the former provide the direct experiences of female managers, the latter are useful to help us understand how female employees make sense of their female supervisors' experiences of gender in relation to management. I consider both to be valuable sources of data to help me understand the gender implications of management.

It has been suggested that for female employees who are positioned at the basic and lower levels of an organisation, female managers could be sources of inside information on the management team. Chih-Lu's female supervisor, for example, revealed details to her about the male managers' attitudes towards gender which were not revealed in their interactions with employees. At that time, Chih-Lu was working for an international IT company. It is an enterprise which claims to have a reputation for gender equality in management policies. Based on her personal experiences as an employee, Chih-Lu did feel that the organisation valued equal opportunities and respected women's rights and interests. She felt that when it came to gender issues at work, most male managers had been generally sensible. However, after being informed about interactions among the managers by her female supervisor, Chih-Lu saw the need to revisit her first impression.

Chih-Lu: She said that, in front of other staff or colleagues, they may seem very [serious and professional] ... However they would tell dirty jokes too. For example, at the kind of social events to which only senior managers are invited, they [male senior managers] would say things like: 'Should we have some "fun" tonight then? Maybe we can find some exotic dancers.' Then my supervisor would interrupt them by saying things like 'If that's the case, hunks for me then.' [...] She would use alternative strategies to [interrupt their conversations] ... And then they would say, 'We were just joking'. Something like that.

It seems that those male managers saw such exclusive occasions for the senior management team as an opportunity to behave without regard for the gender equality policies of the organisation. They would not tell 'dirty jokes' when they were working with other staff. However, they certainly felt it was okay to do so on occasions when only senior managers were present.

During the interview with Pei-Ju, a mechanical engineer, I mentioned a newspaper article referring to various problems caused by so-called 'feminine competition in the workplace' (Chiu 2011). The title of the article could be translated into English as 'Why women persecute women'. According to this article, one of the problems is that female supervisors are too ambitious and usually target other female employees as potential rivals; therefore, they treat them cruelly. Pei-Ju shared her own experience of working with female supervisors.

Pei-Ju: We have women supervisors in our organisation. I would say they treat us well. The things mentioned in that article have not happened. [...] Most of the time, she was willing to give you the opportunity but she would be strict. [...] It would actually be a risky decision for her to support you. She could promote a *nansheng* instead. [...] Today she recruits a *nansheng*. If his performance is good, then fine. If not, she has already recruited a *nansheng*. He has no inconveniences and he is physically strong enough. But if she recruited a *nyusheng*, she would challenge people's assumptions. So we have to understand that she's under pressure. If the *nyusheng* doesn't perform well, then people will think that she [the female supervisor] shouldn't have hired her.

According to Pei-Ju's observation, when it comes to recruitment decisions, female supervisors' professional judgement will be under strict scrutiny. In other words, recruiting a woman would make a female supervisor vulnerable. Her professional reputation would be bundled together with this employee's performance. She would be held responsible for this female colleague's failure. But if she hired a man, then his failure would be his own. It would have nothing to do with her. I would argue that this women's burden could be interpreted as part of the effect of gender categorisation. Women are not only generalised as a homogeneous group with a shared nature, they have to carry the label of women all together. It is very difficult for a female employee to distance herself from the generalised perceptions about other women in the workplace. Moreover, this perception is usually negative.

From my data, it is can be seen that mechanical engineering is not the only profession in which a female supervisor has to be responsible for her female colleagues. As an active member of the LGBTQ community in Taiwan, Shih-Ching has long been aware of gender discrimination in the workplace and has tried her best to fight against it. In her role as a senior media specialist, she now has more power to negotiate and challenge the system in order to enable her sisters to have equal opportunities. However, her higher position cannot protect her from the burden of risk to her own career. Her identity as a lesbian could be used as an excuse to question her leadership if she insists on giving a lesbian applicant a fair chance. She told me that, only recently, she has changed her approach.

Shih-Ching: Actually I … it's only now, I'm willing to carry this burden.

Shih-Ching used the word 'burden' to describe her personally felt responsibility for her female supervisees. She went on to explain this feeling by giving the example of the recruitment and hiring experience of a particular female member of staff.

Shih-Ching: Let me tell you something funny and ridiculous. At my current company, my supervisor is a man. And he always recruits the good-looking ones.
Ting-Fang: You know this by observing or did he just tell you directly …
Shih-Ching: I've observed it. And once he told me bluntly [about his opinion of an applicant], 'So ugly'. […] And we usually do the interview together, then he asks me, 'Who would you pick?' He shows his list to me. Because I know him well, I

know he will choose the pretty ones. So I will choose two or three candidates who I prefer. And I'll tell him, I say 'those three for you to look at, and these three for me to work with'. So, the last three are my people. [...] It's very clear that he only hires those who look pretty. And because he's responsible for the day shift, so those three [picked by him] also work on the day shift. And those picked by me, those 'ugly ones', work with me on the night shift. One of them, the last one we hired, the last place ... um, he wanted to hire someone else but I want to hire this one. [...] He asked me, 'why do you want to hire this one?' I just replied with 'I just want to hire her'. It's actually because I knew that she's a T and I wanted to give her a try.[8] I've never done this before [hiring someone because of knowing she is a lesbian]. 'I want to hire this one.' Then he said 'All right, all right'. And that's it. He said, 'She's your responsibility. I won't care.' I told him, 'you won't even look at her anyway. Also, she will be working with me.' [...] But you know what? He can be really obvious. Even that employee knows that she must have been selected by me. He never talks to her. [...] What I meant is, most of the time, he would say, 'go find your Shih-Ching *jie* [姊]'.[9] [...] For me, she's the very first one that I interviewed and I hired her because she's a T.

Thanks to her managerial position, Shih-Ching has had the chance to observe and participate in the under-the-table negotiation of recruitment decisions. There is plenty of information regarding gender and employment in Shih-Ching's accounts. The first thing I would like to address is the issue of women's appearance. In her inspiring work on the British tourist industry, Adkins (1995) describes how women's appearance determined their employment status. Examining her participants' experiences of work in an amusement park, Adkins argues that 'women workers needed the "right" appearance to be employed' (ibid.: 105). 'Facial display and appropriate clothing' would directly influence what kind of job a woman would be assigned or even whether she would be hired in the first place (ibid.: 105). Shih-Ching's account echoes Adkins' argument by demonstrating how a female candidate's appearance was judged by a male recruitment officer and how he made recruitment decisions based on his own personal and biased appearance criteria.

The negotiation between Shih-Ching and her male supervisor indicates that this organisation did not have an established standard practice of equal opportunity in the recruitment selection process. Therefore, the male supervisor could make sexist comments about female applicants in the meeting. On the other hand, Shih-Ching used this inappropriate recruitment practice as an opportunity to negotiate in favour of the disadvantaged applicant without a discussion of the sexuality issue. Shih-Ching simply continued to press for it. She justified her selection decision by persistent insistence. Moreover, she used her position as a potential supervisor for the applicant as leverage. She stressed her intention to recruit this applicant onto her own team.

At the end of the discussion, Shih-Ching successfully secured a place for this female applicant. At the same time, her male colleague also explained clearly that this female employee would be Shih-Ching's responsibility. He even made sure of this in daily interactions at work by always referring her to Shih-Ching.

Yu-Nung, an activist who used to work in the advertising industry, had similar experiences. She is also aware of the extra burden that a female supervisor who is willing to hire women in that industry must bear.

Yu-Nung: It's not always about recruitment and interviewing. Because I've experienced gender inequality in the workplace, I decided that once I got the power, I would hire *nyusheng*. [laughing] I would do my best to hire as many *nyusheng* as I could. But in this process, I've encountered so many difficulties. [...] I will use my experience in the production company as an example. I even hired female directors. But female directors would *thut-tshue*.[10] But it's not because they didn't have the ability. It's because ... I've worked with some [male] directors who are big names now. When I worked with them, they would also *tuusse* back then and no one would care. Almost everyone would tolerate him as a beginner. [...] If the same thing happened to a *nansheng* and a *nyusheng*, people would judge them differently. [...] You would find that people have high tolerance towards *nansheng*. [...] He could use ten or twenty films to sharpen his skills, but no one would give the same chance to a *nyusheng* [director]. Of course, she would perform less well, because she could not learn from experience, by actually doing it. So I've paid the price for this. If I hire a woman director, I have to take the risk that she will probably *thut-tshue*.

It should be noted that, generally speaking, there are very few female film directors in Taiwan. Yu-Nung's decision to hire women was not only rare but also 'risky'. Like Shih-Ching, Yu-Nung was actually putting her own career at risk by doing so. In addition, Yu-Nung also observed that people judged female and male directors differently.

Male-dominated industries are unfriendly to women not because they are staffed by more men, but because men are regarded as the norm. Women are deprived of equal treatment beginning at the recruitment stage, right through employment and into management. For those women who have broken through the glass ceiling, the fight is still not over. They must do more than just perform their own job well. They also must carry the burden of making sure that all female employees are doing things right. Gender categorisation is not only about judging someone by categorising her or him into a distinct gender group with distinct characteristics, but also about using a group member's behaviour to conclude things about the behaviour of the rest.

CONCLUSION

In this chapter, I have discussed my participants' accounts regarding management practices. These accounts reveal how female employees make sense of their own experiences of these practices and also those of other female employees in relation to their gender. Through this discussion, I have uncovered the gendered and heteronormative assumptions made by organisational management. Thus, gendered and heteronormative management both constructs and reinforces gender segregation and maternal ideologies in the workplace. Moreover, I have suggested that, as social constructions, gender and sexuality are intertwined with each other. One cannot be examined without reference to the other. From the perspective of materialist feminism, Ingraham (1994) proposes a critical reflection on previous gender theories. Ingraham (ibid.) devised the concept of the 'heterosexual imaginary' and argues that it has prevented some feminists from seeing heterosexuality as a crucial part of the construction of gender. Ingraham further argues that 'the material conditions of capitalist patriarchal societies are more centrally linked to institutionalized heterosexuality than to gender'; in addition, 'gender is inextricably bound up with heterosexuality' (ibid.: 204). Although I still have unsettled thoughts about evaluating heterosexuality over gender, I am convinced that heterosexuality is a key concept that can help me to understand the gendered arrangements in the material world. I also agree with Jackson and Scott's

(2010) argument that heterosexuality is privileged in aspects of social life that are not necessarily sexual. It is so normalised that it seems to be 'natural or inevitable' (Jackson 2006: 112). Jackson and Scott (2010: 85) also point out that 'heterosexuality should not be thought of as simply a form of sexual expression', because it is a social institution that has influence extending far beyond people's sexual lives. Heterosexuality is not only produced and reproduced in heterosexual relationships but is actually 'mobilized and reproduced in everyday life' (Jackson 2006: 114). Heteronormativity is deeply embedded in both our sexual and our non-sexual routine activities. As Jackson proposes, it requires 'our continual reaffirmation for its continuance' in the everyday practices that enable the gendered heterosexual order to be sustained (2001: 291). From the above discussions of my research findings, it is clear that the ideology of normalised heterosexuality manifests itself in gendered management in the workplace. Therefore, I am taking a standpoint that the examination of gender in employment cannot be achieved without including the institutional construction of heteronormativity in the picture.

In order to further investigate the gendered heterosexual order in everyday non-sexual and social practices, I will move from organisational management to everyday interactions in the workplace. The analysis will be continued in a discussion of quotidian social practices at work in the next chapter.

NOTES

1. *Nyusheng* [女生] means a young woman or a girl. It can also be a plural noun.
2. The official report indicates that in 2014 there were in total 11,537 personnel in social welfare, 9516 women and 2021 men (Ministry of Health and Welfare 2015).
3. '*Nansheng*' [男生] means a young man or boy. It can also be plural.
4. Since the female and male singular third person pronouns in Mandarin have identical pronunciation, it could not be determined which one Han-Ting had used, and therefore I chose 'she/he' as the translation. The same translation strategy is adopted in other quotes from participants' accounts.
5. This quote is from the official English translation of the article. The complete English translation is available at the official website of the Ministry of Labour: http://laws.mol.gov.tw/eng/flaw/FLAWDAT0201.asp
6. I discuss the hierarchical culture in the workplace further in Chap. 5.
7. *Renfen* [認分] in Mandarin means being aware of and accepting one's own social status and situation.

8. *T* is a lesbian identity. The term is derived from the English word 'tom-boy'. It refers to a more 'masculine' sexual role, while its counterpart *Po* [婆] refers to a more 'feminine' one (Chao 2008). *T* and *Po* are two common terms with lesbian connotations in Taiwan.
9. *Jie* [姊] means an older sister. In Taiwan, it is used to refer not only to those with family relationships but also to women who have superior social status. It is usually used in a casual context.
10. *Thut-tshue* [脱箠] is a Taiyu (or Taiwanese) term. It means to make trivial mistakes.

References

Adkins, L. (1995). *Gendered Work: Sexuality, Family and the Labour Market.* Bristol, PA: Open University Press.

Bacik, I., & Drew, E. (2006). Struggling with Juggling: Gender and Work/Life Balance in the Legal Professions. *Women's Studies International Forum, 29*(2), 136–146.

Brooks, A. (2006). *Gendered Work in Asian Cities: The New Economy and Changing Labour Markets.* Aldershot: Ashgate.

Chao, Y. (2008). Drinks, Stories, Penis and Breasts: Lesbian Tomboys in Taiwan from the 1960s to the 1990s. *Journal of Homosexuality, 40*(3–4), 185–209.

Cheng, L. (2010). Why Aren't Women Sticking with Science in Taiwan? *The Kaohsiung Journal of Medical Sciences, 26*(6), S28–S34.

Cheng, Y., Wu, S., & Wong, Y. [鄭雅文, 吳宣蓓, & 翁裕峰]. (2011). 過勞職災的認定爭議與政策因應: 日本經驗對台灣的啟示 [Disputes and Policy Responses Concerning the Hazards of Overwork and Workers' Compensation: Experiences in Japan and Their Implications for Taiwan]. 台灣公共衛生雜誌 [*Taiwan Journal of Public Health*], 30(4), 301–315.

Chiu, W. [邱文仁]. (2011). 女人何苦為難女人 [Why Women Persecute Women], 自由時報 [*Liberty Times*], August 8. Retrieved August 18, 2016, from http://news.ltn.com.tw/news/supplement/paper/514843

Chou, W., Chen, C., Fosh, P., & Foster, D. (2009). The Changing Face of Women Managers in Taiwan. In C. Rowley & V. Yukongdi (Eds.), *The Changing Face of Women Managers in Asia* (pp. 171–198). Abingdon: Routledge.

Cockburn, C. (1991). *In the Way of Women: Men's Resistance to Sex Equality in Organizations.* Houndmills: Macmillan.

Crompton, R., & Lyonette, C. (2006). Work–Life 'Balance' in Europe. *Acta Sociologica, 49*(4), 379–393.

Evans, J. (1997). Men in Nursing: Issues of Gender Segregation and Hidden Advantage. *Journal of Advanced Nursing, 26*(2), 226–231.

Faulkner, W. (2009). Doing Gender in Engineering Workplace Cultures. I. Observations from the Field. *Engineering Studies, 1*(1), 3–18.

Glover, J., & Guerrier, Y. (2010). Women in Hybrid Roles in IT Employment: A Return to 'Nimble Fingers'? *Journal of Technology Management & Innovation*, 5(1), 85–94.

Guerrier, Y., Ecans, C., Glover, J., & Wilson, C. (2009). 'Technical, but Not Very …': Constructing Gendered Identities in IT-related Employment. *Work, Employment and Society*, 23(3), 495–511.

Guo, J., & Liang, G. (2012). Sailing into Rough Seas: Taiwan's Women Seafarers' Career Development Struggle. *Women's Studies International Forum*, 35, 194–202.

Hartmann, H. (1976). Capitalism, Patriarchy, and Job Segregation by Sex. *Signs*, 1(3), 137–169.

Hioe, B. (2016). Tsai Ing-Wen and Taiwan's Year of the Female Politician? *New Bloom*, February 13. Retrieved August 9, 2016, from https://newbloommag. net/2016/02/13/tsai-female-politician/

Hou, Y. [侯岳宏]. (2013). 未依法定計算方法給付加班費之效力 [The Effect of Overtime Payment not Conforming to the Calculation Method Prescribed in the Act]. 臺北大學法學論叢 [*Taipei University Law Review*], 88, 261–291.

Ingraham, C. (1994). The Heterosexual Imaginary: Feminist Sociology and Theories of Gender. *Sociological Theory*, 12(2), 203–219.

Jackson, S. (2001). Why a Materialist Feminism Is (Still) Possible and Necessary. *Women's Studies International Forum*, 24(3–4), 283–293.

Jackson, S. (2006). Gender, Sexuality and Heterosexuality: The Complexity (and Limits) of Heteronormativity. *Feminist Theory*, 7, 105–121.

Jackson, S., & Scott, S. (2004). The Personal Is Still Political: Heterosexuality, Feminism and Monogamy. *Feminism & Psychology*, 14(1), 151–157.

Jackson, S., & Scott, S. (2010). *Theorizing Sexuality*. Maidenhead: Open University Press.

Lu, L., Gilmour, R., Kao, S. F., & Huang, M. T. (2006). A Cross-Cultural Study of Work/Family Demands, Work/Family Conflict and Wellbeing: The Taiwanese vs. British. *Career Development International*, 11(1), 9–27.

Mies, M. (1998). *Patriarchy and Accumulation on a World Scale : Women in the International Division of Labour*. London: Zed Books.

Ministry of Health and Welfare [衛生福利部]. (2015). 社會工作人員專職人數 [*The Statistics on the Number of Full-Time Social Workers*]. Taiwan. Retrieved August 10, 2016, from https://www.gender.ey.gov.tw/gecdb/Stat_Statistics_DetailData.aspx?sn=AWUNf1023B1vACKQJxIJmQ%3D%3D&d=x6hHAJy%2F6kd5%2FI2WaRjP4Q%3D%3D

Ministry of Labour [勞動部] (2015). 性別勞動統計專輯 [*Report of Gender Labour Statistics*]. Retrieved March 15, 2016, from http://www.mol.gov.tw/statistics/2452/2465/23491/

Munn Giddings, C. (1998). Mixing Motherhood and Academia: A Lethal Cocktail. In D. Malina & S. Maslin-Prothero (Eds.), *Surviving the Academy: Feminist Perspectives* (pp. 56–58). London: Routledge.

Ochiai, E. (2008). Researching Gender and Childcare in Contemporary Asia. In E. Ochiai & B. Molony (Eds.), *Asia's New Mothers: Crafting Gender Roles and Childcare Networks in East and Southeast Asian Societies* (pp. 1–30). Kent: Global Oriental Ltd.

Ochiai, E., Mari, Y., Yasuko, M., Zhou, W., Onode, S., Kiwaki, N., Fujita, M., & Hong, S. (2008). Gender Roles and Childcare Networks in East and Southeast Asian Societies. In E. Ochiai & B. Molony (Eds.), *Asia's New Mothers: Crafting Gender Roles and Childcare Networks in East and Southeast Asian Societies* (pp. 31–70). Kent: Global Oriental Ltd.

Panteli, N., Stack, J., & Ramsey, H. (2001). Gendered Patterns in Computing Work in the Late 1990s. *New Technology, Work and Employment, 16*(1), 3–17.

Phillips, A., & Taylor, B. (1980). Sex and Skill: Notes Towards a Feminist Economics. *Feminist Review, 6*, 79–88.

Ramsay, K., & Letherby, G. (2006). The Experience of Academic Non-mothers in the Gendered University. *Gender, Work and Organization, 13*(1), 25–44.

Sechiyama, K. (2013). *Patriarchy in East Asia: A Comparative Sociology of Gender.* Leiden: Brill.

Smithson, J., & Stokoe, E. H. (2005). Discourses of Work–Life Balance: Negotiating 'Genderblind' Terms in Organizations. *Gender, Work & Organization, 12*(2), 147–168.

Tu, C., & Kuo, A. [涂鉅旻、郭安家]. (2014). 「婦科在女人大腿中討生活」柯又失言 ['Doing Obstetrics and Gynaecology Is Making a Living Between Women's Legs', Ko Made a Gaffe Again]. 自由時報 [*Liberty Times*], 8 September. Retrieved August 10, 2016, from http://news.ltn.com.tw/news/politics/paper/811410

Wang, N. [王能君]. (2012). 勞動基準法上加班法律規範與問題之研究-日本與臺灣之加班法制與實務 [The Enforcement and Practice of Overtime Regulations of Labour Standards Act between Japan and Taiwan]. 臺北大學法學論叢 [*Taipei University Law Review*], *81*, 75–138.

Watts, J. H. (2009). 'Allowed into a Man's World' Meanings of Work–Life Balance: Perspectives of Women Civil Engineers as 'Minority' Workers in Construction. *Gender, Work & Organization, 16*(1), 37–57.

Yen, C., & Wu, Y. [顏振凱、吳詠航]. (2006). 辜:統帥不應讓穿裙子的當 [Koo: 'Commander in Chief Should not Be a Skirt-Wearing Person'], 蘋果日報 [*Apple Daily*], 15 December. Retrieved August 10, 2016, from http://www.appledaily.com.tw/appledaily/article/headline/20061215/3108250/

Yu, A. [余艾苔]. (2014). 陳以真可坐櫃檯惹議,柯P:當市長要有歷練 [The Comment 'Chen Yi-Chen Can Sit at a Counter' Sparked Controversy. Ko: A Mayor Must Have Experience']. 蘋果日報 [*Apple Daily*], 7 September. Retrieved August 10, 2016, from http://www.appledaily.com.tw/realtime-news/article/new/20140907/465283/

Yu, W. (2009). *Gendered Trajectories: Women, Work and Social Change in Japan and Taiwan.* Stanford: Stanford University Press.

CHAPTER 4

'Don't I Have a Brain and Hands?': Negotiating Gender in Mundane Interactions at Work

INTRODUCTION

I was walking around the university on a very hot and humid day, having just gotten my hair cut. It was fairly short and easy to take care of. It was exactly what I needed to survive a typical summer in Taiwan. When I met a colleague in a corridor, she said, in a tone that was full of surprise and even concern, 'Why did you cut your hair so short? What happened to you?' I was quite confused by her questions but still managed to reply honestly: 'Just because hot weather has happened.' It was not until later that day that I realised the connotation of the expression that my colleague 'gives off' (Goffman 1959: 14). In Taiwan, long hair is generally considered the norm for a young woman; it is a way of performing her femininity. If she decides to cut her hair short, it must be because she wants to be not so feminine for some reason. The most clichéd interpretation would be that it was done because of an unpleasant break-up. My colleague was worried about me. She thought something unpleasant had happened to me and that I had had a haircut in order to change my mood. Trivial as it may seem, this incident illustrates that everyday interactions are actually full of traces of gender construction. For my colleague, my short haircut was expressing some kind of symbolic message, and this message was only comprehensible when she read it with the attribution of my gender. It was a gendered and gendering interaction. There is no university regulation that enables this to happen. It is a construction that goes beyond

© The Author(s) 2018
T.-F. Chin, *Everyday Gender at Work in Taiwan*,
Gender, Sexualities and Culture in Asia,
https://doi.org/10.1007/978-981-10-7365-6_4

organisational management or arrangements. This kind of 'trivial' and subtle everyday practice is exactly the subject that I discuss in this chapter.

Although I did not adopt an ethnomethodological approach in conducting fieldwork, this methodology has provided me with useful concepts with which to examine the data. Often regarded as something 'natural', gender is identified by ethnomethodologists as part of the common sense that requires further investigation. Although the concept of gender had not been proposed or theorised at the time, Garfinkel's work indicates that 'sex status' as the 'ascribed object' can only be achieved and sustained by consistent work in everyday life (1967: 133). By studying the case of Agnes, a transexual research participant, Garfinkel illustrates that an individual's 'sex status' is a management project involving conscious calculation. Therefore, Agnes's 'passing' introduced a sociological inquiry: do we all at some level work on our 'sex status' in everyday practices? Reviewing the conventional sociological theories of gender, West and Zimmerman (1987) provide an alternative approach to understanding gender as something a social being does rather than something a social being inherits or 'is'. They propose conceptualising 'gender as a routine accomplishment embedded in everyday interaction' (ibid.: 125).

While I am aware that gender as a 'doing' is perpetuated through institutional management and organisational arrangements, I am convinced that it is critical not to neglect the role of individual practices in everyday life. In terms of the power relationships in knowledge production, focusing on everyday practices is a critical position to take on. Proposing a sociology from a woman's perspective, Smith (1987) has eloquently argued for a method that enquires into the 'everyday/everynight world' and experience. The 'tacit knowledge' situated in women's experiences, which we might not have the 'appropriate language' to speak of, could thereby be revealed, exposed and examined (Smith 1997: 394). Moreover, any attempt to challenge persistent gender inequality cannot be successful without critically assessing those taken-for-granted routines. Kitzinger has argued that, compared with the '"macro" level of oppression', such as gender discriminatory laws, the '"micro" level of oppression' that happens in everyday interactions is 'the most resistant to analysis and political challenge' (2009: 97).

Having discussed gendered and heteronormative organisational management in Chap. 3, I now move on to the general interactions that occurred in my participants' day-to-day working lives. The analysis in this chapter primarily focuses on my participants' accounts of everyday social practices, such as appellations, casual conversation and body language. I demonstrate that, while everyday practices at work are happening in a gendered and heteronormative cultural context, they are also intertwined with the hierarchical social order.

BEING IDENTIFIED AS A *JIE* [姊]

Since 2013, the movement to reconceptualise the legal idea of the family in Taiwan has drawn much public attention. The draft of the *duoyuan chengjia* [多元成家][1] legislation has been proposed and promoted by the Taiwan Alliance to Promote Civil Partnership Rights. Despite disputes about strategic issues, most of the pro-LGBTQ activists and non-governmental organisations (NGOs) are taking part in this movement and have launched campaigns to back up the legal reform. The draft is organised into three sections: marriage equality, the civil partnership system and the multiperson family system. By arguing in favour of expanding and reshaping the legal definition of family, this legal movement has directly challenged the conventional view of familial relationships. Because of this, several groups that support the conventional ideology have attacked the proposed legislation by asserting that it will destroy 'traditional' social values, which they consider worthy of preservation. I was particularly struck by their argument concerning familial appellations. They are against the proposal to change the column of *fu mu* [父母: father and mother] on a personal ID into *shuangcin* [雙親: both parents]. They believe this would prevent children from using the Mandarin appellations of mum and dad to address their parents, and therefore the traditional family values and ethics would be 'broken'. Although the causal relationship between changing the name of an ID column and stopping a certain social practice is confusing, it is obvious that the rhetoric of tradition is being used to argue for the preservation of heterosexual familial appellations.[2] While using the conventional practice of appellation as a legal argument against the reform of marriage rights may seem absurd, it serves to illustrate how adopting familial appellations is perceived as a social norm.

In the Taiwanese context, the social order embedded in everyday interactions depends heavily on hierarchical relationships. Collins points out that 'various kinds of minor conversational routines mark and enact various kinds of personal relationships' (2004: 18). I argue that a comprehensive analysis of everyday routines in Taiwan has to specifically take into account the hierarchical social order. In Taiwan, a social actor is very often allocated complex social relationships which are interwoven like a tight web surrounding the individual. Therefore, any given social encounter could be a rather complex situation for the social actors. It requires them to constantly identify, reassure and construct each other's social positions through day-to-day practices in order to demonstrate proper manners and civilised selves. It would be fair to say that people are constantly reflexive in a relational and hierarchical way. Moreover, this hierarchical relationship is also gendered. This can be illustrated by the appellations used in everyday conversations.

While a senior person may address a junior one by her/his personal name, a junior person should never use a personal name to address someone more senior because it would be regarded as rude and offensive. This appellation system reflects the idea of *beifen* [輩分]. *Beifen* means the order of kinship and generations. It even goes beyond the family context. Take studying at a university, for example; in the UK, it is a generally accepted norm that a university student will address a professor using their personal name. However, in Taiwan it would be regarded as unacceptable or at least uncommon to do so. A proper and polite way to interact with a professor is by using her/his family name and her/his professional title. A less formal way would be to use the family name and the appellation that means teacher (*laoshih* [老師]). Even students are categorised according to their seniority. A senior female student is usually addressed by someone junior as *syuejie* [學姊] and a senior male student as *syuejhang* [學長], while a junior female student is usually addressed by someone senior as *syuemei* [學妹], and a junior male student as *syuedi* [學弟]. The first part of these four terms is the same character, which means learning. The second part consists of words that refer to different siblings. *Jie* means elder sister and *mei* means younger one, while *jhang* means elder brother and *di* means younger one. Through this example, we can see that gender is also a crucial component of this system of *beifen*. It is a system of social order which is constructed and maintained through everyday practices, such as labelling gendered and hierarchical relationships by appellations in general conversations. Moreover, it can be seen that familial appellations are not only used to address family members. They are also widely adopted in everyday social interactions among social actors in non-familial relationships.

The social practice of appellations is so common and taken for granted that there is no law to enforce it, but people adjust their behaviour according to this hierarchical system. While studying at a university in Taiwan, I was often addressed as *syuejie* [學姊: a female senior study colleague] by other MA students in the department. As discussed previously, this is a conventional appellation used to address a female student who is in a class more senior than that of the speaker. However, in my case it was because of my age. I was much older than most of the students in the department, therefore even colleagues who were in my study year addressed me as *syuejie*. I felt there was no need to use this appellation, and sometimes I suspected they were only doing so because they could not remember my name. I tried to convince them to stop addressing me as *syuejie*. I told them several times that I preferred to be addressed by my personal name. However, they found this practice difficult to adopt. One colleague even told me that he would feel awkward if he stopped addressing me as *syuejie*.

Adopting proper appellations to show respect is something to which I became very sensitive as soon as I began my fieldwork, especially when I was interacting with participants who were senior to me. Tzu-Ling was one of those participants. She was in her 50s when we were introduced by a common acquaintance. This acquaintance is a friend of mine and a niece of Tzu-Ling's. My friend is about my age and always addresses Tzu-Ling as *ayi* [阿姨], which means 'auntie' in Taiwanese Mandarin.[3] In other words, we are of the same generation and junior to Tzu-Ling in terms of age, social status and *beifen*. At first I used Tzu-Ling's personal name to address her, just as I did with most other participants, but I soon sensed a slight uneasiness during the conversation among the three of us. I asked Tzu-Ling whether she found it odd for me to call her just by her name, and she replied 'yes, a little bit' and explained that it was because it was obvious that I am of the same generation as her niece. After that, I used the appellation *ayi* to address Tzu-Ling, to indicate our different social statuses.

Considering this specific social and cultural context, I propose that an analysis of appellations in routine social interactions may provide insight into the everyday symbolic activities of doing gender in Taiwan. Through the practice of adopting proper appellations, social actors are constantly identifying, constructing and negotiating their relationships with others in quotidian verbal activities. Based on his observations at an American medical institute, Goffman developed an analysis of symmetrical and asymmetrical rules of conduct, with a focus on deference and demeanour. He argues that 'deferential pledges are frequently conveyed through spoken terms of address involving status identifiers' (1967: 60–61). According to Goffman, the action of addressing a recipient with a specific term is designed to show deference and declare that 'the expectations and obligations of the recipient, both substantive and ceremonial, will be allowed and supported by the actor' (ibid.: 60). In other words, the adopted appellation is a meaningful source for examining the assumed and expected relationship as well as the subsequent interactions between the actor and the recipient. Here, I focus on how familial appellations are used as gendered indicators for social actors in the workplace to negotiate work as well as to make sense of relationships in the workplace.

'It's a Way to Show Respect'

According to my participants' experiences, it seems that using familial appellations to address colleagues is a common practice in the workplace. Although such appellations appear to be less formal than job titles, they could actually be a way to express a sense of respect in the context of workplace interactions. It is an informal strategy to mark the hierarchical differences between social actors in general conversation. Shih-Ching's account of the practice of using appellations in the organisations where she has worked provides a good example. Shih-Ching has pursued a career in the entertainment and media industries. She has worked for several different organisations with a variety of work cultures, some casual and some formal. However, when it comes to addressing a more senior colleague, choosing an appellation that conveys a sense of respect is generally considered necessary.

Shih-Ching: For example, when I worked at a record company, colleagues usually called each other by their names. As for superior staff, we would call ... the supervisor's family name is Kao, we would call him Kao *san* [桑].[4] [...] Just add *san*. We would not, um, use General Manager or other titles. Um, if his position were even higher, then we would use *gong* [公].[5] For example, we would call the Chairman of the Board Chuang *gong*. [...] His family name is Chuang. Then we add *gong*, which means grandpa or old man. We would call him Chuang *gong*.

According to Shih-Ching, the work culture at the record company was fairly casual and relaxed. It was common practice for the employees to call each other by their personal names rather than their job titles. Even so, when it came to colleagues in obviously superior positions, appellations connoting hierarchical differences would still be used. The examples she provided here are *san* [桑] and *gong* [公]. The appellation *san* [桑] is a transliterated loanword with foreign origin. It originated from the Japanese appellation *san* [さん], a title that is adopted to show respect and proper manners towards the addressed, usually someone senior or of superior social status to the speaker. It is generally a gender-neutral term that can be used to address anyone in Japanese. However, in the Taiwanese context, it is more often used to address a man than a woman. The other appellation, *gong*, is very gender-specific. *Gong* is conventionally used to address a male. As an appellation, *gong* has multiple meanings. It is a respectful title for a senior man or a man with eminent social status. It could also be a familial appellation for grandfather, or a married woman's father-in-law. Moreover, it could refer to a title of nobility, mostly in the context of ancient and imperial China. It is a title with a *Fengjian* [封建: Chinese Feudal] connotation. For example, after Chiang Kai-Shek, former president of the Republic of China, died, the KMT government granted him the official title of Chiang *gong* [蔣公] as a political strategy to construct his legacy. This title used to be the formal way to refer to Chiang in every textbook published by the Ministry of Education. As an appellation used in everyday conversations in the workplace, *gong* therefore could convey multiple symbolic meanings. On the one hand, it is a gendered appellation clearly indicating the superiority of the person addressed in terms of social status, seniority or more generally his power within the organisation. On the other hand, the familial relationship implied by this title somehow softens the sense of formality. Instead of using the formal job title as the appellation, *gong* could be perceived as a more subtle and informal term which allows for a potential personal bond between social actors despite the obvious distance created by their differing social status.

Shih-Ching also mentioned several other appellations, all of which, apart from san, are terms that connote familial relations.

Ting-Fang: How about in a Newspaper Agency?
Shih-Ching: We have to use Editor in Chief or *ge* [哥].[6] Li *jie* [姊], Luo *ge* [哥].

It is common practice for people to use familial relational appellations to address colleagues at work in Taiwan, especially to refer to those who are senior or older. This may not be a unique social practice. It can be observed in other societies, such as China. However, the social meaning and interpretation may be very different, according to the accounts of my participants. In his work on the gendered identities of male Chinese migrant workers, Lin uses participants' daily conversations to demonstrate 'the emergence of new extended "family relations"' among workmates 'based on their "real" familial gender relations' (2013: 96). Lin explains that this is a strategy developed by the workers to adapt to the urban workplace setting. On the one hand, it allows them to maintain their masculine identities by constructing 'non-kin familiar social relations at work' (2013: 94). On the other hand, it could be interpreted as a practice designed to build a private social network to help each other. In his investigation of masculinity in China during the post-Mao era, Osburg argues that 'the hierarchical and gendered idiom of brotherhood' is adopted as a business communication strategy to establish 'fictive brotherly relationships' through 'elite privileges' (2016: 158, 159). However, it seems that my participants' narratives manifest a possible interpretation of the practice that is very different from those of the male Chinese migrant workers and non-state elites, and is concerned more with hierarchy than solidarity.

When I asked what appellation she preferred, Shih-Ching expressed ambivalent feelings about being addressed as a *jie*. She admitted it was not easy for her to accept it at first, but gradually she came to find it acceptable and sometimes even expects the respect that the term connotes.

Ting-Fang: When people first called you Shih-Ching *jie*, did you find it difficult to get used to?

Shih-Ching: I would tell them not to do so. [...] Now I've got used to it. But sometimes, people call me *jie* ... for example, I used to tell people don't call me *jie*, but sometimes, you go somewhere. Young people who don't know who I am, they might directly call my name. And then I would look twice at them. I would feel that they have no proper manners. Because, first, I'm not that familiar with you and also it's in the workplace. For me, it's the same. Although I'm relatively old but in my work discipline, if I meet someone senior to me, or if she is more experienced than me, I would call her *jie* with respect.

For Shih-Ching, other than showing respect, *jie* seems to function as an indicator to mark distance rather than to show intimacy or a personalised relationship in the speech act. That is, proper manners indicate proper distance in terms of relationship. Power relationships are a crucial dimension in understanding the proper social distance between social actors and their interactive behaviours. As Goffman argues, 'ceremonial distance' and 'sociological distance' seem to have a common ground (1967: 64). He points out that 'between status equals we may expect to find interaction guided by symmetrical familiarity', while 'between superordinate and subordinate we may expect to find asymmetrical relations' (ibid.). Shih-Ching's account may seem contradictory; however, I argue that it actually demonstrates that using appellations is a normative social practice to indicate the appropriate social distance based on the status relationship between the actor and the recipient, which social actors may find it difficult to subvert. In the latter example, Shih-Ching was offended by the assumed familiarity in her subordinate colleague's act of addressing her by her first name.

Another participant, Chieh-Ming, was more directly critical of the use of senior appellations as a gesture to show respect to colleagues in the workplace. According to Chieh-Ming's observation, it is not always people who are younger than she is that address her as *jie*.

Chieh-Ming: They're not necessarily younger. It might be people who feel that they're less experienced than you are. They feel that it's a way to show respect.
Ting-Fang: How do you feel about it then?
Chieh-Ming: Personally, I feel extremely uncomfortable. [...] I feel that I don't need you to show respect through terms of address. If you respect me, then you respect me. I don't need any formality to verify your respect towards me. Respect doesn't come from my position, my status. It's because we should respect each other, no matter who you are.

Chieh-Ming's account indicates that the hierarchical order in the workplace is multifaceted. Seniority is not always about age differences but could be about work experience. She also revealed her uneasiness about accepting the practice of using familial appellations as a way to show respect to colleagues. She described it as a 'formality'. It seems that, for

Chieh-Ming, ceremonial acts of showing deference are entirely superfluous. She did not perceive her superordinate status in the organisation as a sufficient and necessary condition for being treated with deference by others.

'Don't Play that Trick on Me'

As a familial appellation used to show deference to non-familial social actors, the implications of *jie* invite diverse interpretations. *Jie* is an appellation connoting both hierarchical and familial relationships. The familial connotation may therefore be interpreted as a communication strategy to project a sense of personalised closeness. In the situational context of a workplace, while it marks the recipient as a superordinate woman, the actor may also use this term of address to propose a more personal relationship than that between colleagues or business partners. This increased level of intimacy on the part of the actor may therefore not be welcomed by the recipient, particularly when their social statuses are not equal.

Some of my participants expressed their uneasiness about being addressed as *jie* in the workplace because it implies a less formal relationship. Hsi-Shu, for example, has experience in team coordination and supervising junior colleagues. For this reason, it is not uncommon for her to be addressed as *jie* in everyday workplace interactions. Hsi-Shu told me it is difficult for her to accept colleagues addressing her as a *jie*; moreover, she personally perceives it as improper conduct in the workplace. Hsi-Shu's dislike of the use of familial appellations at work demonstrates her resistance to the personalisation of work relationships.

Hsi-Shu: I always think calling me by my name is just fine.
Ting-Fang: Then what's the reason that you find it difficult to get used to?
Hsi-Shu: Um, don't play that trick on me.
Ting-Fang: (laugh) What trick?
Hsi-Shu: Calling me *jie*. [...] I think she or he is trying to find a way to make our *guanxi* closer, but I think it would make *jiu shi lun shi* [就事論事] a difficult thing to do.[7]

According to the online Mandarin Dictionary produced by the Ministry of Education of Taiwan, the definition of *guanxi* [關係] is 'the joint action between things or individuals' or 'influence, involvement'. It can be generally translated as 'relationship' or 'relation' in English. In speech, it is mostly used as a noun and occasionally an adjective. When this term travels to the West, its meaning is more exclusively defined. For instance, the Oxford Dictionary defines *guanxi* as a noun that means '(In China) the system of social networks and influential relationships which facilitate business and other dealings'. In academia, *guanxi* has conventionally been conceptualised as a distinct practice of business culture in China, particularly in the post-Mao era (see e.g. Wank 1996; Tsang 1998; Lee et al. 2001). Beyond China, *guanxi* also plays an important role in the business world of other societies and communities which share a certain Confucian cultural heritage, such as Hong Kong and Taiwan (see e.g. Davies et al. 1995; Chow and Ng 2004; Hwang et al. 2009; Bedford and Hwang 2013).[8] While *guanxi* has drawn attention as a specific business and cultural phenomenon, its exact definition remains contested (Tsui and Farh 1997). While acknowledging the diverse interpretations of the term, it has been proposed that 'the core idea about *guanxi* involves relationships between or among individuals creating obligations for the continued exchange of favours' (Dunfee and Warren 2001: 192). As a business practice, *guanxi* could be perceived as a specific reciprocal relationship that is deliberately built and managed for personal favours in order to gain business advantages.

Although a substantial amount of academic effort has been expended in studying *guanxi*, it has been suggested that most of the studies limit their scope to the question, 'Does *guanxi* work?' (Dunfee and Warren 2001). Dunfee and Warren argue that most previous studies 'rely upon purely instrumental evaluations of *guanxi* and provide little consideration for ethical concerns' (ibid.: 202). The ethical concerns around the practice of *guanxi* are primarily related to bureaucratic corruption and bribery (Luo 2002; Osburg 2016). Empirical studies that discuss the ethical concerns around *guanxi* or its potential problems are often undertaken in the context of international patron–client relationships or, more specifically, when 'the Western' meets 'the Chinese Asian' (see e.g. Tsang 1998; Hsu and Saxenian 2000; Hwang and Blair Staley 2005; Millington et al. 2005). The investigation of *guanxi* is seldom situated in the context of interactions among colleagues at work, particularly from the perspective of gender. This is a dimension of *guanxi* practice which is revealed in Hsi-Shu's accounts.

'*Jiu shi lun shi*' is a Mandarin idiom which is often used to describe a certain attitude or principle with which to approach things. It means to take the matter on its merits rather than judging it on personal feelings or personal preferences. That is the work style that Hsi-Shu intends to construct and maintain in the workplace. It seems that she is not very interested in building personalised, intimate relationships with colleagues. Furthermore, for her, personalising relationships at work might damage work ethics and prevent team members from interacting professionally. She does not regard *jie*, a familial appellation, as a proper way for colleagues to address her.

For Hsi-Shu, the personalised and yet respectful appellation *jie* serves as an indicator of hidden and nuanced intentions by the speaker. By addressing her as *jie*, the speaker not only projects a personalised relationship but also deliberately grants Hsi-Shu a higher position. In other words, the speaker is constructing a personalised relationship with power differences between them. This is regarded as a communication strategy that is used to ask for personal favours. Therefore, when she hears a colleague addressing her as *jie*, Hsi-Shu interprets it as a 'trick' to request a favour from her. Personalising a relationship means demanding something that would otherwise be out of the question in the context. Therefore, she prefers colleagues to use her personal name. While a familial appellation offers a sense of personalisation, a personal name is regarded as a way to indicate individuality. Moreover, while an appellation is often gendered, the personal name is an option that offers the implication of individuality without addressing the person's gender. It is therefore comparatively gender neutral.

Chia-Chun provided another illustration of how using familial appellations at work is a communication strategy that is used to personalise work relationships in order to persuade colleagues to offer their help. Chia-Chun worked for an insurance company where one of her tasks was to deal with the settlement of claims. She told me that sometimes her colleagues would call her the *yijie* [一姊] of settlement.

Ting-Fang: Have you ever been addressed as *jie*?
Chia-Chun: Oh, sure. *Yijie* [一姊]. The *yijie* of settlements. [...] When you're called that, you know that it means this person is hoping you will solve some problem for her or him.

Yi [一] literally means 'one' or 'the first' in Mandarin. *Yijie* is a term usually used to refer to a woman who performs very well in a specific area. By addressing her as the *yijie* of settlements, Chia-Chun's colleagues were actually referring to her as the top female employee in the settlement of claims. It is a title that connotes praise. For Chia-Chun, it is a flattering gesture with a catch.

Both Hsi-Shu and Chia-Chun regard *jie*, the familial appellation for a senior woman, as a signal notifying them that whoever is using it is asking them for a favour. Addressing a female colleague as *jie*, therefore, is perceived as a deliberate action to place her in a higher position. By doing so, the person adopting this appellation is drawing a line between herself and the person being addressed. The appellation implies a difference in power or ability between them. While it seems to create an invisible distance, the fact that it is also a familial appellation also implies a sense of closeness. In this way, a personalised and, at the same time, hierarchical relationship is implied. It is both distanced and intimate at the same time. Both Hsi-Shu and Chia-Chun are hesitant to accept this personalised appellation because they realise it will be followed by a request for a personal favour. Their concerns reflect an ideal professionalism which treats the workplace as free from personalised relationships. Building up *guanxi*, personalised and reciprocal social networks, has been widely recognised as a common strategy to facilitate business in the commercial world of Chinese communities. But here, both of my participants demonstrate negative feelings about personalising workplace relationships; they seek to differentiate the workplace relationship from the private relationship.

However, Hsi-Shu's experiences suggest that *jie* as a personal yet respectful appellation is adopted as a communication strategy not only to ask for personal favours but also to reject a request. In the interview, she told me that a negotiation tactic that she really has an issue with is *sajiao* [撒嬌].[9] Personally, she found it totally unacceptable in the workplace. She used the case of a male supervisee as an example.

Hsi-Shu: Basically, I don't buy it. I really can't swallow it. I can't, I just can't. [...] He [a male supervisee] would use *sajiao* [撒嬌] as a tactic to solve problems or *shualai* [耍賴].[10] Then I heard it. It made me feel really uncomfortable. For example, I told him, 'You haven't completed this task yet. You might need to hurry up. Could you submit it to me next week?' And then he might say something like, 'Oh no, *syuejie* [學姊: a female senior study colleague], bullying, it's bullying ah'. [...] He was kind of joking. He said that in front of a lot of people. 'Bullying oh, bullying oh. *Syuejie*, please don't do this to me la.'[11]

Ting-Fang:	He would call you *syuejie* in such a context?
Hsi-Shu:	Yes.
Ting-Fang:	He graduated from the same university as you did?
Hsi-Shu:	Bullshit.
Ting-Fang:	Then why did he call you that?
Hsi-Shu:	Kind of a respectful appellation in the workplace.

In her investigation into Chinese language and gender in the urban Taiwanese speech community, Farris (1988) identified *sajiao* as one of the featured gender-marked verbs.[12] The meanings of *sajiao* are defined as: '(1) "to show pettiness, as a spoilt child," and (2) "to pretend to be angry or displeased, as a coquettish young woman"' (ibid.: 301). Farris further argues that native speakers perceive *sajiao* as a communication style that 'spoiled children of both sexes, and young (particularly unmarried) women engage in for certain strategic goals' (ibid.: 302). However, later empirical research has contested the conceptualisation of *sajiao* as a 'female' communication style. Adopting an ethnographic perspective, Yueh (2013) uses the everyday speech data collected in Taipei, Taiwan to illustrate that *sajiao* can be gender-neutral to native speakers. Yueh approaches *sajiao* as 'a babyish form of persuasion' that requires team play by the social actors in the situated context and challenges the conventional categorisation of *sajiao* as 'a women's speech act' (2013: 159, 177). She argues that 'the daily language, the media representations, and the display of gender' have contributed to the discursive construction of *sajiao* as 'the "natural" way women talk and do things' (ibid.: 177).

The example provided by Hsi-Shu about her male supervisee demonstrates that *sajiao* is not a 'woman-only' communication style in her workplace. Male employees adopt it to negotiate work too. As a tactic of persuasion, the purposes of a *sajiao* act could be multiple. In this case, it was used to refuse an order from a more senior colleague. The appellation *syuejie* serves as a component of his speech act. Yueh (2013) identifies several verbal and non-verbal features of *sajiao* performance. One is that the actor is 'portrayed as a helpless, childish, incapable, dependent, or powerless subject' (ibid.: 161). By identifying her as *syuejie*, the supervisee was indicating Hsi-Shu's seniority with a personalised touch. Moreover, the term 'bullying' also serves as a crucial indicator of the power disparity between them. By using this term to interpret the job request from Hsi-Shu, the supervisee therefore rendered himself in a disadvantaged position, or even with a comparatively powerless status.

'You Are Not a mei [妹]'

Through the analysis of my participants' accounts, it becomes evident that while *jie* is adopted as a gendered honorific title in the workplace, it also facilitates tactical interactions to negotiate work. By being identified as a *jie*, a senior female employee is stepping into a personalised relationship constructed by the speaker. Her professional authority and abilities are valued and yet, at the same time, she is targeted as a potential favour provider or as someone to be placated through *sajiao*. In his theorisation of deferential acts, Goffman reminds us that, since the actor and the recipient 'are likely to be related to one another through more than one pair of capacities', 'the same act of deference may show signs of different kinds of regard' (1967: 61). Some other interview data suggests that this honorific gendered appellation could also come with sexual implications. On the topic of being identified as a married and senior female colleague at work, Hsi-Shu mentioned her feeling of being perceived as 'desexualised'.

Hsi-Shu: I feel that we, mature and married women, tend to be desexualised. That is, if you don't try to promote your own femininity, I think that men would tend to treat you ... you're not a *mei* [妹],[13] in short. You're a *jie*, you're a *dajie* [大姊: big sister].[14]

According to Hsi-Shu's personal experience, 'mature and married' female colleagues are regarded as less feminine and less sexually attractive by male colleagues and therefore find themselves being treated in a certain way. In Hsi-Shu's narratives, *jie* is compared with another gendered appellation, *mei* [妹], which is the familial appellation for younger sister. While *jie* is generally used as an honorific appellation that implies a woman's seniority at work, the social and cultural meaning of *mei* as an appellation is more complicated than simply indicating female juniority. It could also be used to refer to a 'chick', particularly when the term is marked by level tone.

   In order to discuss the gendered implications of *mei*, an introduction to the popular Mandarin terms which are commonly adopted to refer to beautiful young women will be helpful. The conventional, and rather old-fashioned, term to describe a beautiful woman is *meinyu* [美女].[15] The literal translation of the term is 'a beautiful woman'. In the early 1990s, a new term, *lamei* [辣妹], emerged in the mass media.[16] It originated from the Mandarin translation of 'Spice Girls', a British pop girl group. In

Taiwan, the official translation of the name of the group is *lamei* [辣妹] *hechangtuan* [合唱團].[17] This could be translated back into English as 'an ensemble of hot chicks'. Since then, *lamei* has become a popular term adopted in speech by the general public to refer to beautiful young women, particularly those who are identified as attractive in a sexy way. In the late 1990s, another term was coined, *jhengmei* [正妹], which has claimed popularity in online social networking platforms and the mass media.[18] It has become a popular term used to refer to 'a gorgeous chick' or 'a cutie'. *Jhengmei* is not only a linguistic creation with cultural connotations but also an economic phenomenon. The commercialisation of *jhengmei* is recognised as a successful marketing strategy (see Wang 2009; Chen 2012).[19]

Yu-Chen's account of attending a male-dominated computing conference conveys the gendered connotations of *mei*.

Yu-Chen: Once I attended a conference, a conference of computer engineers. Do you know how *wuliao* [無聊][20] they [male computer programmers] were? They created a Google file. An openly shared file to mark the location of every *jhengmei* [正妹] at the conference. They drew a picture, one little square mark after another. If they thought a female delegate was a *mei* [妹], they would mark it in red. See how *wuliao* they were? Extremely *wuliao*.

The gendered connotations that can be implied by using the appellations *jie* and *mei* in general, therefore, are more than female seniority or juniority, particularly in a society where a marriage gradient is the norm. In Taiwan, hypergamy and homogamy are regarded as the conventional marriage patterns for women (Yang et al. 2006; Wu et al. 2013). Women are generally expected not to 'marry down'. In their study on assortative mating in Taiwan, Yang et al. (2006) identified education, earnings and age as the three main socio-economic factors in assortative mating; a woman is conventionally expected to find a male partner who is older, better-educated and has better earning capacity than she does.[21] In other words, in a heterosexual relationship, a man is expected to be more advantaged in terms of socio-economic conditions. If a woman is addressed by a man as *jie*, her seniority is labelled and constructed in the interaction. She is identified as the more advantaged one in their relationship.

By examining my participant's accounts, I have shown that *jie*, as an informal and personalised appellation, serves as a speech device that facilitates gendered interactions in the workplace. It is an indicator of the perceived and assumed relationships between the interacting social actors. On the one hand, it is adopted as an honorific appellation to show respect and good manners to senior female colleagues by their juniors. On the other hand, it can also be used for strategic communication purposes. Being referred to as a *jie* means that a female employee is given a superior and advantaged position in an interactive context. A colleague might use it as a tactic to negotiate work by acquiring and constructing a less powerful position for her or himself. Moreover, since *jie* is a gendered term used to indicate not just seniority but specifically female seniority, it can have specific connotations in a heterosexual interaction. While *mei*, the appellation indicating female juniority, is also a term used to refer to 'a beautiful chick', being identified as a *jie* could be interpreted as being perceived as less heterosexually desirable. Being identified and interacted with as a *jie*, therefore, is a gendered categorisation with sexual implications.

Patrolling Gender Boundaries

In Chap. 3, I discussed how gender segregation at work is sustained through organisational management and practices. The gendered division of labour underpins not only the binary structure of domestic/public labour but also the arrangement of work in an organisation. Work is, therefore, gendered. Some tasks are constructed as men's work and others as women's work. Women are employed and expected to fit into this gendered deployment. However, the construction of gendered labour and women as gendered employees in the workplace are not only accomplished by organisational management but also by general interactions among individual social actors. The latter is the theme emerging from my participants' accounts of some interesting (for some, in an annoying way) little episodes about gender in their everyday work. By examining this interview data, I show how my participants are identified and realised as gendered social actors in the workplace. I argue that the symbolic interpretations of their gender are constantly accomplished through general interactions at work. Their labour, bodies and general work practices are constructed as gendered. The meaning of my participants' gender, as well as the meaning of gender as a social category, is therefore negotiated in everyday interactive activities in the workplace.

'But Initials Are More Often Used by Men'

When I interviewed Chih-Lu, she was working in Taipei in the local office of an international corporation. Communicating with colleagues located in other countries was part of the daily routine, and English was the main language used in her organisation. Although it is not compulsory, using an English name is widely accepted as part of the organisational culture. Chih-Lu, however, was one of very few employees who chose to use the transliterated form of her Mandarin name. She had not anticipated that it would be an issue. After her supervisor noticed, she tried on several occasions to convince her to use an English name instead.

Chih-Lu: My supervisor had raised this issue three times. [...] 'Chih-Lu, you don't have an English name?' I said, 'No. I haven't used an English name for a long time, so if you called me by an English name, I wouldn't turn around. I wouldn't know who you were calling.' Then she said, 'Oh, okay'. The second time, she probably said something like 'Uh, but if you don't use an English name, the regional staff might find it difficult to pronounce your name'. And I said, 'I don't think so. Or they can call me C.L. I don't mind people calling me C.L.' Then my supervisor said, 'Oh, right, using initials. But initials are more often used by men.' Then I was like, 'Oh, I'm not sure about that actually'. (laugh) [...] I never interpret it in such a way. All I can say is that she was really 'gender sensitive'. (laugh)

Chih-Lu's supervisor tried to convince her not to use English initials by suggesting that it is usually only men who do so. This was stated as if it were a fact. The supervisor did not provide any evidence to support this statement, and she failed to explain why, even if that were the case, it would be a problem for a woman to use initials simply because it is a practice mostly adopted by men. This example shows how gender is regarded as a sufficient reason for making claims in everyday interactive situations. In other words, the supervisor was expecting Chih-Lu to adopt not only an English name which followed the work conventions of the organisation but also a name which conformed to her gender.

Gender seems not only to serve as a sufficient reason for making assertive claims in general communication, it is also adopted as an appropriate reason to doubt and restrict women's ability to do things. This is shown in Hsiao-Yin's account of a disagreement she had with a colleague about who could and should change the fluorescent tube in their office. Our conversation about the gender ratio among the staff in her workplace turned into a discussion of the gendered allocation of general tasks in her workplace.

Hsiao-Yin: I really can't stand it. Previously, we had this maintenance problem about lights. [...] There was one time, I said, 'the light keeps flickering'. The new fluorescent tube was there in our office, but no one wanted to change it. I said, 'Can someone let me use her or his desk as a ladder? I'm going to change the fluorescent tube.' Then she said, 'Don't do it. Just wait for the maintenance guy.' I said, 'Wait til when? It keeps flickering. I really feel uncomfortable. I can do it. I know how to do it.' However, she still insisted that it was not okay. [...] Then she asked her boyfriend [who was also working in the organisation but in a different department] for help. [...] There's only one male staff member in our office. On occasions like this, for instance, when something needs to be repaired or fixed, she would use a demanding tone, probably because she is quite senior. She would say [to the male employee], 'You change it'. I feel like, if I was him, I would feel, 'What the ...?' Everyone is capable of changing the light. It's really weird that she didn't allow me to do it.

Hsiao-Yin's willingness and her ability to change the fluorescent tube were rejected. On the other hand, her colleague's suggestions were problematic for Hsiao-Yin. It seems that the colleague was insisting on having a man change the tube. At first, her colleague tried to convince her to wait for the maintenance staff to do the repair. After that was declined, the colleague then turned to her boyfriend. Moreover, according to Hsiao-Yin's observation, she often asked the only male staff member to take care of similar tasks when he was present. This suggests that, for Hsiao-Yin's colleague, changing the fluorescent tube is a man's task. This incident is a good example of how the meaning of a gendered body is constructed in everyday interaction in the workplace. Being perceived and interacted with as women, my participants were expected by other individuals at work to behave accordingly. Sacks points out that social categories are 'inference rich' and that 'a great deal of the knowledge that members of a society have about the society is stored in terms of these categories' (1989: 272). Gender is therefore used and reinforced as a sufficient reason to allow or forbid a social actor's actions.

'I Feel that a Woman Is...'

As a female computer programmer, Yu-Chen was accustomed to people reacting with doubt and even shock when they found out her profession.

Yu-Chen: Or people would say, 'You're a *nyusheng*'. I said 'Yes'. 'You can do programming?' 'Yes.'
Ting-Fang: So it's kind of obvious that they think it's a men's thing?
Yu-Chen: Yes. Some people would even ask, 'How come you, a *nyusheng*, want to do programming?'
Ting-Fang: What did you reply to that?
Yu-Chen: I said, 'Who says a *nyusheng* can't do programming? Don't I have a brain and hands?'

What annoyed Yu-Chen the most is not that people find it unusual to meet a female computer programmer, but that they inappropriately question her career choice simply based on her gender. Working in the IT industry, which is widely acknowledged to be male-dominated, Yu-Chen faced negative assumptions and doubts about her occupational abilities not only from individuals when she first met them, but also from male colleagues with whom she worked. They had the idea that working with a female colleague is a bother because she can never work like a man does. For example, they assumed that a woman would be less strong physically than a man, so would be unable to carry a desktop tower on her own. And that would be problematic for them.

Yu-Chen: They probably feel that ... um ... a woman doesn't have enough strength to carry a desktop tower. [...] But I don't think that's always the case. For instance, recently my company had a refurbishment. We had to move things around. I carried two towers on my own. [...] But you know, sometimes, it's not about whether a woman can actually do it or not, but how they [men] feel about it. Sometimes a male colleague would say 'I feel that a woman is blah blah blah ...' And I would just tell him, 'I feel you should eat shit'.

The fact that Yu-Chen demonstrated sufficient physical strength could not really change her male colleagues' stereotypical opinion of women. This suggests that the ability of a female employee is predetermined by her gender and has nothing to do with her actual work performance. A woman is deemed to be weaker than a man and therefore less qualified. Facing this type of obvious gender discrimination, Yu-Chen could not resist fighting back with sharp and very direct comments. Since the speaker justified his sexist remark by reference to his feelings, Yu-Chen then delivered her reply using a similar sentence structure and logic to ridicule it.

For Yu-Chen, building up and maintaining an image as one who never holds back her opinions is something worth working on. She told me that being a direct person in the workplace saved her time because she could say whatever she wanted to, just cut directly to the point. In addition, it also made rejection much easier. However, while she never hesitated to give a piece of her mind to anyone making inappropriate assumptions about a female programmer, her directness gained her a reputation of 'being just like a man'. This can be observed in the way she was addressed by her colleagues. Yu-Chen has a nickname, Aki. Rather than just calling her Aki, her colleagues would add *ge* [哥: elder brother] after the nickname.

Yu-Chen: Everyone in my department calls me Aki *ge* [哥:an elder brother].
Ting-Fang: Aki *ge*?
Yu-Chen: They said that 'except for your appearance, you're basically a man. Take off your camouflage!'
Ting-Fang: (laughs) How so?
Yu-Chen: Probably because I don't talk like a *nyusheng*. I don't talk in a euphemistic way.

Yu-Chen has made a tremendous effort to show that computer programming is not and should not be a male-only occupation; a woman can also do it and do it well. However, while she survives her female-unfriendly workplace by employing a strategy of not holding back her opinions, this is interpreted as her not being feminine, rather than her colleagues realising there is something wrong with the male-dominated culture. By categorising Yu-Chen as a man-like female computer engineer, her colleagues reassure themselves that men are the norm in this workplace. The structure of gender duality is thus reaffirmed. Women who survive the male-dominated work culture and achieve a professional career in it are often labelled as not feminine. If you clearly do not fit the stereotype of woman, then you must be a man or like a man. An example is Margaret Thatcher; when she became prime minister, she was described as 'an honorary man' (Pringle 1994: 120). This is both praise and a negative comment. Her ability and success were accepted because she was 'like a man'. Therefore, she was also devalued as being 'not woman enough'. Ultimately, male masculinity and male identity are still the norm in politics, as in many workplaces.

'If a Nyusheng Participates, We Might Have Bad Luck'

Gender discrimination in everyday interactions not only undervalues women's professional ability in the male-dominated workplace but may also deprive women of the opportunity to perform certain tasks. Pei-Ju, a mechanical engineer, shared her thoughts about the tremendous pressure that a female employee can face in a male-dominated workplace. For example, there exists a superstition that if a woman goes onto a worksite or construction site, she will bring bad luck and something will go wrong. This presented her with a dilemma. On the one hand, she needed on-site experience to demonstrate her professional ability and skills. On the other hand, she risked being blamed if anything went wrong.

Pei-Ju: Yep. That is, you (as a *nyusheng*) being in a tunnel … for example, when we go down the tunnel at night and then other people would tell you … 'He has no bad intentions.' He would say, 'Um, but if a *nyusheng* comes, we might have bad luck'. He had no bad intentions. Most of the *nansheng* [男生: men] that we are facing have good intentions. If he had bad intentions, then it would be easy to deal with. But his intentions are good.

Ting-Fang: So the reason why he said this …

Pei-Ju: He sincerely thought so. […] He wanted to persuade you, to give you advice. 'There is no rule saying that you have to go. Would you like not to come?' He worried that you would be censured. Then what kind of dilemma are you facing? On the one hand, if you don't go, you miss an opportunity to gain experience. And then this experience would … people would use it to prove your disqualification. There are certain places that you couldn't go. […]

	This kind of evidence is not in words. It's a kind of ... when you want to be promoted, the fact that you don't have certain experience ...
Ting-Fang:	Um, it would not be stated on your résumé, but ...
Pei-Ju:	Yep, but people would identify you as, for example, you can't work solely on your own. It would be taken into consideration. On the other hand, if you go, you would feel the pressure. What if ... actually there is always a chance that the machine might suddenly break down. But if other people [go] and you don't, it breaks down. People would think it just happened today. But if you go and the machine indeed breaks down, they would feel 'Wow, the superstition is [true]'. [...] Really, they're all well-intentioned. But good intentions are even more horrible. Because of their good intentions, you have to reject or go against them in a delicate and tactful way.

Pei-Ju was aware that the career path she had chosen would not be female-friendly, and she prepared herself for and indeed experienced all kinds of hostile situations. She does not mind to have a serious argument about gender equality with any individual who has an opinion about female mechanical engineers. However, in the interview Pei-Ju emphasised more than once that she found 'well-intentioned' gender discrimination to be the most difficult kind to deal with. The discouraging words from her male colleagues were meant to be a kind reminder, or even a thoughtful suggestion. They wanted to prevent Pei-Ju from being blamed for an unsuccessful performance. As a member of the mechanical engineering team, even though she had acquired competent professional ability and qualifications, Pei-Ju was treated by her male colleagues as a gendered colleague who required extra care or who should be excused from certain tasks. In this way, a female mechanical engineer is categorised as a different kind of team member from the 'ordinary male one' because of her gender. Her gender is perceived as a special situation which requires their understanding and sympathy in work arrangements. Pei-Ju's story about her personal dilemma indicates how everyday symbolic exchanges contribute to sustaining the ideology of the gendered division of labour. Even though she is not necessarily labelled through verbal communications, her identity as a female staff member is constantly identified and constructed in everyday work practices.

'They Would Belittle You, Infantilise You'

While the previous discussion primarily relates to interactions between my participants and their colleagues, Yu-Nung's experience shows another interactive dimension at work. When she was working in the TV and film industry, Yu-Nung noticed that clients would praise female and male staff differently. She used a presentation experience as an example. While she was in her thirties, on one occasion she presented a commercial proposal to a male-dominated organisation which had a strict hierarchical system. Most of the high-ranking staff members were attending the event. After the session, Yu-Nung was invited to have an informal meeting with the chief. When she entered the room, the chief was seated in the main chair while all the other staff members were standing to the side. Yu-Nung approached the chief, chose the seat next to him and asked him directly for his comments about her proposal. Later that day, following a conversation with a male staff member who was in charge of her reception, she realised that her action might have surprised other members of the organisation.

Yu-Nung: He said, 'Eh, you, a *siao nyusheng* [小女生:little girl]'. He said it like that. 'You, a *siao nyusheng*, didn't you feel nervous or intimidated when you met with our chief and talked to him?' [...] I don't think it was the first time for them [to meet a woman who works in this industry], but strangely enough ... the reason why I use this example is that, in my area, when they talk about a *nansheng*, they say 'you're a talented young man'. If it were a *nyusheng*, they would belittle you, infantilise you, but at the same time appreciate you. It feels like they really appreciate and admire you but in a reluctant way. So they infantilise you, then they feel balanced.

It seems that the staff member was impressed by her frank attitude when she was facing the powerful and formidable chief. However, instead of expressing more straightforward praise of Yu-Nung's bold and confident meeting appearance, he delivered it as a question and addressed her as *siao nyusheng*, a little girl. He was showing his appreciation but at the same time undermining her professional authority by placing her in an infantilised position. Yu-Nung then linked this experience to others she had had in the industry. This was not the first or only time that she was addressed as a 'little girl' by male clients or work partners, even though she was clearly an adult woman with a professional and managerial title. According to Yu-Nung's observation, while a young male staff member would be described as 'a talented young man', a young female staff member would more often be described as 'an interesting little girl'. In this case, compared with 'talented', 'interesting' is a word that denotes less recognition of an individual's professional abilities.

I have presented my participants' accounts of common interactions at work in order to discuss how female employees are constantly reminded of their membership of the category of women in everyday routines. These experiences of gender categorisation constitute an important part of the 'gendered reality' of their everyday working lives (see Stokoe 2006; Hester and Francis 1997). Membership categorisation has been identified as an important aspect of doing gender in everyday social interactions (see Stokoe and Smithson 2001; Stokoe 2003, 2006). Adopting an ethnomethodological approach to studying gender and language, Stokoe proposes membership categorisation analysis as a useful tool to investigate gender and language in everyday social occasions. She argues that it is important to investigate 'how gender categories are routinely occasioned to accomplish some action' in 'mundane moments of interaction' (Stokoe 2006: 488). It is within the 'situated accomplishments of local interaction' that 'the routine gendering of social life gets "done"' (ibid.: 468). Also, it is through 'people's social and moral categorization practices' that gendered order is routinely achieved (Stokoe 2003: 4). Through an examination of the interactive episodes shared by my participants, the related 'normative conceptions' and 'cultural knowledge' about gender are therefore manifested. In her pioneering study on language and sexual politics in the case of a murder interrogation, Maria T. Wowk argues that 'gender is tacitly used as a background scheme for the performing of some "other" actions' (1984: 76). Her analysis reveals that, by facilitating 'commonsense reasoning' about men and women in his defence, the murderer was actually blaming the victim for the outcome of his own criminal act (ibid.). In the case of my participants' experiences, their gender is assumed to be a valid cause of dos and don'ts within their routine work performances. They are constantly perceived and treated as gendered beings by colleagues, supervisors and clients. As female employees in the workplace, my participants are expected to perform everyday work tasks in ways that 'fit' their gender. Working as a woman therefore means working as a member of the gendered social category, women.

INTERACTING HETEROSEXUALITY

I was once asked by an acquaintance why 'homosexual people' always have to be so 'sexually explicit'. Knowing that I am a supporter of gay rights and have joined the Taipei Pride several times, she regarded me as a proper candidate for this discussion and expressed her enquiry in a sincere tone. She told me that she would be more than willing to support gay rights if only the campaign could be much more low-key and not 'full of sexual stuff'. I cannot recall my response exactly, other than that I tried my best to engage in the conversation without unleashing the sarcastic remarks on the tip of my tongue.

It is not surprising that minorities are easy targets for stigmatisation. For non-heterosexual groups, the label 'sexual deviant' is always quickly applied. While heterosexuals can easily pass as 'normal' human beings, lesbians, gays and sexual minorities are often perceived as the sexualised other. The demonstration or presentation of homosexuality is thus easily perceived as excessively sexual. On the other hand, because heterosexuality is identified as the norm, it is so 'natural' that people often ignore it in everyday life. It is this 'unnoticeable' but actually ubiquitous heterosexuality in social life to which I now turn.

'They Feel the Need to Know Your Plans About Children'

In Chap. 3, I discussed how the marital and relationship status of a prospective employee is considered an issue to be investigated during the recruitment process. From the interview data, it appears that this is also an issue in everyday and mundane social interactions. One of the common experiences among my participants is that they are quite often asked about their heterosexual relationship status. 'Do you have a boyfriend?' 'Are you and your boyfriend going to get married soon?' 'Do you two plan to have children in the near future?' From the wording of these questions, it is clear that only heterosexual relationships are considered. The reasoning behind these questions assumes that heterosexuality is the person's only possible sexual orientation. In addition, these questions touch on the personal aspects of their lives. However, they are often posed by people with whom they do not necessarily share private information. It is as though heterosexual life is so normal, it is a perfectly acceptable subject to chat about with someone you do not know well. Hsi-Shu's account is a clear example.

Hsi-Shu is married and has no children. Her status as a married and childless woman seems to offer her colleagues sufficient reason to engage in social conversations regarding her pregnancy plans. In our interview, Hsi-Shu clearly expressed her annoyance about this constant prying in the workplace.

Hsi-Shu: During the past three years, my colleagues have constantly asked me why I don't have children. They keep asking me that. 'How come you haven't had any children yet?' But for what reason should I exchange such *wuliao* [無聊] information with my colleagues?

Hsi-Shu used the term *wuliao* to describe the information her colleagues were seeking. For her, having a conversation about her pregnancy plans is boring, mundane and nonsensical. She has no intention of sharing this part of her personal life with individuals in the workplace. She regards it as a meaningless social activity. Hsi-Shu continued to provide further details of the enquiries that she received.

Hsi-Shu: They feel the need to know your plans about children, or 'do you want to have children?' 'Do you plan to have one?' 'Are you taking Chinese herbal medicine?' 'You can't have anything chilled or cold (if you want to get pregnant).' I feel that people in the workplace care a lot ... not only the workplace actually. People are very interested in whether other people are going to get pregnant or not. [...] It's like today you ... um, it's like something as *wuliao* as the question 'What time did you wake up this morning?'

Hsi-Shu used the question of the time one woke up as an analogy to demonstrate how mundane she felt the questions regarding her pregnancy plans were. It seems that a woman's pregnancy plans are regarded as a proper conversational topic in general social interaction. It is as common as if they were asking about something routine, and they seem not to be aware of intruding on her personal and private life. I argue that this commonness is based on the ideology of heterosexual marriage. It should not be overlooked that Hsi-Shu's personal and private life is perceived as a heterosexual one. The fact that she married a man guaranteed her the position of having a 'normal life' as a member of the group of 'normal people'.

What is not clear from the English translation is that the 'you' in these enquiries is always in the singular form. The questions were posed to Hsi-Shu specifically. In other words, it was regarded as solely Hsi-Shu's 'problem' that she does not have children in her married life. They did not mention her husband at all. In fact, Hsi-Shu's colleagues went beyond prying into her intentions and plans about pregnancy, and offered specific suggestions for ways to overcome the 'problem'. According to their suggestions, her body was assumed to be the problem which was preventing her from conceiving. It seems that everyone felt able to have a say about this part of her personal life, even in the workplace.

Our daily social lives are actually filled with heterosexualised details. Heterosexuality is regarded as the norm; therefore, it is often neglected by social actors. Moreover, it is powerful enough at the symbolic level to disguise it as something else. That is, people are able to talk about heterosexuality without labelling it as heterosexual. Hsi-Shu provided a very impressive example of this. She told me that socialising with colleagues is not an easy task for her. One of the reasons is that she feels that her colleagues tend to pry into other people's personal lives, especially their sexual lives. However, they seem to be unaware that they are doing so.

Hsi-Shu: They [His-Shu's colleagues] like to discuss others, other *fuci*'s [夫妻][22] sex life. For example, did you keep your legs in a higher position [during or after sex]? [...] I will be totally honest with you here. I think if someone cares about other *fuci*'s sexual life by being concerned about whether they have children or not, that kind of thing, it's like assuming that having children is only about giving birth. 'Why have you not got pregnant?' Are you ever aware that maybe they don't enjoy their sex life? This kind of thing is funny. If you care about their sex life ... It actually is. You ask her about her sexual position, ask if she adopts a certain position or not. This is discussing other people's sex life. But basically, married women in Taiwan are not willing to discuss their real sex life. You're actually talking about others' bloody sex life but you're not willing to discuss the core of that sex life. Sex is a topic that is always obscure in the workplace, but having children is not. It's so strange.

Hsi-Shu feels that, although her colleagues were talking about sex in an explicit way, they thought they were talking about a normal part of married life: conception. In this case, talking about conception in a heterosexual marriage is regarded by Hsi-Shu's colleagues as not talking about sexual activity. Moreover, they did not realise they were intruding into a very personal and private part of another person's life. In his analysis of 'cultural heterosexism', Brickell argues that 'heterosexuality is positioned as normative' and 'a social order typified by heterosexuality is said to be essentially neutral' (2005: 101). While homosexuality is recognised and marked as 'an illegitimate occupier' or invader, heterosexuality is simply invisible (ibid.). Hsi-Shu's account serves as a very revealing example to demonstrate how 'ordinary people' convey the 'normativeness' and invisibility of heterosexuality in the common talk-in-interactions (ibid.).

'What's Up? You Getting Married?'

A heterosexual personal life is regarded not only as an appropriate and common conversational topic but also as a good symbolic resource to fill in the blanks or avoid an awkward moment in a conversation. Here is an example provided by Chih-Lu.

Chih-Lu:	[...] it might be because for him it's a subject for chatting.
Ting-Fang:	So he might feel that it's a safe and proper topic?
Chih-Lu:	Yes, I think it's very likely. You know, when I was planning on leaving the job, I told Jason first. [...] When I went to his office, there were many people around, interns for example. I think he wanted to let people know that it wasn't something serious. It's a subconscious behaviour. So when he stood up, he said. 'What's up? You getting married?' Like that.

Chih-Lu's colleague used a question about her marital status as a strategic move to ease the potential tension among other colleagues even though it was totally out of context. In her work on conversational practices, Kitzinger examines how heterosexuality is 'produced and reproduced in everyday talk-in-interaction' (2005: 221). She argues that using heterosexual reference terms is one of the common practices in our daily conversations. By doing so, people not only position themselves in heterosexual relationships with others but also take part in the construction of the heteronormative world. Kitzinger's work reveals the nuanced doing of gender in daily symbolic exchanges. Examining the data I collected, the construction of heteronormativity in social interactions at work is also evident. The normality of heterosexuality is constructed by appropriating it in everyday conversation.

'He Asked His Wife to Make the Call'

It has been suggested that the workplace is often desexualised (Bruni 2006). However, to avoid something requires first knowing exactly what to avoid. If desexualisation includes preventing any social practice that may be interpreted as sexual, individuals in the workplace could only successfully achieve this by first being aware of what could be interpreted as sexual. In other words, constructing a desexualised workplace probably requires the participants to be sensitive to and reflexive about sexuality. Therefore, it might be fair to say that, while individuals intend to desexualise their behaviour, their consciousness of this is actually a social product of sexualised consciousness. The experiences of my participants indicate that their own desexualisation of the workplace is partly accomplished by differentiating the ways in which they interact with same-sex or 'opposite-sex' colleagues.

When I asked about her leadership style, Hsi-Shu disclosed that the way in which she interacts with her supervisees varies according to their gender. She felt that, as a female supervisor, she could show her appreciation towards her female supervisees with a sense of intimacy through verbal cues and body language. On the other hand, if it were a male supervisee, she would interact with him in a different manner. She would not interact with him in an intimate way.

Hsi-Shu: [...] But when gender intersects with hierarchy, it would be very different. Female supervisor, male supervisor, male supervisee or female supervisee, I feel there is something different. It's very subtle. First, in the case of same sex, no matter if it's about someone in a higher or lower position, I feel that there is something you can go beyond. It's a kind of care, from the higher one to the lower one. It could be more natural. It's true. For example, he is my male supervisee. No matter what, I would never put my arm around his shoulder.

> When he performs well, I could not interact with him in an intimate way. But if it's my female supervisee ... when everyone performs well, I would talk to her in an intimate way.

Hsi-Shu's account indicates that she would take gender into consideration when expressing her appreciation of her supervisees. For her, in the case of same-sex interactions, there is something that she can 'go beyond'. It is a kind of intimacy that she would only express to her female colleagues through both physical gestures and verbal utterances. The physical and emotional distances can be closer. On the other hand, she feels that she should distance herself more from her male colleagues. Thus, gender serves as a baseline to determine what kind of action to adopt and also for interpreting whether it is proper or not. It is a kind of gender order that is embedded in the minutiae of everyday interactions. As the interview continued, Hsi-Shu revealed that sexuality matters in her reasoning behind this pattern of interaction.

Ting-Fang: Would it be different because of sexual orientation?
Hsi-Shu: If he was gay?
Ting-Fang: Yes.
Hsi-Shu: I might hug him. It is possible. (laugh)

Hsi-Shu's reasoning is very much based on the heterosexualised concept of gender. It seems that to interact intimately with an 'opposite-sex' colleague in a professional setting is inappropriate unless this colleague is not heterosexual. Hsi-Shu's account provides meaningful material for reflecting on the desexualisation of office scenarios. In a society where heterosexuality is assumed to be the norm, the desexualisation of the workplace is actually deheterosexualised. And it is done by being extremely aware of boundaries with people of the opposite sex.

Che-Yuan's assessment of her supervisor as a decent man reveals that avoiding heterosexual interactions with female employees in the workplace is a crucial principle in constructing this decent style of supervision.

Che-Yuan: It's very obvious that he would keep his distance. Even when we wear low-necked dresses, I can trust him without a doubt. He's not one of those people who would come close to you when you wear a low-cut top. He's not that kind of person. He's very, very decent. He would never

chih doufu [吃豆腐],[23] even verbally. There was one time,
when a colleague was eager to put out a message. It was
late, probably around 11 p.m. or midnight. She put out the
information from home. However, it was inaccurate. Our
supervisor was very, very angry. He was very angry when he
saw that. However, it was very late, so he didn't call that
female colleague. He asked his wife to make the call and ask
what was going on. So when it comes to male–female relationships, he keeps the boundaries clear. So everyone trusts
him very much. Because in that aspect, he is a very decent
person.

From Che-Yuan's narrative, we can see that the desexualised interaction is accomplished when the social actor is heterosexually sensitive. Her
male supervisor was clearly aware of the social boundaries between himself
and his female supervisee. He avoided any 'inappropriate' interactions. In
the case of *chih doufu*, he was avoiding any gestures or verbal occurrences
with sexual connotations. As for the late-night call, he was avoiding having
a private conversation with the female colleague.

'Why Didn't You Travel with Your Husband?'

Hsi-Shu often feels that her colleagues show too much interest in her private and personal life. For her, the annoyance stems from her colleagues
not only being nosy, but also voicing their opinions about her life.

Hsi-Shu: [...] I don't let people at work pry into my life. However, for
example, I bring lunch to work, and then they say, 'Oh, is it
made by your husband? Is your husband good at cooking?'
This superficial stuff is okay, but the real everyday life of ours,
I don't want to reveal it to them. For instance, there was one
time I travelled with a female friend. Then, they [colleagues]
said, 'It's so strange. Why didn't you travel with your husband?' 'Why it was not with your husband?' 'How come you
didn't go with your husband?' 'Why did you travel alone?'
[...] Generally speaking, apart from our honeymoon, I have
always travelled with my friends. Then every time, people
would be very, you know, incredulous and question me a lot.
I have been very confused. Why can't I travel with friends?

It is interesting to see how coupledom is constructed differently in different conversations. On the issue of pregnancy, the husband was dismissed, but when it came to social activities such as travel, he was regarded as the wife's 'natural' companion. Hsi-Shu's colleagues seemed to suggest that since she was a married woman, her husband should be her travel partner instead of her friend. They assumed there must have been a reason for his absence on the journey and therefore Hsi-Shu had to travel with her friend instead. Their questions and comments demonstrate the assumption that a heterosexual couple should act as a pair in everyday social activities. In their enquiry into sexuality and sexual relations in the later modern era, Jackson and Scott point out that, despite some shifts and developments in sexual diversity, 'the heterosexual couple remains enshrined as the normative form of adult sexual relationship' (2004a: 236). Heterosexual coupledom is still regarded as the norm and its features are even being adopted into other sexual relationships. 'Long-term', monogamous and 'stable' are now the standard to define all acceptable relationships. (ibid.: 237). The establishment of heterosexual monogamy is not just about the sexual or intimate parts of a couple's life or, in Klesse's words, 'the hegemony of the core couple as the only valid script for erotic and intimate relationships' (Klesse 2014: 73). It also includes the social aspect. As Jackson and Scott argue, 'the centrality of monogamous sexual-romantic relationships not only encourages us to de-prioritize our friendships, but also structures how we socialize with friends' (2004b: 155). An analysis of Hsi-Shu's account of the recurring and annoying interactions in her workplace has revealed how heterosexual coupledom is expressed on everyday social occasions. In the case of a married woman's travelling companion, her husband is assumed to be the prioritised candidate, rather than her friend.

Conclusion

In this chapter, I have used my participants' accounts to show that everyday social interactions in the workplace are both gendered and heteronormative. By examining common social practices, I have shown that the construction of gender and heteronormativity at work is accomplished not only through organisational management but also through everyday social activities. I used the social practice of gendered appellations to analyse the construction of gendered relationships in everyday interaction. While addressing each other with the so-called proper appellations shows respect and good manners, it is also a social practice that constantly labels normative relationships in everyday conversations. This normativity is aligned with the hierarchical and gendered social order. In addition, based on my participants' stories about day-to-day conversations with their colleagues and business partners, I have suggested that gender duality is maintained and constructed in commonplace encounters. The normativity of the gendered social order is constantly accomplished and patrolled through our daily social actions and interactions. Moreover, the construction of this gendered social order is intertwined with the normativity of heterosexuality. My participants have provided accounts of how heterosexuality is seen as a 'normal' and 'natural' part of life. However, their experiences also show that the gendered social order is not necessarily an absolute one but a relationship to be negotiated. I discuss this further in Chap. 5, as well as how it can be challenged.

NOTES

1. *Duoyuan* [多元] means 'diversity'. *Chengjia* [成家] means 'having a family' or 'establishing a family'.
2. However, it should be noted that this convention is very much Han-centred and a fairly new creation in Taiwanese society. Take the personal practices in my family, for example: the appellations for mother and father have only been adopted in my generation. My mother used to address her mother by her personal name. And my grandmother used *yia*, an appellation which it is speculated has an indigenous root, to address her mother.
3. It should be noted that in Mandarin, *yi* [姨] as a familial appellation is specifically used to refer to a maternal aunt.
4. *San* [桑], an appellation showing respect, is a loanword originating from the Japanese language. Taiwanese Mandarin has borrowed a substantial number of Japanese words since the Japanese occupation (1895–1945). Although importing words from Japanese was tightly controlled by the KMT government, which came to Taiwan in 1945, many loanwords have survived the regulation and are commonly used in everyday conversations (see Chung 2001). *San* is one example. These words have become a distinct characteristic of Taiwanese Mandarin.
5. Gong [公] is a term used to refer to a senior and respected man.
6. *Ge* [哥] means older brother in Mandarin.
7. '*Guanxi*' is included as an English word in the Oxford Dictionary, so here I followed the Hanyu Pinyin convention. *Jiu shi lun shi* [就事論事] is a Mandarin idiom which means to take the matter on its merits. The literal meaning of *jiu* [就] is 'according to' or 'focus on'. *Shi* [事] is a noun which refers to a thing or a serious matter. *Lun* [論] is a verb which means to discuss.

8. It should be noted that establishing reciprocal social networks as a business practice is not necessarily a unique Chinese social and cultural phenomenon. Research suggests that there are similar concepts or practices in other cultures, such as '*rapporto clientelare*' in Italy and '*blat*' in Russia (see Orru 1991; Michailova and Worm 2003).

9. *Sajiao* [撒嬌] is a Mandarin term which is difficult to translate with an equivalent English word. The meaning of this term could be generally understood as acting in a spoiled and childlike way. Further details will be discussed in the following analysis.

10. *Shualai* [耍賴] is a Mandarin term. It means being shameless and sly. As a social act, it is often performed in a childish way.

11. 'Ah' [啊], 'la' [啦] and 'oh' [喔] are common final particles in colloquial speech in Taiwan. The usage of sentence final particles and prolonging these words has been identified as one of the verbal features of the *sajiao* style of communication (see Chuang 2005; Yueh 2013).

12. Similar concepts can be found in other societies, such as *amae* [甘え] in Japan and *aegyo* in Korea. It has also been suggested that even in cultures or societies that do not have a term for this communication style, there may still exist a similar social practice (see Yueh 2013).

13. *Mei* [妹] is the Mandarin word referring to a younger sister.

14. *Da* [大] literally means 'big'. In this context, it is added in front the appellation to emphasise the seniority of the referred individual.

15. The first character of this term, *mei* [美], means 'beautiful'. *Nyu* [女] means 'a woman' or 'women'.

16. *La* [辣] is an adjective to describe hot and spicy food in Mandarin. It can also be used to describe someone who is sexually attractive.

17. *Hechangtuan* [合唱團] is the Mandarin term for ensemble.

18. It is suggested that *jhengmei* is an abbreviation of *jhengdiande* [正點的] *meimei* [妹妹] (Wu 2011). *Jhengdiande* (or *jhengdian*) is a Mandarin slang term. It could be understood as 'hell of a good' in English. *Meimei* means a younger sister. But when it is pronounced with a rising intonation, it is usually used to refer to a young woman or girl.

19. Despite the fact that *jhengmei* has been a notable cultural and economic phenomenon, it seems that it does not attract much academic attention. There are only a very few studies on it.

20. *Wuliao* [無聊] is a Mandarin term which has several meanings. In this context, it means boring, mundane and nonsensical. This term is generally used to describe a behaviour that is meaningless.

21. It has been suggested that with the expansion of higher education and improvements in women's earnings and labour participation, there are emerging changes as well as persistence in the pattern of women's hypergamy in Taiwan. For example, Yang et al. suggest that 'it seems that downward marriage in one aspect tends to be compensated by hypergamy in another aspect' (2006: 4).

22. *Fu* [夫] means 'husband' in Mandarin. *Ci* [妻] means 'wife'. *Fuci* [夫妻] is the common gendered term used to refer to a married couple.
23. *Chih doufu* [吃豆腐] literally means 'eating tofu'. *Chih* [吃] means 'eat'. *Doufu* [豆腐] is tofu. The phrase is commonly understood to mean an act of unpleasant dalliance or sexual harassment.

REFERENCES

Bedford, O., & Hwang, S. L. (2013). Building Relationships for Business in Taiwanese Hostess Clubs: The Psychological and Social Processes of Guanxi Development. *Gender, Work & Organization, 20*(3), 297–310.

Brickell, C. (2005). The Transformation of Heterosexism and Its Paradoxes. In C. Ingraham (Ed.), *Thinking Straight: The Power, the Promise, and the Paradox of Heterosexuality* (pp. 85–106). New York: Routledge.

Bruni, A. (2006). 'Have You Got a Boyfriend or Are You Single?' On the Importance of Being 'Straight' in Organizational Research. *Gender, Work & Organization, 13*(3), 299–316.

Chen, S. [陳聖光]. (2012). Show Girl 的美麗與哀愁 解讀高學歷正妹的另一種途徑 [The Beauty and Sorrow of Show Girls: An Alternative Interpretation of Highly Educated *Jheng Mei*]. 性別平等教育季刊 [*Gender Equality Education Quarterly*], *59*, 110–119.

Chow, I. H. S., & Ng, I. (2004). The Characteristics of Chinese Personal Ties (guanxi): Evidence from Hong Kong. *Organization Studies, 25*(7), 1075–1093.

Chuang, T. I. (2005). The Power of Cuteness: Female Infantilization in Urban Taiwan. *Stanford Journal of East Asian Affairs, 5*(2), 21–28.

Chung, K. S. (2001). Some Returned Loans: Japanese Loanwords in Taiwan Mandarin. In T. E. McAuley (Ed.), *Language Change in East Asia* (pp. 161–179). Surrey: Curzon Press.

Collins, R. (2004). *Interaction Ritual Chains*. Princeton: Princeton University Press.

Davies, H., Leung, T. K., Luk, S. T., & Wong, Y. H. (1995). The Benefits of "Guanxi": The Value of Relationships in Developing the Chinese Market. *Industrial Marketing Management, 24*(3), 207–214.

Dunfee, T. W., & Warren, D. E. (2001). Is Guanxi Ethical? A Normative Analysis of Doing Business in China. *Journal of Business Ethics, 32*(3), 191–204.

Farris, C. S. (1988). Gender and Grammar in Chinese: With Implications for Language Universals. *Modern China, 14*(3), 277–308.

Garfinkel, H. (1967). *Studies in Ethnomethodology*. Cambridge: Polity Press.

Goffman, E. (1959). *The Presentation of Self in Everday Life*. Reading: Cox & Wyman.

Goffman, E. (1967). *Interaction Ritual: Essays on Face-to-Face Behavior*. New York: Pantheon Books.

Hester, S., & Francis, D. (1997). Reality Analysis in a Classroom Storytelling. *British Journal of Sociology, 48*(1), 95–112.

Hsu, J. Y., & Saxenian, A. (2000). The Limits of Guanxi Capitalism: Transnational Collaboration Between Taiwan and the USA. *Environment and Planning A, 32*(11), 1991–2006.

Hwang, D. B., & Blair Staley, A. (2005). An Analysis of Recent Accounting and Auditing Failures in the United States on US Accounting and Auditing in China. *Managerial Auditing Journal, 20*(3), 227–234.

Hwang, D. B., Golemon, P. L., Chen, Y., Wang, T. S., & Hung, W. S. (2009). Guanxi and Business Ethics in Confucian Society Today: An Empirical Case Study in Taiwan. *Journal of Business Ethics, 89*(2), 235–250.

Jackson, S., & Scott, S. (2004a). Sexual Antinomies in Late Modernity. *Sexualities, 7*(2), 233–248.

Jackson, S., & Scott, S. (2004b). The Personal Is Still Political: Heterosexuality, Feminism and Monogamy. *Feminism & Psychology, 14*(1), 151–157.

Kitzinger, C. (2005). 'Speaking as a Heterosexual': (How) Does Sexuality Matter for Talk-in-Interaction? *Research on Language and Social Interaction, 38*(3), 221–265.

Kitzinger, C. (2009). Doing Gender: A Conversation Analytic Perspective. *Gender & Society, 23*(1), 94–98.

Klesse, C. (2014). 'Loving More Than One': On the Discourse of Polyamory. In A. G. Jónasdóttir & A. Ferguson (Eds.), *Love: A Question for Feminism in the Twenty-First Century* (pp. 63–76). New York: Routledge.

Lee, D. J., Pae, J. H., & Wong, Y. H. (2001). A Model of Close Business Relationships in China (Guanxi). *European Journal of Marketing, 35*(1/2), 51–69.

Lin, X. (2013). *Gender, Modernity and Male Migrant Workers in China: Becoming a 'Modern' Man*. London: Routledge.

Luo, Y. (2002). Corruption and Organization in Asian Management Systems. *Asia Pacific Journal of Management, 19*(2–3), 405–422.

Michailova, S., & Worm, V. (2003). Personal Networking in Russia and China: Blat and Guanxi. *European Management Journal, 21*(4), 509–519.

Millington, A., Eberhardt, M., & Wilkinson, B. (2005). Gift Giving, Guanxi and Illicit Payments in Buyer–Supplier Relations in China: Analysing the Experience of UK Companies. *Journal of Business Ethics, 57*(3), 255–268.

Orru, M. (1991). The Institutional Logic of Small-Firm Economies in Italy and Taiwan. *Studies in Comparative International Development, 26*(1), 3–28.

Osburg, J. (2016). Corruption, Masculinity, and Jianghu Ideology in the PRC. In L. Kam (Ed.), *Changing Chinese Masculinities: From Imperial Pillars of State to Global Real Men* (pp. 157–172). Hong Kong: Hong Kong University Press.

Pringle, R. (1994). Office Affairs. In S. Wright (Ed.), *The Anthropology of Organizations* (pp. 115–123). London: Routledge.

Sacks, H. (1989). Lecture Six: The MIR Membership Categorization Device. *Human Studies, 12*(3/4), 271–281.

Smith, D. E. (1987). *The Everyday World as Problematic: A Feminist Sociology*. Boston: Northeastern University Press.

Smith, D. E. (1997). Comment on Hekman's 'Truth and Method: Feminist Standpoint Theory Revisited'. *Signs, 22*(2), 392–398.

Stokoe, E. H. (2003). Doing Gender, Doing Categorization: Recent Developments in Language and Gender Research. *International Sociolinguistics, 2*(1), 1–12.

Stokoe, E. H. (2006). On Ethnomethodology, Feminism, and the Analysis of Categorial Reference to Gender in Talk-in-Interaction. *The Sociological Review, 54*(3), 467–494.

Stokoe, E. H., & Smithson, J. (2001). Making Gender Relevant: Conversation Analysis and Gender Categories in Interaction. *Discourse & Society, 12*(2), 217–244.

Tsang, E. W. (1998). Can Guanxi Be a Source of Sustained Competitive Advantage for Doing Business in China? *The Academy of Management Executive, 12*(2), 64–73.

Tsui, A. S., & Farh, J. L. L. (1997). Where Guanxi Matters: Relational Demography and Guanxi in the Chinese Context. *Work and Occupations, 24*(1), 56–79.

Wang, Y. H. (2009). 'Posing into Being': An Exploratory Study of Taiwanese Girls' Self-Portraiture Online. In N. Capentier et al. (Eds.), *Communicative Approaches to Politics and Ethics in Europe* (pp. 179–192). Brussels: ECREA.

Wank, D. L. (1996). The Institutional Process of Market Clientelism: Guanxi and Private Business in a South China city. *The China Quarterly, 147*, 820–838.

West, C., & Zimmerman, D. H. (1987). Doing Gender. *Gender & Society, 1*(2), 125–151.

Wowk, M. T. (1984). Blame Allocation, Sex and Gender in a Murder Interrogation. *Women's Studies International Forum, 7*(1), 75–82.

Wu, Y. [吳永佳] (2011). '正妹經濟學' [*Jheng Mei* Economics], *Cheers, 119*, November [Online]. Retrieved September 4, 2016, from http://www.cheers. com.tw/article/article.action?id=5028034

Wu, L., Yeh, H., & Tsay, R. [巫麗雪, 葉秀珍, & 蔡瑞明]. (2013). 遇見另一半: 教育婚配過程中的介紹人與接觸場合 [Meeting the Other Half: Matchmakers and Settings of Contact in Educational Assortive Mating]. 台灣社會學 [*Taiwanese Sociology*], *26*, 147–190.

Yang, C., Li, D., & Chen, K. [楊靜利, 李大正, & 陳寬政]. (2006). 台灣傳統婚配空間的變化與婚姻行為之變遷 [Assortive Mating in Taiwan: Changes and Persistence]. 人口學刊 [*Journal of Population Studies*], *33*, 1–32.

Yueh, H. I. S. (2013). Body Performance in Gendered Language: Deconstructing the Mandarin Term Sajiao in the Cultural Context of Taiwan. *Journal of Theories and Research in Education, 8*(1), 159–182.

CHAPTER 5

'I Feel You Should Eat Shit': Picturing the Agency of the Misfit Self in the Workplace

INTRODUCTION

In Chaps. 3 and 4 I discussed gendered and heteronormative practices in institutional arrangements and everyday interactions in the workplace. I argued that these practices are deeply embedded within a cultural context that values hierarchical social order and reciprocal relationships. I also presented my participants' accounts of how they make sense of these practices and their reactions to the social encounters that disqualify or discriminate against female employees. These episodes not only demonstrate the gendered and heteronormative aspects in the workplace but also provide details about female employees' experiences of negotiation when they are disadvantaged by social and cultural factors in a working situation. Those details have motivated me to enquire into the mobilisation of agency and the construction of the social self. In this chapter, I explore these themes further and present my analysis of them.

I start with my approach to theorising the social self. Through undertaking and reviewing a reflexive reading of the work of George Herbert Mead, I propose my own method of understanding the concept of 'the self' in the context of Taiwan. In Mead's work, language plays an essential part in his thinking on the sociality of 'the self'. Since I am working on research data that was generated in a different linguistic context from Mead's, there are theoretical concepts that I have to consider before I move on to link the theory with my data.

© The Author(s) 2018
T.-F. Chin, *Everyday Gender at Work in Taiwan*,
Gender, Sexualities and Culture in Asia,
https://doi.org/10.1007/978-981-10-7365-6_5

In the second half of this chapter, the focus is on the construction of the social self during the process of negotiating gender. I examine the emerging social self in my participants' accounts and argue that, while the strategies they have adopted may vary, there is one common element across my participants' narratives: a reflexive self that does not fit into the generalised community in a given situation. In the analysis, I point out that the realisation and construction of this misfit self may play an important role in the mobilisation of agency and, therefore, make negotiation possible.

Theorising the Social Self

The analysis in this chapter derives its theoretical framework from sociological ideas about social selves in an anglophone knowledge system, especially the work of Mead. In presenting my critical reading of Mead's theory of 'the self', my aim is to develop an approach that is useful for examining the contextual details of my research data. I first explain my understanding of Mead's ideas about the sociality and reflexivity of 'the self', then discuss the potential problems and benefits of adapting his theory to a non-anglophone context.

Mead's Theory of the Self

Mead conceptualises the self as deeply embedded within sociality, and his version of sociality is tightly intertwined with reflexivity. For Mead, the self can only come to exist in a particular historical and social context. According to him, 'the self is something which has a development' and it occurs 'in the process of social experience and activity' (1934: 135). In other words, Mead sees the self as the ongoing development of an individual living in a society. As an individual's social being continues, the construction of the self carries on. Moreover, this socialisation takes place in relation to other social beings. The sociality of the self is mobilised by the numerous interactive events that happen during an individual's life. The self is something that is acquired and continuously constructed through the interactions between a social being and others.

By emphasising the interactive social element, Mead cultivates the connections between sociality and reflexivity in agency. For Mead, reflexivity originates from the ability of an individual to have an objective view of her/his own being in a given situation. He argues that 'reason cannot become impersonal unless it takes an objective, non-affective attitude toward itself; otherwise we have just consciousness, not self-consciousness' (1934: 138). In distinguishing self-consciousness from consciousness, Mead proposes that learning to evaluate one's own behaviour in such a way that one 'becomes an object' to oneself is an essential part of the socialisation that triggers reflexive psycho-social activity. By putting her/himself in an objective position, an individual is able to adopt other individuals' attitudes towards her/him in a specific social context. She/he examines her/his own experiences and behaviour from the perspectives of other people who are also taking part in that context. An individual then becomes both subject and object. As Jackson explains, 'reflexivity here denotes the dialogic interplay between self and other, the capacity to see ourselves as subject and object, to engage in conversations with ourselves' (2010: 126).

Mead uses grammatical concepts as theoretical tools to explain this psycho-social activity. In his words, 'the "I" reacts to the "self" which arises through the taking of the attitudes of others. Through taking those attitudes we have introduced the "me" and we react to it as an "I"' (1934: 174). By distinguishing the 'I' from the 'me', Mead is theorising the reflexivity of the self. This reflexiveness is the main component in Mead's version of agency. It 'drives the development of the reflective intelligence, that is, the capacity of actors to critically shape their own responsiveness to problematic situations' (Emirbayer and Mische 1998: 971). While differentiating the 'I' from the 'me' provides a comprehensive explanation of Mead's theorisation of agency, it would be oversimplifying his idea to view 'I' and 'me' as two distinct and independent aspects of a social being. Since Mead's version of reflexive sociality is a process that is deeply situated within the interactive context, it would be a partial reading if we neglected the aspect of time and the relational element in it. 'In Mead's work there is no assumption of a primitive pre-social "I". Rather, the "I" is only ever momentarily mobilised in dialogic, ongoing interplay with the "me"' (Jackson 2010: 128). Both 'I' and 'me' are temporal products in a historical and social situation. In any given moment, a reflexive social being is both object and subject; for that reason, the individual is both the 'I' and the 'me'.

Rethinking Mead's Ideas in the Context of Taiwan

Mead states that 'the language process is essential for the development of the self'; therefore, his theorisation of the self relies heavily on language or symbolic activity (Mead 1934: 135). Since the language of the original data for this research is not English, even though Mead's theorisation of the concept of the self is inspiring, I feel that it would be too blunt to adopt his ideas to examine my participants' accounts without considering the linguistic context of my data. Due to the linguistic differences, I have to locate alternative symbolic signals in order to develop my own approach to reflexivity.

Unlike in English, personal pronouns in Mandarin do not have subject forms and object forms (see Table 5.1). The personal pronoun stays the same. Its character and pronunciation do not change. Take the first person singular pronoun in Mandarin, *wo* [我], for example; it only has one form. No matter whether it is put in the subject or object position in a sentence, *wo* [我] is the only word that can be used. Moreover, although in Mandarin the second and third personal pronouns have female and male written forms, they all have the same pronunciation, but the male pronouns can be used in a neutral way. Therefore, it is possible to talk about a third party in a conversation without addressing his or her gender. This is one of the many cultural conditions that enable the very 'sociological moment' described in Chap. 1 to happen. My colleague could not figure out the gender of my friend by the Mandarin pronoun that I used. If it were a conversation in English, I would have to use a gendered pronoun to refer to my friend.

Table 5.1 Personal pronouns in Mandarin

Number	Person	Gender	Personal pronouns
Singular	1st	Female/male	我 [*wo*]
	2nd	Female	妳 [*ni*]
		Male/female	你 [*ni*]
		Polite	您 [*nin*]
	3rd	Female	她 [*ta*]
		Male/female	他 [*ta*]
		Animal	牠 [*ta*]
		Neuter	它 [*ta*]
Plural	1st	General	我們 [*women*]
	2nd	Female	妳們 [*nimen*]
		Male/female/general	你們 [*nimen*]
	3rd	Female	她們 [*tamen*]
		Male/female/general	他們 [*tamen*]
		Animal	牠們 [*tamen*]
		Neuter	它們 [*tamen*]

Mead suggests that a crucial part of reflexivity is to view oneself as both subject and object. Since there are no differences between the subject and object form of a personal pronoun in Mandarin, one may infer that a narration in Mandarin is less reflexive than one in English. Furthermore, the fact that a person can be addressed without indicating his/her gender may give the impression that verbal communication in Mandarin is less gendered. That is, people probably do not care about gender very much in daily conversation.

Are Mandarin symbolic activities less reflexive and less gendered than those in English? In order to answer this question, other linguistic features and cultural factors need to be considered as well. I will demonstrate that, although it might be inappropriate to directly copy the reflexivity theory proposed by Mead and apply it to the Taiwanese context, this does not mean that reflexivity is not a useful analytical tool for this research. I propose that different cultures engage in different symbolic activities, which demonstrate different models of reflexivity. I will discuss this in two parts.

Firstly, I would like to point out that lacking gender indications in verbal communication is not equivalent to practising gender-neutral communication. The conversation that I had with my colleague is also a good example to illustrate that, even though we might talk about a person without indicating her/his gender, this does not mean that gender is forgotten or neglected in Mandarin symbolic activities. My colleague did care about the gender of my friend or she would not have asked about it. In addition, even when people do not ask the gender question, this does not mean they are interacting with others in a gender-neutral way. They probably just make assumptions about people's gender or, in Kessler and McKenna's (1985) terms, make 'gender attribution' without asking.

I would like to use a riddle to illustrate this. It is a riddle about relationships. A father and his son had a traffic accident and were sent to the casualty department of a hospital. The son was badly injured and needed an operation immediately. However, the on-duty surgeon took one look at the injured son and refused to operate. The surgeon said: 'I can't perform an operation on this patient. He is my son.' Who is this surgeon?

The 'clever' and 'humorous' answer to this riddle is that the surgeon is the mother. This riddle probably sounds dull and silly to people who believe in gender equality and women's rights. For them, this riddle is not a riddle at all and there could be more than just one correct answer. However, some people do need a few minutes to figure it out. The main twist of this riddle relies on the gender stereotyping of occupations. When the riddle is told in Mandarin, the speaker can avoid indicating the surgeon's gender even when pronouns are used. The 'surprising cleverness' of the answer depends on the audience not thinking that a woman could be a surgeon. The audience is expected to assume that being a surgeon is a 'male' occupation and therefore that the surgeon is a man; moreover, that he is a heterosexual man. While the riddle itself can be told in a gender-neutral way, that is, the language of the narrator may not contain any obvious gendered clues, such as gendered pronouns, this does not necessarily prevent people from making assumptions about the gender of the characters in the story.

The point that I am trying to raise here is that, while the available linguistic resources may differ, for example in English and Mandarin, this does not mean that the speaker of one language is necessarily less reflexive than the speaker of another. I believe that each language system has its own linguistic indicators and tools for an individual to generate agency within any symbolic interaction. Therefore, even though we are thinking in different linguistic contexts, Mead's thoughts on the relational and reflexive aspects of 'the self' have provided a useful map for me to develop my own approach.

Secondly, similar to many other societies, relationships play an important role in quotidian social life in Taiwan. However, Taiwanese society has its own distinct attributes. In Taiwan, a relationship is often gendered and hierarchical. Everyday social interactions usually take place within a specific system of social order. As I discussed in Chap. 4, the conventional appellations used in everyday life illustrate this. The nature of an interpersonal relationship is expected to be established and maintained according to the social positions that the participating individuals have acquired in society. Moreover, their interactions are also expected to be practised accordingly. Under such circumstances, an individual's self-consciousness ordinarily evolves through placing herself in the system of social relations. In other words, when the social being is calculating the possible, available and appropriate action in a given situation, she has to take the social relationships among the participants into consideration. For this reason, I argue that an individual's agency in the context of Taiwan cannot be fully deciphered without acknowledging the relationships within which an individual is immersed.

I am convinced that Mead's theory of reflexivity has advantages that shed light on the investigation of my participants' experiences in negotiating gender. Accessing agency as a philosophical concept, Emirbayer and Mische propose a conception of agency that 'is intrinsically social and relational'. They see the merits in Mead's theoretical framework and emphasise its relational element. From their point of view, 'agency is always a dialogical process by and through which actors immersed in temporal passage engage with others within collectively organized contexts of action' (1998: 973–974). They point out that, in Mead's conceptualisation of agency, 'the capacity for imaginative distancing' plays an important role (ibid.: 971). I am in sympathy with their point of view and I will further argue that this practice of distancing is not only about distancing an individual from her/himself but also about distancing her/himself from the generalised other, or sometimes from specific others.

Cultivating the Relationship Between 'the Self' and 'the Community'

According to Mead, 'one has to be a member of a community to be a self' and 'the process out of which the self arises is a social process which implies interaction of individuals in the group, implies the pre-existence of the group' (1934: 162, 164). The self emerges with a sense of realisation and assessment of the relations between the individual and other social beings in a given context. However, being aware of other social members does not mean that an individual will necessarily always adopt the attitudes of these others. As Mead indicates, 'we are not simply bound by the community'; there are 'critical situations' in which an individual may speak up and against a community (1934: 168). Deploying agency and being reflexive means that 'we are engaged in a conversation in which what we say is listened to by the community and its response is one which is affected by what we have to say' (1934: 168). The result of this conversation is not predetermined. It is relational, responsive and momentary, for the self is always in a state of transformation from subject to object and vice versa. In Elliott's words, Mead's conceptualisation of the self is 'at once individuality and generality, agent and recipient, sameness and difference' (2008: 32).

When agency is understood in terms of examining the relationship between the self and a community, it is crucial not to neglect the complexity of identity. A social being often has connections with and memberships of more than a single social group. Gender, race, class, occupation, hobby—there are numerous social categories with which a social being can identify herself in a given historical moment. Since agency is a process involving dialogue between an individual and herself in relation to other social beings, it is important to consider any possible conflict between the groups with which the individual identifies and the individuals with whom she is interacting at that moment. It is entirely possible for an individual to react against a community with which she/he interacts. Mead points out that 'the only way in which we can react against the disapproval of the entire community is by setting up a higher sort of community which in a certain sense out-votes the one we find' (1934: 167–168). Although I am less assertive than Mead, I do think that the potential conflicts and competitions among the multiple identities that a social being could have is one of the factors enabling an individual to 'react against' a community. Identity, like agency, is a product of social relationships. Lawler points out that 'the notion of identity hinges on an apparently paradoxical combination of sameness and difference' (2008: 2). This sense of sameness and difference comes from an individual's social experiences. 'Identity needs to be understood not as belonging "within" the individual person, but as produced between persons and within social relations' (ibid.: 6). The relational aspect of the self therefore provides a point of intersection for looking at agency through the construction of identities.

Reading Mead's words about the possible confrontational self, I then contemplated my participants' symbolic interactions with people in the workplace, especially those moments of defiance. I could not help but think that there is probably no better data informing me about agency than the narratives of the 'critical situations' in my participants' accounts. They were not only providing information about how gender inequality still prevails in the workplace; they were also telling me stories about how they struggled with it. They were offering me narratives about how they behave and who they are in relation to other individuals in the workplace. 'Identities can be understood as being made through narratives' (Lawler 2008: 11). Perhaps the interviews I conducted with my participants were both a research process and a social practice of doing identities. I asked about their experiences, their thoughts and their points of view. At the same time, through the conversations, I was also sharing mine. We were generating not only data but also narratives about ourselves. Conducting this research was itself a process of symbolic interaction.

A GENDERED SELF THAT DOES NOT FIT IN

It is probably not a surprise that most of my participants had experienced moments when they felt they did not really quite fit into their workplace, since the overall working culture in Taiwan is still very much gendered and heteronormative. When the working culture is not friendly, critical situations become a part of everyday life. A self that is distanced from the generalised community at work therefore appears in the data. Before I move on to discuss this emerging self, I have to clarify this claim a bit more in order to prevent the potential generalisation of female employees in Taiwan. I am aware that there are limits to the representativeness of my data. My interpretation and analysis are confined by the scope of this project and the experiences of my participants. Therefore, I have no intention of painting with a broad brush here. The misfit self that I am discussing is not a product that can be used to understand every interaction at work or every female employee's story in Taiwan.

During the early stages of fieldwork, my attention was focused primarily on the instances of gender inequality in my participants' accounts. I did not pay much (or any) attention to their utterances relating to the construction of 'the self'. It was only after my interview with Siang-Yun that I put the first note about 'the self' into my fieldwork journal. Siang-Yun works in the banking industry. As a member of the front-desk staff, she is required to wear a uniform during working hours. She shared a story about how she and her colleagues use changing clothes as a strategy to distinguish work time from private life. This inspired me to think about the boundaries and construction of 'the self' in the workplace. I then started to pay attention to the traces of the social self that were appearing in my participants' accounts. Gradually, as the interviews moved on, I started to see the hierarchical structure into which their stories were fitting. I saw their personal struggles within that structure, and I realised that my participants were telling stories about 'the self' within their interactive situational engagements in the workplace. However, I only realised much later that 'the misfit self' could be a theme to discuss in this monograph.

This epiphany was delivered in a collaborative way, when I participated in a semi-social and semi-academic event for PhD researchers. We were asked to do an academic version of speed dating. We had to introduce our own research project to others in small groups within a very short period of time. I had a printed slide with me to show my colleagues a quote from one of my participants.

Yu-Chen: But you know, sometimes, it's not about whether a woman can actually do it or not but how they feel about it. Sometimes a male colleague would say 'I feel that a woman is blah blah blah …' And I would just tell him, 'I feel you should eat shit'.

When I presented the quote, almost all of my colleagues gasped. One asked 'did she really say that?' My colleagues were surprised at the language Yu-Chen used and the bluntness of her attitude. It was even suggested that I should definitely use this sentence as the title of one of my chapters. From their feedback, I realised that my participant's reaction was probably unusual. But why is it regarded as unusual? Is it because she is a woman and thus is expected to be gentle and polite in her words? Is it because she works in a male-dominated workplace, and people assume that she would feel intimidated and avoid direct conflict with her male colleagues? The questions that are raised by this sense of unusualness have lingered in my thoughts ever since. Maybe it is actually an enquiry that cannot be fully answered without looking at the intersection of gender, race and cultural hegemony. Considering that Asian society is usually understood through a lens of dichotomy and viewed as the opposite, and sometimes even a homogeneous, entity to 'the Western', I could not help but suspect that it is surprising because it is unexpected to encounter an 'Asian woman' who speaks out and gives a piece of her mind. I am aware that it is indeed part of Asian culture that women are usually compelled to conform to an image of submissiveness and that the harmony of interpersonal relationships is usually positively valued.

Although I am still pondering what perceptions contribute to this sense of the unusualness of Yu-Chen's words, I do feel the intellectual necessity to present experiences and practices that do not fit into that assumed standard. I am interested in what makes my participants 'dare to' express their opinions in an unconventional way. In short, I believe my participants' 'unusual' narratives are meaningful material to challenge stereotypes about both 'Asian culture' and 'Asian women'. Moreover, they may provide insights into women's agency in the 'critical situation' of gender inequality.

Before presenting the analysis, I would like to devote some attention to explaining the change of writing style in the following sections. In the previous two chapters, I have presented my participants' accounts in categories. I managed to find common themes in their experiences and developed a categorisation to examine them. However, in this chapter I adopt a different strategy, focusing on five participants' stories and presenting each person's narrative about 'the self' individually. I feel that, even doing qualitative research, I am often haunted by quantitative thoughts. During the early stages of my data analysis, one of the main strategies that I adopted was trying to categorise my participants' accounts. I located possible themes through repeatedly reading the transcripts and identified the emerging themes by the frequency of their appearances. During this screening process, data that did not seem 'representative enough' would be filtered out. However, a lack of representativeness does not necessarily mean that those unusual, uncommon, different bits are irrelevant to this research. I found it difficult to abandon the idea that this data might be meaningful in its own way, and my participants' accounts of the 'misfit self' are part of this.

I hope that, through the change in writing style, I can present my participants in a different way. I would like to present them as real people with background details. Those details may seem irrelevant to the analysis, but I think they are useful in enabling readers to visualise them as real human beings. I know my analysis has a limit. To avoid only capturing a fragmented glimpse of my participants, I require the help of my readers' imaginations. And I hope that this alternative writing style can provide some material to facilitate that imagination. I have borrowed Mead's theories to elucidate my view on reflexivity. It is a momentary process, and the results emerged in an interactive context. Although my writing strategy for this chapter is to focus on specific participants and present them one by one, I did not intend to categorise them as 'participants with reflexivity' and label the rest as being without. Rather, my intention is to provide a just portrait of the participants. By presenting background information about the interview and details about their characteristics, I aim to provide the reader with a vivid image of my participants. Balancing between the intended strategy and accessibility for the reader, I think it would be impractical to present every single participant in this way and therefore I have selected five participants in order to analyse their agency in this chapter. However, this does not mean that there is no sign of a misfit self in other participants' accounts.

I am still not sure what rationales lay behind my colleagues' surprised reactions to Yu-Chen's account, but I would like to interpret their gasps as a sign of being challenged by something unexpected. I hope that the 'not so typical' narratives provided by my participants can serve as useful material to defy the stereotypical impressions about women in Taiwan and

women in general. In one of her talks, Adichie (2009) warns of the consequences of only hearing a single story about a certain ethnic group. She
identifies the single story as a dangerous narrative because it confines our
imagination and therefore shapes our understanding of minorities. 'It robs
people of dignity. It makes our recognition of our equal humanity difficult.
It emphasises how we are different rather than how we are similar.' We
need stories that are different from one another in order to fertilise our
sociological recognition and imagination of the 'empirical reality' (Plummer
2001: xi). As Plummer argues, the world we live in is a 'plural world' which
is 'constituted through multiple refracted perspectives' within which meaning is constantly negotiated (2001: xi). Otherwise, we might be lured into
accepting what Narayan identifies as cultural essentialism. We might accept
the idea that '"actual cultural differences" correspond very neatly to the
"packages" that are currently individuated as "separate cultures" or manifest themselves as evenly distributed across particular "cultures"' (Narayan
1998: 102). Having presented and discussed gender inequality at work
from the perspectives of both institutional and everyday interactional practices, I hope that this shift to introducing the misfit self will offer, if not
justifiable, then at least substantial representations of my participants. I
discuss their agency by investigating the different kinds of misfit self that
are constructed in their narratives.

'I Am Very Forthright and Blunt'

The analytical part of this chapter begins with Yu-Chen as the first case
study, because her account was the source of one of my important epipha-
nies during this project. Yu-Chen and I met up at a French restaurant in
Taipei. The restaurant was almost fully booked that evening. We could
only manage to get counter seats. The atmosphere there was vibrant and
lively. We had to speak loudly in order to hear each other. It was not a
short interview and we did talk a lot. We were concentrating on the conversation rather than the food, and we were still having our entrée when
the main courses were served. The speed at which she spoke was remarkable. Her voice was not exactly loud but she made every word audible. She
was articulate without using fancy expressions. It was a fun interview. I was
fascinated by all the stories that Yu-Chen told me.

My original intention was to confine our discussion to full-time working experience only. But I soon realised this was obviously a silly idea.
Gender and work was of course the core subject of the interview and I

managed to link every question I asked to it. However, Yu-Chen's narrative went beyond that. I would not say that she digressed. I did find the peripheral information meaningful in terms of academic value. These accounts brought forth a sensible and necessary personal history which helped me to understand how she experienced gender at work and how she interpreted those experiences. The 69-page interview transcript is almost a mini memoir. The stories she shared with me go back to her days as a high school student.

She related an incident of sexual harassment when she was working a holiday job during high school. Her immediate reaction was to give the offender a slap. Yu-Chen said she had not told her colleagues about the incident because she was '*shao bu geng shih* [少不更事]',[1] otherwise she would definitely have 'made a big thing of it' and let other people know about it. There is a previous version of self in Yu-Chen's narratives. The 'young self' is described as comparatively immature and inexperienced compared with the self she is now. This sense of comparison entails a personal history of transformation. Having more experience as a social being within society is delineated as the key to transformation. The current self that Yu-Chen is constructing has grown out of the self of the past. In her narratives, the constructions of the current self and the past self are interdependent. The social meaning of one only manifests itself when the other is presented. It would be an oversimplification to view them as two different versions of self that are completely detached from one another.

I proposed a hypothetical question to Yu-Chen. I was curious as to whether, if she were to encounter any gender discrimination or sexual harassment in her current organisation, she would trust the official procedures and file a complaint. She replied with a positive answer.

Yu-Chen: I don't care whether it would be handled properly. But at least I would report the problem.

She suggested that her mistrust of the complaint procedure would not prevent her from reporting the case. For Yu-Chen, making a formal complaint has its own significance. Along with this answer to my hypothetical question, her accounts of the way she approached other issues at work persuaded me that she would stand up for herself and defend her rights. Her insistence on taking action on problems in the workplace that concern her is one of the characteristics of Yu-Chen's narrations that I would like to highlight, along with a sense of directness.

Yu-Chen: Oh, I am very forthright and blunt. I would say, 'it's none of
            your bloody business'.

That statement sums up my impression of Yu-Chen. When she talked,
it was her style to come to the point and never suppress her own opinions.
However, her direct attitude comes with a price. She shared her thoughts
about the merits and disadvantages of being a direct person in the
workplace.

Yu-Chen: For me, there are more pros than cons as a direct person in
            the workplace. Of course, the downside is that people would
            say, 'you have a bad attitude. You're overbearing and aggres-
            sive.' But, on the other hand, I can save a lot of time. Also, I
            can always just say no to whatever I want to reject.

Clearly Yu-Chen's bluntness and directness are not personal characteristics that stem from ignorance of social expectations. She knows that
other people might hold a negative opinion of her interactive style. There
is a reflexive evaluation about her preferred way to communicate. For
Yu-Chen, being labelled as 'overbearing and aggressive' is the price she
probably has to pay in order to enjoy the freedom to decline nonsense
requests directly. Yu-Chen's account shows an alternative form of self-
image management. For her, having a negatively valued social image is a
useful strategy to survive the workplace. The importance of expressing her
opinion freely outweighs her desire to avoid stigmatising judgements from
others. In the reflexive process, maintaining face for her colleagues seems
not to concern Yu-Chen very much.
     Yu-Chen is very aware of her 'differences'. Keeping one's mouth shut
is the most popular survival strategy in her company, and mainstream
communication is conducted in a less direct way. There are not many
people like her, as she would express her opinion without holding back.
Moreover, being an ambitious female computer engineer, she knows she
is definitely not a member of the majority in the IT industry.

Yu-Chen: There's usually this chain reaction of shock. You're a com-
            puter engineer?! You're a woman?! You've been working for
            how many years?!

Yu-Chen has surprised many people she has met on business occasions
merely by being present, as if a woman and a computer engineer are two

opposite identities that cannot coexist. The fact that she is a female computer engineer does not guarantee her membership of both identity categories. She is one of a kind because she is a woman in a male-dominated workplace and also because she always makes her voice heard in all kinds of disadvantaged circumstances. In Yu-Chen's narratives, we see that a misfit self is constructed in the context of a challenging workplace. Her deviance is not merely something determined by the mainstream others but is also a construction of her own agency.

'I Can't Work in a Place Where I Can't Be Who I Am'

Yu-Nung's career trajectory covers several fields. She started out in the entertainment industry, mainly film production and commercials, and then later gradually moved into the area of social work. When I interviewed her, Yu-Nung was in her 40s and held a managerial position in an organisation. Her experiences in different industries had enabled her to observe different working cultures in different workplaces. She was surprised when I mentioned that the Gender Equality in Employment Act has been in effect since 2002. At that time she had already acquired a managerial position in a production company and, as she recalled, policy on gender equality was never included in the management agenda. This was not because there were no gender issues in the company, but because people simply did not realise it was something they should be concerned about. She clearly remembered an incident that illustrates how sexist her colleagues could be. She was working as a supervisor, one step down from the Chief. Production was a male-dominated sector in the industry, and there were only a few female employees in the organisation. On one occasion, when a male colleague appeared to be upset about something, he suddenly expressed his anger by muttering about working under a woman. Yu-Nung suspected that he was referring to her. She was astonished when she heard his grievance. He was among the colleagues whom Yu-Nung would socialise with outside of work, and she thought they had developed a good working relationship. She had not realised he held a grudge against her and, most of all, had problems working with a female supervisor.

Her position as a high-ranking female supervisor provided Yu-Nung with many opportunities to experience and observe incidents of gender inequality in the organisations where she worked, especially in the business negotiation process. She had more than once felt threatened by hints of physical violence from male colleagues.

Yu-Nung: Another case, this is also about a male colleague. The accounting record he made was a total mess. It was out of line. So I said to him, 'you might have made a mistake. I suggest you take it back and correct it'. Then he handed it in again, but it was still the same. So I circled out the problematic parts and asked him to make corrections. He then threatened to beat me up. [...] He didn't say so but acted like he was about to physically attack me.

Ting-Fang: [...] How did you handle it after what had happened?

Yu-Nung: I insisted, asking him to make corrections. (laughs)

This was not the only occasion when Yu-Nung sensed threatening signals from a male colleague. Once, in a meeting over a managerial issue, she was not convinced by a male colleague's argument and therefore expressed her own opinion on the matter. The meeting turned into a heated debate. Failing to gain an advantage in the verbal contest, the colleague attempted to bring closure to the discussion by imposing emotional pressure on her. He banged on the table with his hands. However, his intimidating tactic did not bring about the outcome that he desired.

Yu-Nung: After he banged on the table, I banged on the table too. I said to him, 'Don't ever think that you're the only one who dares to do that. I can do it too. So what?'

Banging on the table and yelling at colleagues were not part of Yu-Nung's communication style. However, in this exchange, she decided to do so in order to show that she would not be silenced by that kind of threat. She noticed that a slight look of surprise crossed her colleague's face. He probably had not anticipated that she would fight back or adopt his tactics. Not every male colleague that Yu-Nung has worked with has used the assumed 'male' physical advantages in an attempt to intimidate her, but those who have done so are all male. None of them actually threatened to attack her physically or enact violence, but they obviously intended to force her to keep quiet by displaying physical strength. A loud voice and intimidating body language are commonly used tactics in such a scenario.

According to Yu-Nung's experience, attempts to silence women are not limited to male-dominated workplaces, but can also occur in an organisation where women are in the majority and which claims a reputation for gender equality. She told me about a management meeting in which the discussion was about a proposal on flexible working hours for female employees with children, who are more likely to arrive late to work because of unforeseen family issues. Yu-Nung supported this policy while a male colleague in a high-ranking position was opposed to it.

Yu-Nung: I think it's a reasonable request. Based on the beliefs of our organisation, even if it might cause some managerial troubles, I think we should still do it because this is the price we should pay. We have to care about gender equality. He then said, 'I also have to take care of my children'. What he meant was that he is also a person with children. [...] I asked him, 'If there is something wrong with your kids, who is usually the one taking care of it, you or your wife?' Then he showed me the kind of face that he wanted to beat me up. [...] In that meeting, no one dared to argue with him on that proposal, only I did.

This male colleague tried to argue against the proposal by identifying himself as a parent who managed to show up at work on time and did not ask for special treatment. He was blind to the male privilege he enjoys in a gendered society. After Yu-Nung poked holes in his logic, he clearly displayed a hostile attitude towards her.

Based on the episodes she told me about, I am convinced that Yu-Nung is not afraid of confrontation in the workplace. If a heated debate arose on any business matter, she would be ready for it. She would express her opinion and hold her ground as long as it was a reasonable one. An essential part of her stories about speaking up in conflict situations is the narrative of cherishing herself the way she is. Yu-Nung values being who she is over maintaining harmonious relationships with colleagues at work. Although she did recognise that maintaining good relationships is one of the key strategies for a successful career in Taiwan, she confessed that she had only recently become aware of this. She attributed this delayed awareness to her personal life philosophy.

Yu-Nung: In fact, in general, I feel that a human being is always solitary. This has been my life philosophy.

Because of this philosophy, Yu-Nung did not recognise the need to maintain good relationships in the workplace. She even borrowed a phrase from a pop song and described herself as 'a lone wolf'. Therefore, Yu-Nung left me with the strong impression that she holds a fairly individualistic interpretation of her existence as a social being. She also informed me that she is a person who cherishes herself quite a lot. When I asked if she had any office survival strategies to share, Yu-Nung replied with the following.

Yu-Nung: My own observation is that I don't have any strategies. If an individual can survive, then survive. If she/he can't survive, then just don't. Didn't I tell you? Being who I am is very important. I am *bi jhou zih jhen* [敝帚自珍].[2]

I had no idea what this phrase meant, so Yu-Nung explained it word by word. *Bi jhou zih jhen* [敝帚自珍] is an idiom. The literal meaning is to value one's own shabby broom. It is a metaphor often used to describe things that have no value but are cherished by the owner. Yu-Nung used this idiom to express her feelings about herself.

When I asked Yu-Nung what had been her key consideration when she decided to quit her previous job, she told me about a conversation she once had with a friend about her determination to leave.

Yu-Nung: I said that I'm not happy. I can't be who I am here. Because she asked me why I wanted to go, and I said because I'm not happy. I told her that. I said that I can't work in a place that makes me unhappy. I can't work in a place where I can't be who I am.

For Yu-Nung, being who she is was a crucial part of working life. She will choose to leave an organisation if she finds the workplace to be a hostile or unfriendly environment for her. I feel that Yu-Nung has accepted the premise that everyone is a unique individual, so there is no point in suppressing one's characteristics in order to survive the workplace. She recognises herself as a unique individual and cherishes this uniqueness.

'Colleagues from Other Departments Thought I Was Still Single'

The sound of a typical weekend evening in urban Taipei was the auditory background to my interview with Hsi-Shu. It was a Saturday evening and Taipei was busy as usual. We met up in the underground shopping mall in

Taipei Main Station area. Our original plan was to find a restaurant and conduct the interview while we ate dinner, but we had underestimated how crowded it would be during the weekend. It seemed it would be impossible to find a nice place to eat without having booked first. We had to compromise and in the end found a less crowded restaurant. A waitress informed us that, because it was a holiday and a busy time, we could only have the table for one and a half hours. I immediately thought, 'It won't be enough time!', so we decided to continue our interview on the underground street. Hsi-Shu and I were moving from shop to shop. Our conversation was a mixture of serious discussion on gender issues and casual talk about items in the shops. The recording perfectly captured the sounds of the environment as well as our conversation.

The recorded audio file starts with Hsi-Shu's thoughts on things that are unfair for women in the workplace. Hsi-Shu was critical. She has a sociological academic background and is very aware of gender inequality in the workplace. Her narrative started with these words: 'Anything is about gender. Because we live in this society, everything is about gender.' She told me about her personal experiences and her observations of the unequal treatment of men versus women and that of married versus single women. Then our conversation gradually turned into a discussion about the gossip culture at work. As a married woman, she had noticed that people seemed to assume that it was socially acceptable to ask a married female employee questions about whether or not she would be having children. Personally, Hsi-Shu found the subject boring and felt annoyed by this kind of social interaction.

Hsi-Shu: Take me, for example, I've been asked why I don't have children for three years. Colleagues keep asking me, 'why do you still not have children?' But why should I exchange such boring information with my colleagues?
Ting-Fang: This is nothing to do with your work.
Hsi-Shu: But they just like asking it. They need to know whether you plan to have children. 'Do you want to have children?' 'Are you preparing to have one?' 'Have you tried Chinese herbal medicine yet?' 'Don't eat anything chilled.' I feel that indeed in the workplace in Taiwan, people to some level care a lot about ... not only in the workplace, I feel the same [in other social domains], people care a lot about other people having children or not.

Hsi-Shu did not understand why other people cared so much about her parenthood plans. She used the word 'care' to describe the motivation for their curiosity. This indicates that asking a married woman about her parenthood plans seems to be widely accepted as a proper topic for chit-chat. But for Hsi-Shu, it is personal information which she does not want to share.

Ting-Fang: Do you feel that they think it's a common topic for casual chatting?

Hsi-Shu: Of course. It's like, eh, like 'What time did you get up this morning?' that kind of simple and boring question. [...] It's like, 'Eh, is it raining over there?' It's a boring question. 'How come you haven't had children yet?' 'Do you want to get pregnant? Do you have plans for it? But I think you can.' I don't even know where this suggestion comes from.

Ting-Fang: What was your reply to this kind of question?

Hsi-Shu: Mm, I just said, 'I don't want to'.

During the interview, Hsi-Shu more than once described the gossip about parenthood plans as boring. She did not understand why people showed so much interest in other people's plans around pregnancy and having children. She also did not understand why people felt comfortable offering advice that she had not requested. Hsi-Shu found it very difficult to get used to this type of social interaction. Despite her disgust, she did not try to sidestep these offensive questions but provided honest and direct answers. Unfortunately, this did not put a stop to her colleagues' questions.

Hsi-Shu: They would tell you, they would talk to you from the perspective that having children completes your life. I've heard more than ten people tell me this. If not from elderly people then study mates, friends, colleagues. 'Life can only be completed with children.'

Although Hsi-Shu has never withheld her opinion on this issue, her calm and direct answer seemed unable to assuage her colleagues' 'care'. Hsi-Shu did not give in, either. The discourse adopted by her colleagues failed to convince her. The colleagues did not sustain 'a standard of consideration' and did not care about Hsi-Shu's personal feelings or her 'face' (see Goffman 1967: 10). When information control in a conversation becomes a task that is too difficult to achieve, an alternative strategy has to be adopted. Hsi-Shu's response has been to distance herself from 'caring colleagues'. Her management of information control begins before social contact occurs. It starts with the selection of suitable social actors with whom to socialise. Based on her previous experience, Hsi-Shu has concluded that people who have children tend to adopt the discourse that children complete a woman's life, and therefore she has more recently tried to avoid interacting with them. Hsi-Shu labels herself as a *cianfujhe* [潛伏者], a lurker, at work because the social culture in the workplace does not fit her. She finds it difficult to participate in the gossip culture at her workplace and has made an effort to avoid being the subject of gossip. One of her strategies is to keep her personal life and her emotions private. The clear distinction that she makes between her work and her personal life means that she hides some parts of her personality.

Hsi-Shu: I can tell you, I only show less than 30% of my personality at work.

Besides the gossip culture, she also finds it wearisome to try to blend in with the married female employees. In Chap. 4, I presented Hsi-Shu's accounts to illustrate that interactions in the workplace are often gendered and heteronormative. According to her observations, heterosexuality is often normalised in daily social interactions at work. Hsi-Shu is married. By observing other married female employees, she realised that she behaves differently from them. For example, she noticed that their talk is always centred on either children or husbands. She said that, because she has not changed the way she socialises, colleagues from other departments assumed that she is still single. As for those colleagues who knew her marital status, they assumed that her husband would occupy all of her private time and that he would be her plus-one at any social event. If he did not show up, it would be regarded as unusual and she would be asked to explain and provide a proper excuse for his absence.

Hsi-Shu: For example, I visited Nepal. I was travelling with a girlfriend. They [her colleagues] then said, 'Ah? It's strange. Why wouldn't you go with your husband? Why didn't you go with your husband? How come you didn't travel with your husband? Why did you travel on your own?'

In the workplace, Hsi-Shu tries to distance herself from most of her married female colleagues. By doing so, she is actually distancing herself from the typical image of a married woman and the related gendered culture.

In the interview, Hsi-Shu disclosed her awareness that she did not fit people's ideal of a married female employee. In spite of this, she has no intention of changing the way she acts. The deviant and misfit self also emerges in her narratives of self-portrait. I asked Hsi-Shu for suggestions on how to depict her in my monograph. The following is her answer.

Hsi-Shu: You should seriously describe me as a middle-aged, 34-, 35-year-old person who still thinks of herself as in her twenties. Also, this person, this participant, is undertaking a project of body transformation and dedicating her efforts to moving out of her comfort zone, in both personal and working life. She is getting into a mid-life adventure, although inside she is a teenage girl.

By body transformation, she meant that she was very enthusiastic about keeping up a good exercise routine at the gym. She emphasised that there is a younger person inside her. She recognised herself as a middle-aged woman but with a young spirit. Just as she refuses to act like a married woman, Hsi-Shu also refuses to see age as a limitation on her choice of lifestyle. Her account therefore constructs a self that intends to live outside the assumed social categorisations that might be ascribed to her.

'Tongzhi Have to Fight Hard'

Every interview, with every participant, was distinctive, but the one I conducted with Shih-Ching is definitely going to stay in my memory for a very long time. The interview as a whole was a unique experience for me. I managed to meet most of my participants in public spaces, including Shih-Ching. However, this one took place not just in a public space but actually in a public venue where a demonstration for a campaign was taking place.

We were sitting on Katakalan Boulevard.[3] This is the main road in front of the Presidential Office Building. An LGBTQ organisation called Taiwan Alliance to Promote Civil Partnership Rights (TAPCPR) was holding an event there to promote the Family Diversity Legislation Campaign. The

title of the event was *ban jhuo* [伴桌]. The literal meaning of the first character, *ban* [伴], is 'partner'. The second character, *jhuo* [桌], means 'a
table' or 'a dining table'. The term was invented by the organisers. It was
used as the theme of the campaign because it has a homophonic twist
relating to a conventional wedding custom. Its pronunciation is identical
to that of another Chinese term, *banjhuo* [辦桌], which is the common
translation for the Taiwanese custom *bando*. *Bando* is a distinct cultural
practice in Taiwan. The literal meaning of *bando* could be understood as
'doing a table of delicacies for guests' (Chen and Huang 2011: 101). It
was originally a Taiwanese term and was then adopted into the Standard
Mandarin in Taiwan. *Bando* plays a crucial part in various cultural ceremonial practices, such as weddings, funerals and showing hospitality or gratitude to significant guests. On the occasion of a wedding, conventionally
the bride, the groom and the groom's parents would invite relatives and
friends to a *bando*, in this case a wedding banquet, which usually has more
than one table of guests. The campaign event was organised in the format
of a wedding banquet to promote the idea of civil partnership.

Shih-Ching and I both attended the event to show our support, and we
conducted the interview while it was going on. The background sound in
the recording is the speech of the main organisers on the stage. We sat at
the side of the boulevard, at a certain distance from the main stage, in
order to hear each other clearly. I had my digital recorder with me, while
Shih-Ching had a cigarette between her fingertips. It seemed natural,
given the event, for us to have a conversation about LGBTQ communities
and LGBTQ movements in Taiwan. Shih-Ching expressed her views
about why gay communities have stronger bonds and ties between them
compared with lesbian communities. Rather than expressing despair or
pessimism, however, I felt that her words grew out of an expectation of
pushing the lesbian movement forward.

Shih-Ching is not the only participant in this study who identified herself as a lesbian; however, she is certainly one of the few who allowed me
to record the fact and include it in the research data. She is very forthcom-
ing about her sexual identity, or 'non-heterosexual identity'. During the
interview, she emphasised more than once that her sexuality was not a
sensitive issue that had to be concealed. She assured me that it would be
totally fine to include information about her identity as a lesbian in my
research data. Her assurance made me recognise her trust in me both as a
friend and a researcher, along with the weight of research ethics. From her
feedback on the transcript, I know that she is discreet about anything

involving her friends' and colleagues' privacy. She proposed deleting interview segments that might reveal the identities of individuals whom she mentioned. She explained to me that her concern was not for herself but for other people whom she has known.

Shih-Ching told me fascinating stories about her work experiences and career trajectory. Those accounts cannot be fully comprehended without knowing that she identifies as a member of the lesbian community in Taiwan. I do not mean that her sexuality somehow determines every aspect of her life. Rather, her narratives are enriched with details and perspectives that can only be acquired by an insider. She used to manage a *T*-bar and therefore has made close observations of social scenes in the community.[4] She told me that things have changed. In the old days, the lesbian circle was, in her words, 'very conservative'. There were only certain gendered roles available. You had to be either a *T*, a 'masculine' lesbian, or a *Po*, a 'feminine' lesbian. Otherwise, you would be mocked and marginalised in the community. It is very different now. She feels that, when it comes to gender, individual expressions and variations are very much appreciated and celebrated nowadays.

She is not uncomfortable about revealing her sexual identity in the workplace. According to Shih-Ching, the entertainment and media industry has been comparatively friendly towards individuals who do not exactly follow the social norms. It is not uncommon to work with individuals who have come out about their sexuality. However, this does not mean that gender equality prevails in the industry. Occupying a mid-managerial position, Shih-Ching has access to a decision-making framework that is inaccessible to general personnel. She has observed serious management problems that hinder gender equality in the organisation. Take the recruitment process, for example; she has noticed the discriminatory comments made by other supervisors which I discussed in Chap. 3. In addition to fighting for young lesbian applicants to have equal opportunities in the recruitment process, Shih-Ching also fights against discrimination in everyday working circumstances.

Shih-Ching: For instance, it's simply, there are people who would talk behind people's backs. They would say, 'that gay person is blah-blah-blah …', something not nice at all. I would tell them directly, 'don't talk about people like that behind their backs. If you have guts, then just say those things in front of them. Don't do that behind people's backs.' And I would say, 'she/he is gay and so what? How about me? Why don't you criticise me, then?'

Their 'deviant' sexualities have situated lesbian and gay employees in a vulnerable position in terms of hostile social encounters. They are easily targeted and labelled with their 'gayness' even if it is not the main point of the malicious gossip. Shih-Ching would not tolerate this kind of discriminatory comment and would intervene. She found such comments offensive, as well as the way in which the speakers targeted their victims. She noticed that their discrimination was actually two-fold. One form was obviously sexual discrimination, while the other form was much more nuanced. By targeting a gay or lesbian employee who had less power in the workplace, they were discriminating against people according to not only their sexuality but also their position in the organisation. She expressed her disapproval of such behaviour by calling the gossips cowards. She indicated that talking behind people's backs is not a fair game to play. She also pointed out the absurdity of their gossip, as though being gay is something wrong by its very nature. Then she proposed herself as a subject for their verbal abuse. By doing so, Shih-Ching stated her identity as a lesbian and made the whole thing personal to her. She intended to make the bullies understand that if they were targeting gay colleagues that meant they were targeting her as well. As a senior staff member with managerial status and a truculent attitude, she would not be an easy target for them. Her description of how she managed the situation illustrates her awareness of the hierarchy, work culture and power relationships in the workplace.

Shih-Ching has learned to use her power to defend other employees with minority or disadvantaged backgrounds or less favourable characteristics. She is doing this both for equality and for pragmatic reasons. She sees value in employees who do not strictly comply with mainstream rules.

Shih-Ching: I feel, when I select employees … that is, during recruitment, I usually avoid hiring those who seem to be too submissive. Because I think that it's not a job for submissive individuals. You have to be flexible and spontaneous in order to do this job well.

Shih-Ching prefers to work with people who dare to challenge authority for righteous causes. She interprets this as a personal quality that a professional should have. This preference also implies that, as a supervisor, she expects her team members to be able to work independently rather than following orders from her. She told me that her supervision style is actually not typical of the industry. Most supervisors still prefer the more 'submissive' type of employee. They incline towards a more hierarchical relationship between themselves and their supervisees. She knows the value of 'deviant colleagues' because she identifies herself as one of them.

Shih-Ching: I'm easily infuriated, or I should say, infuriated by things that are unfair or unjust. I would take the risk of saying whatever I want to say. [...] Many of my supervisors have told me that I can be very difficult. If I insist on something worth fighting for, I don't care who my opponent is.

While she acknowledges the stubborn part of her personality, Shih-Ching does not think this is the sole reason for her career success. She is aware that she could not have progressed in her career without the support of previous supervisors who respected and appreciated her characteristics. Therefore, she is trying to do the same to help newcomers. She knows what a difference a supervisor can make in the workplace. In Shih-Ching's opinion, the level of friendliness towards LGBTQ staff depends on the work culture of an organisation. Therefore, a supervisor with managerial power has the ability to shape it for her supervisees. Although the whole of society is more friendly and 'tolerant' towards LGBTQ individuals than it used to be, it can still be quite difficult for them to survive in the workplace without support from the organisation and their supervisors.

Shih-Ching: I think it depends on different companies and supervisors. For instance, there are quite a few children of my friends who still face the dilemma of hiding their identities.

For Shih-Ching, having a successful career is not simply about personal accomplishment—it is also a path to social change. The higher an individual can climb on the career ladder, the more she can do for the community. Work has its transcendent value in the personal and the political. Shih-Ching identifies this as one of the most important strategies to improve the situation of *tongzhi* in Taiwan.

Shih-Ching: Yes, power is crucial. So *tongzhi* [同志] have to fight hard and work hard. That is, when you make it to a higher position, there are more things you can do. Then you can make a lot of things better.

'I Think the Fact that I Did Gender Studies Should Be Mentioned'

Among the questions I would usually ask a participant towards the end of our interview was how she would prefer to be described in my thesis. Chih-Lu answered that it was important to her personally that I should mention her academic background and that she had earned an MA in Gender Studies. I agreed because I felt it would be impossible to depict her accurately without introducing this piece of information about her. I have known Chih-Lu for quite some time and she never shies away from speaking up about her opinions on gender and never hides her identity as a feminist. While some of my participants, such as Hsi-Shu, were practising information control to conceal certain aspects of their personalities and personal life at work, Chih-Lu on the other hand has been very open about her background in gender studies and feminism. This has sparked several interesting social interactions in the workplace. One of these was a conversation during a job interview. A member of the interview panel was a representative from the human resources department and she (or he) proposed a question that amused Chih-Lu.

Chih-Lu: She/he asked me, 'Are you a feminist who puts feminism into practice?' And I said, 'Eh? Of course, is there any other kind?' (laughs) And she/he continued, 'Oh, is that so? How would you practise it, for example?' I said, 'For instance, if I feel I am able to do something, I won't let my gender be a constraint influencing my decision to do it or not.' She/he then responded like, 'oh …'. I was thinking, eh? So is there a particular kind of feminism in the world that doesn't involve any practice at all? What does that even mean? (laughs)

It seemed hilarious to Chih-Lu to even think about the idea that there is a kind of feminism that does not advocate and promote the actual application of the knowledge itself. For her, being a feminist means to practise the feminism to which an individual relates. It is both a way of knowing and a way of doing. She identified herself as a feminist who challenges the imposed gender constraints on individuals by taking action personally and encouraging others to do the same. Her honest attitude about her background and identity also had a significant effect on her everyday social interactions at work. Chih-Lu is known as THE feminist in the office.

Ting-Fang: Would you let your colleagues know that you're a feminist?

Chih-Lu: I would. I would let my colleagues know. And, I think someone doesn't have to say she's a feminist, it only needs her to say that she was doing gender studies, then people will naturally have certain stereotypical impressions about this individual.

In everyday interpersonal encounters Chih-Lu has sensed that some of her colleagues might find her or her interest in feminism and gender issues intimidating. She once mentioned to a colleague that she has been a member of a reading group for quite some time. The colleague first showed strong interest until she realised it was a reading group that focuses on gender.

Chih-Lu: She then said, 'Eh, I thought if it was another kind of reading group, I might be able to join. But if it's about gender then ... it seems not ... I'm very patriarchal, I'm very ... I have a happy life in the patriarchal system.' My response was, 'Oh, okay. I didn't intend to invite you anyway.' (laughs)

The colleague seemed to be trying to quickly draw a line between herself and Chih-Lu to show their different opinions on gender. On the other hand, Chih-Lu's response and her tone while telling this story informed me that she personally feels fine about that line. She even offered a reply that reinforced it. Chih-Lu does not mind her colleague expressing her point of view about gender because she is doing the same. Her response was given in a way that accepted her colleague's distancing herself from the reading group but also rejected her participation. Through that brief social encounter, they were both displaying their membership of different social groups. It is probably fair to describe the interaction as smooth and without obvious conflict. However, there is certainly a potential for tension in it. Goffman defines a 'team' as 'any set of individuals who cooperate in staging a single routine' (1959: 85). This does not mean that individuals in the same social setting are necessarily interacting as a team. For Goffman, a team is a social group with a specific purpose for their social interaction. The teammates would depend on each other to 'sustain a definition of the situation' (ibid.: 92). Chih-Lu and her colleague might have formed a social group in that specific context. However, it is obvious that, according to the narrative provided by Chih-Lu, neither she nor her colleague had any intention of continuing or extending that social interaction. It is as though neither of them had any desire to form a team or conduct a 'team performance' (ibid.: 88). If they performed anything together in that interaction, it was to inform the other that they do not share a common interest and that their views on gender are very different.

Chih-Lu also observed that, when her background in gender and feminism was regarded as a useful professional skill set, her name became a symbolic tool in other colleagues' social interactions. She was once assigned an administrative job on the committee for gender equality in an organisation. While she was doing that job, her colleagues tended to perceive her as an expert in and arbiter for gender equality. Chih-Lu's name would appear in their conversations as a device to interrupt a potentially gender-unfriendly social interaction.

Chih-Lu: My colleagues would say, 'shouldn't we report this to Chih-Lu? Shouldn't we ...', 'What you said would make Chih-Lu angry' ... etc. So it's kind of having this branding effect.

It is interesting to see how Chih-Lu's colleagues referred her as an authoritative figure in casual conversations. This is a communication strategy that involves a designated audience in the interaction. Chih-Lu might have been in the vicinity, but she did not necessarily take part in that interaction. By bringing up her name in the conversation, the colleague was actually including Chih-Lu in the interaction. This seems to be a subtle way to indicate that there was a problem with the interaction. Somebody might have said or done something to make that individual uncomfortable. They then used Chih-Lu as a proxy to express their feelings and thoughts. Instead of saying that she herself disapproved, the individual brought up Chih-Lu's name as a communication strategy to send a message of disapproval.

Chih-Lu: Probably that's the case. Or she doesn't dare to say anything, but other colleagues would say, 'if you keep acting like this, I'll tell Chih-Lu'. It's actually not a bad thing.

Far from being annoyed, Chih-Lu felt totally fine with her colleagues using her as a shield in their struggle against everyday gender inequality. Rather than treating her as a token, she felt they were finding subtle ways to create alliances. The individual who used Chih-Lu as an excuse to interrupt the flow of the interaction in which she was involved was actually demonstrating that her stance was similar to Chih-Lu's. That individual might not feel comfortable fighting against other social actors on her own. Chih-Lu was then recognised and portrayed as a strong but not necessarily present ally. Chih-Lu's narratives suggest that, while it may be stressful to be a token in the workplace, there is also a liberating side to being the different one in the workplace.

THE MISFIT SELF AND SOCIAL CONTROL

While I was drafting the analysis in this chapter, I found that, along with words, shapes kept drifting through my thoughts. I pictured the flow of social interactions as a constantly changing mosaic composed of countless pieces. Each piece was a moment of social encounter. Among them, there were some peculiar ones. Instead of taking a regular shape and connecting seamlessly with the others, they created extra parts, or holes, that did not quite fit the overall picture.

The sense of a different self, a self that does not fit into the generalised other or specific others, emerges from my participants' accounts. This peculiar social self that they were narrating sparks its agency with the light of strangeness. In those specific moments, my participants are social actors who seem to represent what Simmel (1950) identifies as 'the stranger'. According to Simmel's conceptualisation, a stranger, in a sociological sense, is a social actor who is both near to and remote from a particular group in terms of human relations. A stranger is 'an element of the group itself' while her/his position 'as a full fledged member involves both being outside it and confronting it' (ibid.: 402–403). Through their narratives, my participants show that, in the defining encounters, they recognise and embrace their deviance in relation to other social actors; moreover, they challenge and interfere with the presumed rules of social interaction. I have shown that hierarchical relationships are generally valued and maintained at work in Taiwan. However, despite how oppressive and suppressive this may seem, it is exactly within this social and cultural context that a misfit self emerges and declares its agency in the negotiation of gender. As Simmel proposes, in the absence of shared commitments with the group, a stranger is in the position of 'a positive and specific kind of participation'; it is participation with objectivity and freedom (ibid.: 404). I argue that, in realising their 'misfitness', some of my participants are provoked into speaking up. Acknowledging their deviance, they have developed alternative social skills to deal with the 'normal' and gendered work culture in daily life. I hesitate to claim that my participants have expressed 'a voice which is more than the voice of the community', but I am certain that they have expressed different voices (Mead 1934: 168). Furthermore, I argue that this voice of the misfit has a significant sociological significance in challenging the social control that is maintained in and through everyday practices.

In his discussion on social control and the social self, Mead argues that 'social control is the expression of the "me" over against the expression of the "I"' (1934: 210). That is, social control is revealed when the social actor acts in accord with society in a way that echoes the presumed expectations of others in the community. An individual must positively respond to the attitude of 'organized others' in order to maintain her membership status in a social group (ibid.: 199). To be 'me' is therefore a sensible situational strategy to secure a position as a community member. On the other hand, the selected cases I have presented bring forward another dimension of the discussion. It seems that my participants sometimes adopted alternative interactive actions other than the sensible one. In those defiant moments, they did not regard themselves as sharing common membership with others and resisted conforming to others' expectations. My participants were showing a defiant attitude through expressive interactions.

Expressive interactions are subjected to social control. In theorising about 'face-work', Goffman points out that face is not only a social project about the management of an individual's own social image but also involves work on sustaining others' (1967: 5). In a face-to-face social encounter, an individual may adopt what Goffman defines as a 'line', 'a pattern of verbal and nonverbal acts' (ibid.). The confidence to adopt a regular act to interact socially comes from the presumed understanding of both the situation and the roles of the participants in it. It is an act resulting from reflexive evaluation. According to Goffman, 'face' is 'the positive social value a person effectively claims for himself by the line others assume he has taken in a particular contact' (1967: 5). That is, a social actor tends to interact with other individuals in a presentable way in order to obtain their approval and acknowledgement. This presentability is accomplished by attending to concerns about proper interactive social manners and therefore undertaking anticipated social behaviours. By doing 'face-work', social actors are conducting ritual exchanges that are arranged through 'expressive order'. Hence, each social encounter provides a stage for the participants to collaborate in an act that is intended to 'maintain a specified and obligatory kind of ritual equilibrium' (Goffman 1967: 45). This sense of obligation is driven by emotions such as shame that derive from morality in a society. As Goffman (1967) indicates, the moral rules determine how an individual will evaluate her/himself and her/his fellow participants in an encounter. Interaction rituals therefore channel social control into quotidian social practices. Examining the concept of face in the social context of China, Qi points out that, as a social image, it is 'a complex but efficient force of social control in social interactions, which includes incentives and sanctions enforced through both subjective and socially current perceptions and expectations' (2011: 290). There is a connection between face-work and structural social control in a society.

While there is a self-regulation aspect of face-work, this does not necessarily mean that all the practices in every social interaction are patterned and no alternative possibility is available. Goffman points out that, if an individual 'were not a ritually delicate object, occasions of talk could not be organised in the way they usually are' and therefore this person could cause trouble if she/he did not reliably 'play a face-saving game' (1967: 31). It seems that Goffman identifies those social actors who fail to play along with collaborative face-work as 'troublemakers', because their acts prevent daily conversation from proceeding smoothly. When I was sorting out the quotes from my participants in this chapter, it was difficult to avoid the conclusion that my participants would probably be labelled as 'troublemakers' according to that definition. While this is a possible and easy conclusion to draw, I argue that there is an alternative interpretation if my participants' accounts are understood in the context of social control.

In a social context in which heteronormative and gendered interaction is considered to be the normal pattern, the expressive order is 'naturally' expected to be maintained according to this pattern. In other words, when gender equality is not regarded as common sense within an organisation, it will not be included in the rules of interactional ritual. Therefore, my participants find themselves to be deviant in everyday social life in the workplace. They may be viewed by their colleagues as offenders against the assumed expressive order. However, I would like to analyse the situation from the standpoint of my participants. For them, the other party in the social encounter is the offender, the one whose verbal or non-verbal acts have overstepped the line of mutual respect in the social contact. Moreover, since there is a conflict between the two parties' recognition of what kind of line should be delivered in the interaction, my participants' action of 'challenging' would usually be ignored or even perceived as interrupting the expressive order. Therefore, they have to deliver a stronger and more persistent message. Their 'outrageous' acts are provoked by the refusal of other social actors to initiate the corrective process defined by Goffman. Since their challenge is dismissed and there is no 'offering' from other social actors in the given situations, my participants are actually challenging the assumed interactive rules by disrupting the expressive order in their daily lives at work.

Something that is condemned as anti-social does not necessarily have an anti-social agenda within it. In her study on self-identified shy individuals, Scott (2005) provides an in-depth dramaturgical analysis of shyness as an identity and a situational status. The common stereotypical interpretation of shy people's behaviour is that they are not quite socialised, or even anti-social. Investigating the social self that moves back and forth between backstage and frontstage, Scott points out that shy people are actually 'highly sociable and committed to team interaction but feel excluded from the common stock of background knowledge on which other people rely' (2005: 108). While Scott's participants develop skills to prevent interactional flaws and therefore manage their 'awkwardness', my participants have come up with strategies for asserting their deviance. Their accounts indicate that while they are aware of the social rules, and they know that the expected performance of certain social roles is a fundamental part of reflexivity, conformity is not the only possibility. They have presented an alternative sociality derived from the agency of the misfit self. By constructing a gendered deviant self that is different from others in everyday social interactions, my participants are challenging the social ideology of gender. They are contesting the assumed moral rules embedded in quotidian practices, which are very much gendered.

Of course, it would be reckless to announce that a dramatic social turn on gender is happening. However, it is also inattentive to dismiss the potential signs of upcoming social change. While I was examining my participants' accounts of their expressive interruptions, I found myself in a place from which I was able to contemplate the linkage between their everyday experiences and the structural context. If the gendered social order in the workplace has been challenged, I would argue that the female employees who have mobilised these moments of negotiation of gender should receive the credit. By doing gender, one is also taking the opportunity to challenge or modify the given gendered social rules, because every social action of doing is a potential negotiation.

NOTES

1. *Shao bu geng shih* [少不更事] is a phrase that is used to describe a young and inexperienced individual. *Shao* means young. *Bu geng shih* means inexperienced in social life.
2. The term *bi jhou* [敝帚] literally means a worn-out broom. *Zih* [自] means 'self'. *Jhen* [珍] means 'cherish'.
3. Ketagalan is the official romanised term for the name of a Taiwanese indigenous community. It is not a Mandarin term but an aboriginal one and is used as the name of the Boulevard.
4. In Taiwan, '*T*' is used to refer to a 'masculine' lesbian. It can be understood as the 'bulldyke' in the English context. A *T*-bar therefore is a bar whose targeted consumers are 'masculine' lesbians.

REFERENCES

Adichie, C. N. (2009, July). Chimamanda Ngozi Adichie: The Danger of a Single Story [Video file]. Retrieved September 24, 2016, from https://www.ted.com/talks/chimamanda_adichie_the_danger_of_a_single_story

Chen, K., & Huang, D. [陳貴凰&黃穗華] (2011). 呷飽、呷好、呷巧、呷健康——臺灣辦桌菜單品項演變之研究 [Eat, Eat Well, Eat Cleverly, and Eat Healthfully: Study on the Development of Menu Items in Taiwanese Banto]. 餐旅暨觀光 *[Journal of Hospitality and Tourism]*, 8(2), 97–126.

Elliott, A. (2008). *Concepts of the Self* (2nd ed., Rev. and Updated ed., Key Concepts). Cambridge: Polity Press.

Emirbayer, M., & Mische, A. (1998). What Is Agency? 1. *American Journal of Sociology, 103*(4), 962–1023.

Goffman, E. (1959). *The Presentation of Self in Everyday Life*. London: Penguin.

Goffman, E. (1967). *Interaction Ritual: Essays on Face-to-face Behavior* (1st Pantheon Books ed.). New York: Pantheon Books.

Jackson, S. (2010). Self, Time and Narrative: Re-thinking the Contribution of G. H. Mead. *Life Writing, 7*(2), 123–136.

Kessler, S. J., & McKenna, W. (1985). *Gender: An Ethnomethodological Approach.* Chicago: University of Chicago Press.

Lawler, S. (2008). *Identity: Sociological Perspectives.* Cambridge: Polity.

Mead, G. H. (1934). *Mind, Self and Society from the Standpoint of a Social Behaviorist.* Chicago: University of Chicago.

Narayan, U. (1998). Essence of Culture and a Sense of History: A Feminist Critique of Cultural Essentialism. *Hypatia, 13*(2), 86–106.

Plummer, K. (2001). *Documents of Life 2: An Invitation to a Critical Humanism* (2nd ed.). London: Sage.

Qi, X. (2011). Face: A Chinese Concept in a Global Sociology. *Journal of Sociology, 47*(3), 279–295.

Scott, S. (2005). The Red, Shaking Fool: Dramaturgical Dilemmas in Shyness. *Symbolic Interaction, 28*(1), 91–110.

Simmel, G. (1950). *The Sociology of Georg Simmel* (Translated from German by K. H. Wolff). New York: The Free Press.

CHAPTER 6

Conclusion

OVERVIEW

With its impressive economic transformation and distinct gender patterns in employment, Taiwan has attracted sociological research proposing enquiries about and answers to patterns of women's employment. The established scholarship primarily concerns women's roles in the transformation and how their social status has been influenced by the economic shifts, as well as the relationship between women's labour-market participation and social conditions of gender inequality. Previous studies have shown that women's labour-market participation in Taiwan has been consistently high. However, this steady employment pattern has not resulted in gender equality in the workplace. Gender inequality and gender discrimination at work still shadow employed women's situation in the workplace. Moreover, it has also been revealed that, in spite of their high labour-force participation, women are still the main providers of gendered labour in the domestic sphere. While previous research has provided insightful analyses to help us understand women's employment in Taiwan, there are still many unanswered questions. Considering the emerging changes and shifts in social conditions and government policy, I have proposed that further inclusive and thorough investigation into women's working lives in Taiwan is required.

After reviewing the established scholarship, I have proposed my own conceptual framework for gender and work in Taiwan as an 'East Asian'

© The Author(s) 2018   199
T.-F. Chin, *Everyday Gender at Work in Taiwan*,
Gender, Sexualities and Culture in Asia,
https://doi.org/10.1007/978-981-10-7365-6_6

society. Inspired by ethnomethodological and symbolic interactionist approaches, in this study I chose to approach gender as a social construction which is accomplished in everyday practice by social actors with reflexivity. In other words, I adopted the perspective of 'doing gender' and viewed it as neither a compulsory doing nor a free doing, but a social construction involving reflexivity, interactions and relational practices. In order to conceptualise work, I drew on contemporary sociological and feminist studies to expand my perspective on women's work and the social institutions of gendered labour. Although the primary focus of this study is women's experiences in the workplace, I was convinced that it would be important to be aware that the labour demands imposed on women are often gendered and transcend the boundaries of employment. In regarding Taiwan as an 'East Asian' society in the global market of knowledge production, I proposed to recontextualise the country in order to recognise its similarities with other societies in the region as well as its differences. I was particularly concerned with the cultural legacy of Confucianism. Confucianism may be seen as a distinct characteristic of East Asia; however, this cultural feature should be comprehended within the specific historical and political context of each society. Like South Korea and Japan, Taiwan has its own unique interpretation and practice of Confucianism. The legacy of Confucianism in Taiwan is a historical result of the Kuomintang's government policy and political institutions during the Cold War era. Certain Confucian ideologies were deliberately promoted to serve the regime's purposes. This historical and political background entails debates that contest and challenge this cultural heritage. I therefore advocated a perspective that acknowledges the localisation of Confucianism as well as the negotiation of resistance in the East Asian context.

While reading previous studies enriched my understanding of employed women's situation in Taiwan, the execution of this project enabled a reflexive examination of this understanding. Through writing about the methodology and research process of this study, I revealed the stories of the planned, the expected and the surprising, unanticipated parts of my research journey. The original plan and design of this study underwent constant modification before and even after my fieldwork. The feminist perspective on the researcher–participant relationship and the conceptualisation of research ethics served as fundamental anchors during the process of modification. The actual interactions between me and my participants also challenged my original conception of this study. From participant recruitment to interview practices, the unforeseen experiences I had in the research field enabled me to ponder the nuanced details and complexity of ethical conduct. There is no universal formulation of ethical conduct considering that every participant is a unique individual and every interview is a unique social encounter in a specific situation. The complex and diverse exchanges that I had with my participants also made me aware that research data was generated in a highly interactive process. The multilingual nature of the interview data and the international aspect of this study posed difficult yet meaningful questions relating to data preparation. It turned out that the preparation work was far more complicated than transcribing; it also included translation, romanisation and negotiation with my participants. The multiple tasks involved in data preparation demanded that I take on multiple roles in this study. I was the transcriber, the translator and also the researcher, which led to my having concerns about the power relationships between a researcher and her participants, and reflecting upon these. Moreover, due to my flexible approach to the fieldwork, the data I gathered was full of surprises. The interactive and reflexive fieldwork became the initial stage of data analysis. My thoughts and reflections generated in the research field served as the starting point for me to ponder the analytical themes.

My discussion of the data analysis was organised into three parts. Firstly, I focused on the gendered and heteronormative management practices within organisations. By examining my participants' accounts of their work experiences, I argued that female employees tend to be regarded as homogeneously marriage-oriented and family-oriented and are therefore assigned certain jobs and positions accordingly. For instance, the biased and sexist practices of recruitment showed how gendered and heteronormative organisational practices prevented women from fulfilling their career ambitions in male-dominated industries or from attaining positions and jobs that were perceived as more suitable for men. Those who survived the recruitment process had to face other management practices that disadvantage women, such as gendered work arrangements and the gender pay gap. Due to heteronormative ideology, women were categorised by employers as suitable or unsuitable employees based not only on their gender but also on their marital and relationship status. I argued that those gendered and heteronormative organisational management practices therefore contributed to gender segregation both within and between industries. According to my participants' experiences, it was suggested that gender segregation also existed in workplaces where female employees were in the majority. I also discussed how my participants made sense of those management practices and how their career orientation and work strategies were influenced accordingly.

I then moved on to discuss everyday mundane interactions in the workplace that sustain the heteronormative and gendered social order. Examining my participants' accounts of day-to-day working life, I discussed how gender was accomplished in social actions such as adopting appellations, casual conversation and body language. It was suggested that using familial appellations to address colleagues is a common practice in the workplace, especially when referring to those who are more senior or older. I argued that this practice reflects the ideology and social institution of gendered social hierarchy. By adopting appellations which are perceived as proper in a given situation, individuals constantly identify, confirm and negotiate each other's social positions in everyday communications. Informal and personalised appellations serve as speech devices that facilitate gendered interactions in the workplace. While a gendered honorific appellation is adopted to show respect and good manners to senior female colleagues by their juniors, it may also be used for strategic communication purposes. In the case of using *jie* as an appellation, it was revealed that a gendered term indicating not just seniority but female seniority could have specific heterosexual connotations. When identified and interacted with as a *jie*, a female employee is categorised as a gendered being, with specific sexual implications. On the other hand, the analysis of other general social exchanges suggested that employed women's gender is assumed to be a valid cause of dos and don'ts within their routine work performances. They are perceived and treated as gendered beings by colleagues, supervisors and clients. My participants are expected to perform everyday work tasks in ways which justify and demonstrate their membership of the gendered social category, women. I further discussed how the gendered social order in quotidian social practices is intertwined with the normativity of heterosexuality. It was revealed that heterosexuality is constructed through mundane interactions as a 'normal' and 'natural' part of life. Moreover, my participants' experiences also show that the gendered social order is not necessarily an absolute one but a relationship to be negotiated.

In the final part of the data analysis, I advanced the discussion on my participants' negotiation of gender by investigating the agency of the social self. Taking inspiration from sociological theories proposed within anglophone academia, particularly the work of Mead (1934),

I developed my own conceptions of reflexivity and agency in the linguistic, cultural and social context of Taiwan. I argued for the importance of acknowledging gendered and hierarchical relationships when examining the agency of a social being situated within the social context of Taiwan. Pondering Mead's ideas about the self, the community and identity, I then contemplated the symbolic interactions depicted by my participants. Focusing on interview data concerning moments of defiance, I suggested that a social self that is distanced from the generalised community at work was appearing in the narratives of some of my participants. Their accounts showed that, while they were aware of the social rules and the expected performance of gendered beings as a fundamental part of reflexivity, they did not see conformity as the only possibility. Their experiences presented an alternative sociality derived from the agency of the misfit self. By constructing a deviant self that is different from others in everyday social interactions, my participants are challenging the assumed rules embedded in quotidian practices, which are very much gendered.

I am aware that the findings of this study cannot offer a definitive or complete picture of employed women's experiences of gender in contemporary Taiwan. My sample is rather small, as is usual in qualitative research. In addition, my participants were obviously a distinct group of employed women who have similar backgrounds and their own attitudes towards gender at work. The experiences they shared cannot therefore be used as research material to produce a generalised understanding of gender and women's employment in Taiwan. This is a result that I anticipated, considering the fieldwork approach that I adopted. My personal social network and feminist stance had a significant influence on the recruitment and sampling. Applying the snowballing technique in the recruitment process meant that my social network was the foundation for the initial outreach. About half of the participants were directly approached and recruited by me. They were individuals with whom I had established personal relationships prior to this study. They were recruited from the social strata to which I had access. Examining my participants' backgrounds, we can see that there are several shared indicators. Most of my participants were living and working in major cities in Taiwan, mostly Taipei. Their occupations fell within the spectrum of white-collar and highly professional jobs. They were mostly Mandarin and Taiyu (Taiwanese) speakers. They were well educated and had obtained degrees from either colleges or universities. In other words, this study presented the experiences of women with certain social and cultural capital. In addition, I did not conceal my identity as a feminist and the purpose of this feminist study was fully disclosed to all potential participants. I therefore realised that my own academic and political stance might have served as a filter to screen out any individual who held a different viewpoint about gender equality at work from mine. Although there was no deliberate selection, I did realise that this was a consequence of the selection process, indicating the limitations of this study.

While acknowledging the limitations of this study in terms of representativeness, I argue that the limited but specific scope can also be a virtue of this feminist exploration. The accounts shared by my participants describe not only their experiences but also their critical opinions about gender inequality in the workplace. My participants are women with critical eyes and critical minds. It is exactly because of their sharp gender awareness that this study has been able to examine some of the nuanced details embedded in everyday mundane practices at work. As a researcher, I was primarily the one generating the analytical discussion. However, without my participants' contributions, it would have been impossible for me to do so. As Smith points out, taking up 'the standpoint of women' does not necessarily mean to 'imply a common viewpoint among women' (1987: 78). I have no intention of generalising all women's experiences of gender at work in Taiwan. On the other hand, I would like to emphasise the value of bringing in my participants' accounts in order to avoid presenting a homogenised version of women's experiences and to challenge the existing homogeneous imagination on the matter. To emphasise the differences among women and recognise the diversity of women's experiences has been a major concern for feminist researchers (see Letherby 2003). The scope of this study is limited, but also specific. In other words, this study may only provide a small fragment but I argue that it is also a significant and meaningful piece of the whole picture.

On the issue of specificity, I would like to emphasise that this study is a historical production regarding the development of my participants' social lives. As Stanley and Wise argue:

> social life is not 'a text' in the strict sense of the word, something fixed and inscribed, but is rather both dynamic and interactional, and in it the 'texts' of social action are always available to be 're-written' as verbal accounts negotiated and remade again and again. (1993: 216)

I am aware that the accounts shared by my participants should not be viewed as eternal testimony about their lives. The analysis in this study is based on the interview data generated through interactions between my participants and me in the research field. The time and space of the field-work therefore shaped the historical conditions of my investigation. The participants' experiences of gender at work will have continued to expand after our brief encounters. It is reasonable to anticipate that they will have new thoughts and new interpretations about gender at work in Taiwan. It is evident that they do. During our communication about the confirmation of the transcripts, there were participants who informed me of new updates regarding the events they had shared in the interviews. Even after the data preparation period, some participants still kept in touch with me and occasionally shared the latest 'interesting' episodes that had happened in their workplaces. Some messages expressed further concerns about gender equality in Taiwan; others delivered revised views regarding the working culture in organisations. There were also participants who suggested that I should do a follow-up study to discuss changes and updates in their careers. Through these exchanges, I have gained an awareness of the historical situatedness of this study and therefore of the potential for future research on the subject of women's experiences of gender at work.

New Enquiries Emerging from Social Change

Because of this research project, work became a common topic of conversation when I socialised with friends and acquaintances. I was like a walking sociological magnet who attracted people to talk to me about their worries and complaints relating to their jobs. From their sharing, I have observed that there is a newly emerging dimension of social interaction in the workplace: instant communication via mobile devices. One obvious example would be usage of the mobile application LINE. LINE is a proprietary application that was designed and developed for instant communications. Although it supports most electronic devices, in Taiwan it is primarily used with smartphones. Among all the messaging applications, such as WhatsApp and Facebook Messenger, LINE is the most popular instant communication application in Taiwan, dominating the country's market (Alpeyev et al. 2016). When I was undertaking field-work in 2013, this application was already popular. At that time, it was used more for private and personal communications than for office activities. In other words, users would mostly contact individuals in their social networks about non-work-related matters. However, by the time I visited Taiwan again in 2014, the application was being widely used for workplace communication. It had become a common practice to use the built-in settings to create a messaging group which included every individual in a working team within an organisation. Colleagues used it to send office documents and discuss work. Supervisors regarded it as a work platform and delivered task demands on it. It seemed to be a virtual space to accommodate all the general interactions at work outside of the physical environment of a workplace. While the gendered and heteronormative social practices that have been discussed in this study can also be observed within this virtual communication platform, it also brings forward issues that require further sociological investigation. I have heard complaints about interacting with colleagues and supervisors via instant messaging applications. A friend once told me that, although she felt uncomfortable about the interactions within the group, she was hesitant to leave it. Everyone in her office was a member of the group, so it would be seen as odd for her to leave. In addition, quitting the group would prevent her from accessing information exchanges. The setting of the virtual group creates a specific communication scenario and it requires users to develop new strategies of negotiation.

New developments have emerged not only from the personal dimensions of social life but also from Taiwanese society as a whole. The vibrant civil society and political shifts have hinted at potential changes in relation to gender and women's employment. The most dramatic event to occur during the period after my fieldwork and before the completion of this project was the Occupy Movement. On the night of 18 March 2014, after the KMT, the ruling party at the time, unilaterally passed a trade pact with China, hundreds of students and activists stormed into Taiwan's parliament, the Legislative Yuan (see Ho 2015; Rowen 2015; Yang 2017). As the news spread through online social networking platforms and the media, this action drew the attention of the general public. After the initial move, thousands of individual supporters gathered outside parliament to put pressure on the KMT government. This then raised the curtain on an occupation which lasted for 24 days. The movement was not a sudden outcry from civil society. Prior to this occupation, there had been several large-scale protests and demonstrations against administrative conduct and pushing for changes in the policies of local and central government, such as the protest against the demolition of Losheng Sanatorium, the campaign for marriage equality and the diversification of family structures, and the protest against media monopoly (see Yang 2007; Chien 2012; Liu 2015).

Although the mainstream media identified it as a 'student movement', the backgrounds and social statuses of the protesters were actually rather diverse. According to their systematic survey (n = 989) on the demographic portrait of the movement, Chen and Huang (2015) found that the majority of the sit-in protesters outside the Legislative Yuan were individuals in their 20s and 30s with diverse backgrounds in terms of study field and occupation. The findings of this study suggested that 44% of the sit-in protesters were non-students and about 51% were women.

I happened to be in Taiwan when this event took place and I also participated in the movement as a sit-in protester. According to my observations, a substantial number of protesters were women with full-time jobs. Some of my participants were among them. They might not have been able to stay on the scene all the time, like some of the students, but they did their best to spend their own time after work to support the movement. On weekdays, they would go to the Occupy site after finishing their day in the workplace. They would sit on the street and have their dinner there. They would leave around midnight to rest before the next working day. At the weekends, they would spend more time there. They were not the main organisers and they seldom caught the media spotlight. However, they formed one of the many forces that enabled this movement to be sustained. During the Occupy Movement, the area surrounding the parliament was turned into a space for public lectures, political debates and discussions. Organisations from civil society provided support and brought their own concerns into this movement. They organised campaign activities to address various social issues requiring the public's attention and awareness. The individual sit-in protesters outside the parliament were their audience and potential supporters. Take my participants, for example. After the Occupy Movement, many of them joined voluntary organisations and kept an eye out for updated information about social movements. After the Occupy Movement, the crowd of supporters might have disappeared from the site, but many individual supporters have devoted themselves to other civil society activities. The movement therefore sustained and reinforced the momentum of civil society. This momentum was part of the force that contributed to the change of ruling party in 2016.

On 16 January 2016, the official result of the presidential election was announced. Taiwan had elected its first female, and its first unmarried, president, Tsai Ing-Wen. While the international media praised it as a historic moment for the country and even for global gender politics, feminists and activists in Taiwan recognised that it was more the beginning of a new battle in a new era than a landmark indicating the achievement of gender equality. During the presidential campaign, Tsai had promised that a government under her lead would value the principles of gender equality and human rights. An obvious indicator is her public endorsement of same-sex marriage. Moreover, there are at least two specific aspects of Tsai's politics which may have a direct influence on employed women's situation. One is her labour policy, and the other is the national care plan. On the issue of labour policy, Tsai has made six promises: to raise the minimum wage, to reduce working hours, to secure rights and welfare for atypical employment, to support young and older employees, to provide care for industrial injuries and to encourage the organisation of unions (Yen 2016). In terms of the national care policy, Tsai was the only candidate who emphasised the role and responsibility of the state in the issue of care. Her party, the DPP, has proposed a care policy which covers childcare, long-term care and women's employment in order to respond to concerns about the gendered labour of care imposed on women within the domestic sphere. She clearly advocated that the new government should change the current political norm that family is regarded as the main institution to provide care (Tan 2015). Thus, Tsai's government will propose new policies to bring changes to working conditions and family labour arrangements. These changes might lead to new enquiries into women's employment trajectories, and their experiences of gender, both in the workplace and in the domestic domain.

While a new government has been formed, civil society in Taiwan has not paused but continues to push for change. After the occupation of parliament, the momentum of the social movement has been diverted into other social issues. Among these, the labour movement is particularly vigorous. For example, there has been an exciting labour-movement development that was primarily initiated by women. On 24 June 2016, the flight attendants of China Airlines (CAL, a Taiwanese airline) achieved a historic strike. Since flight attendant is considered to be an occupation for women, and they are indeed the major labour provider in this occupation, it would be fair to say that it was a strike primarily organised by women. It was the first strike ever in the airline industry in Taiwan and was reported as 'one of the largest strikes of Taiwan's post-martial law period' (Hioe 2016a). Several thousand flight attendants used this industrial action to protest against the company's management policy, which clearly infringed on their labour rights. The management had announced a change in the report-to-duty location without a discussion with the cabin crews. This change would have directly affected the calculation of flight attendants' working hours. By doing so, the company would not only reduce flight attendants' rest time but also require them to work more shifts. Through management practices, the company was aiming to legitimise excessive working hours. As a consequence, the scheduled on-duty hours of a flight attendant could be extended from 174 hours per month to 220 (Shan 2016).

Since May 2016, the Taoyuan Flight Attendants' Union has represented the flight attendants' concerns and demands; however, the management of the company has continued to ignore the problem and failed to engage in negotiation. Moreover, CAL's management even handled the protest with contempt. A senior manager suggested that the company could easily find substitute labour by recruiting new staff (Hioe 2016a). Some retired flight attendants publicly defended the company by accusing the current employees of discontent and ingratitude.

After going through the formal procedure, the union decided to undertake industrial action and announced that the strike would begin on 24 June 2016. This decision brought a remarkable triumph to the history of the labour movement in Taiwan. The flight attendants identified their protest as a battle for reasonable rest time. They issued a statement to confront the criticisms of their employer and the retired flight attendants as well as to declare their stance.

> First, we would like to use this statement to address a few words to future flight attendants. No matter if it is 2030 or 2040, no matter how labour conditions will be, if one day you decide to initiate industrial action or demonstrate on the street, we promise you with today's decision and action, we will never be the substitute labour for the employer. We will never ask you to be content. We will never accuse you of damaging the company's image and dignity. Because we know that employees are the most important assets for a company. When the rights of the employed are being ignored, the we of today and the you of tomorrow have the responsibility to challenge the unfairness, including confronting a union that refuses to speak for the workers. [...] Having time to rest has become so difficult for employees in Taiwan. This strike is a battle for rest time. [...] The Taoyuan Flight Attendants' Union is willing to be the vanguard in this battle. We will let the capitalists and the government know that Taiwan has to say farewell to the era of excessive working hours and overwork.[1]

On 24 June, several thousand CAL workers gathered in front of the Taipei branch headquarters of the company. They blocked traffic and occupied the main street. In the evening of the same day, representatives from the company agreed to accept all the union's demands.

This successful strike in the airline industry has inspired and encouraged unions across the nation to fight for labour rights (Liang 2016). It is a move that may lead Taiwan's labour movement into a new era. Will this momentum within civil society be sustained and keep female employees at the forefront? How will the growing labour movement change the work situation for employed women? To what extent and in what aspects will it influence women's employment? These are all questions prompted by the recent shifts and changes, and they deserve further observation and investigation.

Moreover, the discussion about sexism sparked by this successful strike shows that, for female employees, the negotiation of work is often tangled up with the negotiation of gender. While support from the general public has been identified as a crucial factor in this triumph, it was a support tainted with gendered perceptions of female flight attendants. In Taiwan, flight attendant is a gendered occupation. It is regarded as a job for young and attractive women. This industrial action led by flight attendants was therefore widely described as the most '*jheng*' [正: an informal term for 'pretty' or 'beautiful'] and '*siang*' [香: fragrant] strike in history. There were online forums that displayed photo collections of the female flight attendants at the protest site. These female employees were perceived as projecting an image of ideal feminine labour providers in the airline industry. While there were concerns that the sexualisation of the protesters might undermine the seriousness of the industrial action, some commentators argued that the gender capital possessed by these 'young and attractive' employees was a crucial factor contributing to the success of this industrial action (see Hioe 2016b; Lu 2016).[2] The conventional 'sweaty' strikes by workers with 'older' bodies and poorer socio-economic backgrounds are still struggling to gain public support.

New shifts and changes in social actors' personal lives and the wider society are keeping women's employment in Taiwan a current sociological issue. I argue that a sociological approach to female employees' everyday experiences of gender is indispensable and could offer valuable insights into this issue.

Sociology of Everyday Life and Women's Experiences of Gender

This feminist study is my initial academic attempt to participate in the production of the sociology of everyday life with a specific focus on employed women's experiences of gender. The sociology of everyday life is recognised as a 'well-established tradition within sociology' in the anglophone and European academy (see Kalekin-Fishman 2013; Neal and Murji 2015). The 2015 Special Issue of *Sociology* is evidence that this sociological tradition has remained strong, with exciting enquiries into and discussions about various aspects of social life. The collection of research presented in this special issue also demonstrates that this body of knowledge is progressing in its development through investigating everyday life in various societies.

While the sociology of everyday life seems to have secured its position and caught the international spotlight, research on everyday life is still struggling to claim a seat at the table of social science in Taiwan. There are limited search results for studies investigating everyday life in Taiwan. This is not to say that no local research attempts have been made. One interesting development in the local scene of social science studies has a potential twist regarding everyday social life and the everyday social world. This undercurrent was steered by a group blog, GUAVA Anthropology [芭樂人類學].[3] Their homepage states that 'GUAVA anthropology covers things that are Grotesque, Unabashed, Apostate, Virid, and Auspicious about anthropology [*sic*]'.[4] The main organisers and the writers are anthropologists working at academic institutions. The English translation of the blog's name only provides a partial meaning of the original term. The original Mandarin characters, 芭樂 [*bale*], are actually a transliteration of the name of the fruit, guava, in Tai Yu [the Taiwanese language]. The term has different meanings in different contexts. It can be the name of the fruit, Taiwanese guava. It can also be used as an adjective to describe things, such as in '*bale* tickets', the Taiwanese term for bad cheques (see Salmonsen 2015). In addition to articles about their own research projects, the blog entries also cover trendy issues that have caught the public's attention. For example, the blog once posted an article providing an anthropological analysis of a popular break-up story circulating on social networking sites. One interesting feature of the blog is the writing style they adopt and the language they use. The writers seem to be aiming for a balance between academic writing and everyday common language. As in the title of the blog, it is an attempt to bring together the academic and the contextual localness.

The appearance of this blog began a trend among social scientists in Taiwan. New group blogs have been established for other disciplines, including Sociology at the Street Corner [巷仔口社會學], Kam-A-Tiam Forum of History [歷史學柑仔店] and The Poli-Sci Market [菜市場政治學]. Like GUAVA Anthropology, these blog names all imply specific cultural twists. Take Sociology at the Street Corner, for example: the original Mandarin title is a combination of two terms. The first part, 巷仔口 [*hang-a-khao*], is a Taiwanese term which literally means 'around the corner of an alley'.[5] The second part is the Mandarin term for sociology. *Hang-a-khao* Sociology therefore suggests a sociological view that concerns the local social events happening in ordinary individuals' lives. It is a research standpoint that values the common, the local and the everyday.

I propose that women's experiences of gender can provide crucial and valuable insights for the sociological knowledge production concerning everyday life in both global and local settings. This feminist study is my first contribution to this scholarship. With this project as my initial academic engagement with ethnomethodology, symbolic interactionism and feminism, I have demonstrated that the intersection of these perspectives is valuable in contributing to the critical inspection of gender inequality in everyday practices. In researching women's experience of gender in the workplace, this study has revealed and examined the gendered routine practices which disadvantage women in employment organisations. The empirical findings also have policy implications. In terms of legal provisions, Taiwan might have shown significant achievements, but writing the principles of gender equality into legal articles is not equivalent to achieving gender equality in routine managerial practices and individual social interactions. Detailed and sensible guidelines and rules of conduct are needed in order to actually exercise gender equality in every social action within institutions.[6] In addition, I have shown that ethnomethodology and symbolic interactionism as a theoretical framework have the capacity to accommodate situational and contextual specificities within particular societies. As an intellectual traveller with the intention of challenging the knowledge boundary between 'the East' and 'the West', I have developed and proposed an approach of theorising through reflective contemplation. My critical analysis is founded on the basis of contemplating the local, the contextual and the situational.

To Add a Final Word

On one occasion I shared my impressions of social psychology with a first-year undergraduate seminar. It was the first session and I was a tutor trying to persuade the group members that a module exploring social interactions was not at all intimidating, even though they would be reading about theories. I said that if I had to pick one word, and one word only, to describe the subject that we would spend a term exploring, it would be 'mundane'. That comment triggered light laughter in the room. Of course, I did not mean the mundane 'mundane'. It was a comment that came with quotation marks. I meant to explain that the theorisation of social interactions can help us to see through the mundane camouflage of everyday routines and reveal the perplexing, the fascinating and the critical.

This study is my personal quest within that process of 'seeing through', and during the journey a phrase struck me that will guide my further exploration. The phrase is '*wuliao*' [無聊; boring in a nonsensical way], a Mandarin term that appears several times in my data. It was used by different participants, but in similar symbolic contexts. They used it to describe boring and annoying social encounters that often have specific gendered and gendering implications. Those narrated situated moments are my intellectual inspirations. '*Wuliao*' therefore serves as a perfect keyword to describe what I have been examining through this empirical research on women's experiences of gender and I intend to use it as my academic compass for a considerable time.

Notes

1. The original statement is in Mandarin. It can be accessed at: http://www.coolloud.org.tw/node/85746
2. The conceptualisation of gender as capital possessed by a social actor has similarities with Hakim's idea of erotic capital. Hakim (2010, 2011) identifies seven gendered and sexual qualities of an individual as personal assets. She also argues that women can use this asset to negotiate power and confront gender inequality. Hakim's work has been seriously contested by feminist researchers (see Green 2013; Warhurst 2012).
3. The blog can be accessed at: http://guavanthropology.tw
4. This is the official English translation provided on the blog.
5. 巷仔口社會學 [Sociology at the Street Corner] can also be translated as 'Street Corner Sociology'. It is probably a reference to the classic ethnographic work, *Street Corner Society*, by William Foote Whyte (1943).

6. For instance, in the UK, guidelines have been developed for recruitment and job interviews to prevent openly discriminatory questions being asked, as these would be illegal.

REFERENCES

Alpeyev, P., Nakamura, Y., & Leung, A. (2016). Has Japan's Most Popular Messaging App Peaked? *Bloomberg*, [online] 11 July. Retrieved September 25, 2016, from http://www.bloomberg.com/graphics/2016-line-ipo/

Chen, W., & Huang, S. [陳婉琪, & 黃樹仁]. (2015). 立法院外的春吶: 太陽花運動靜坐者之人口及參與圖象 [Outcry Outside the Legislature: A Portrait of Sunflower Movement Sit-in Demonstrators]. 台灣社會學 [*Taiwanese Sociology*], *30*, 141–179.

Chien, T. [簡至潔]. (2012). 從「同性婚姻」 到 「多元家庭」-朝向親密關係民主化的立法運動 [From 'Same-sex Marriage' to 'Pluralistic Family Arrangements': The Legislative Movement for Democratic Intimate Relationships]. 台灣人權學刊 [*Taiwan Human Rights Journal*], *1*(3), 187–201.

Green, A. I. (2013). 'Erotic Capital' and the Power of Desirability: Why 'Honey Money' Is a Bad Collective Strategy for Remedying Gender Inequality. *Sexualities, 16*(1–2), 137–158.

Hakim, C. (2010). Erotic Capital. *European Sociological Review, 26*(5), 499–518.

Hakim, C. (2011). *Honey Money: The Power of Erotic Capital*. London: Penguin.

Hioe, B. (2016a). The China Airlines Strike and Street Occupation: A Historic Day for Taiwanese Labour? *New Bloom*, [online] 24 June. Retrieved September 25, 2016, from http://newbloommag.net/2016/06/24/china-airlines-occupation-strike/

Hioe, B. (2016b). The Debate About Sexism in the China Airlines Strike. *New Bloom*, [online] 24 June. Retrieved September 25, 2016, from http://newbloommag.net/2016/06/24/debate-sexism-china-airlines-strike/

Ho, M. S. (2015). Occupy Congress in Taiwan: Political Opportunity, Threat, and the Sunflower Movement. *Journal of East Asian Studies, 15*(1), 69.

Kalekin-Fishman, D. (2013). Sociology of Everyday Life. *Current Sociology Review, 61*(5–6), 714–723.

Letherby, G. (2003). *Feminist Research in Theory and Practice*. Buckingham: Open University Press.

Liang, Y. (2016). Taiwan Unions Buoyed by China Airlines Success. *TheNewsLens*, [online] 4 July. Retrieved September 25, 2016, from https://international.thenewslens.com/article/43460

Liu, C. [劉昌德]. (2015). 自己的傳播權自己救: 近十年媒體改革運動中的公民參與 [Fighting for Our Communication Rights: Civil Engagement in Media Activism over the Last Decade]. 台灣人權學刊 [*Taiwan Human Rights Journal*], *3*(1), 121–133.

Lu, S. (2016). 「我們願意打前鋒,終結過勞時代」華航空服員罷工現場看見性別與階級問題 ['We are Willing to be the Vanguard to End the Era of Overwork': Examining the Gender and Class Issues at the Protest Site of the CAL Strike]. 女人迷 [Womany], [online] 24 June. Retrieved September 25, 2016, from http://womany.net/read/article/11035

Mead, G. H. (1934). *Mind, Self and Society from the Standpoint of a Social Behaviorist*. Chicago: University of Chicago.

Neal, S., & Murji, K. (2015). Sociologies of Everyday Life: Editors' Introduction to the Special Issue. *Sociology, 49*(5), 811–819.

Rowen, I. (2015). Inside Taiwan's Sunflower Movement: Twenty-four Days in a Student-occupied Parliament, and the Future of the Region. *The Journal of Asian Studies, 74*(1), 5–21.

Salmonsen, R. (2015). Guava Anthropology Meets Savage Minds. *Savage Minds*, [online] 14 September. Retrieved September 25, 2016, from http://savageminds.org/2015/09/14/guava-anthropology-meets-savage-minds/

Shan, S. (2016, June 1). CAL Employees Protest Policy Change. *Taipei Times*, [online]. Retrieved September 25, 2016, from http://www.taipeitimes.com/News/taiwan/archives/2016/06/01/2003647631

Smith, D. E. (1987). *The Everyday World as Problematic: A Feminist Sociology*. Boston: Northeastern University Press.

Stanley, L., & Wise, S. (1993). *Breaking Out Again: Feminist Ontology and Epistemology*. London: Routledge.

Tan, Y. [覃玉蓉]. (2015). 性別不平等:各黨總統候選人長照政見中的那頭大象 [Gender Inequality: The Elephant in the Presidential Candidates' Care Policy]. 網氏/罔市女性電子報 [*Bongchhi Newsletter*], [online] 19 October. Retrieved September 24, 2016, from http://www.frontier.org.tw/bongchhi/archives/28717

Warhurst, C. (2012). Catherine Hakim, Honey Money: The Power of Erotic Capital. *Work, Employment & Society, 26*(6), 1036–1038.

Whyte, W. F. (1943). *Street Corner Society: The Social Structure of an Italian Slum*. Chicago: The University of Chicago Press.

Yang, H. (2007). A Study of Issue Activation and Response Strategy: Textual Analysis of the Issue of Demolishing Lo-Sheng Sanatorium [online]. MA Dissertation, Shih Shin University. Retrieved September 23, 2016, from http://libetd.shu.edu.tw/ETD-db/ETD-search-c/view_etd?URN=etd-0125108-105322

Yang, C.-L. (2017). The Political Is the Personal: Women's Participation in Taiwan's Sunflower Movement. *Social Movement Studies*. https://doi.org/10.1080/14742837.2017.1344542.

Yen, C. [顏振凱]. (2016). 「勞工政見絕不退讓」蔡英文:希望勞動節勞工不再傷心陳情 ['No Compromise in Labour Policy', Tsai Ing-Wen: Hope Workers Will Never Have to Propose any Petition on Labour Day]. 風傳媒 [*Storm Media*], [online] 28 April. Retrieved September 24, 2016, from http://www.storm.mg/article/110395

Glossary

ayi	阿姨	maternal aunty
banjhuo or *bando/ banto*	辦桌	preparing a table of delicacies for guests
beifen	輩分	the social order of generation
bi jhou zih jhen	敝帚自珍	to describe things that have no value but are cherished by the owner
Chiang *gong*	蔣公	the honorific form to address Chiang Kai-Shek
chih doufu	吃豆腐	an act of unpleasant dalliance or sexual harassment
cianfujhe	潛伏者	lurker
dajie	大姊	big sister
duoyuan chengjia	多元成家	a campaign that aims to diversify the legal definition of a family
fu	父	father
fuci	夫妻	married couple
fuyang	扶養	to bring up, to raise and to support
ge	哥	older brother
gong	公	an appellation for senior and respected men
guanxi	關係	relationship
guoyu	國語	the Standard Mandarin in Taiwan
han	漢	a term referring to a type of Chineseness
hwa	華	a term referring to a type of Chineseness
jhengmei	正妹	a cutie; a gorgeous chick
jie	姊	older sister
jiu shi lun shi	就事論事	to take the matter on its merits
lamei	辣妹	hot chick

© The Author(s) 2018
T.-F. Chin, *Everyday Gender at Work in Taiwan*,
Gender, Sexualities and Culture in Asia,
https://doi.org/10.1007/978-981-10-7365-6

lamei hechangtuan	辣妹合唱團	Spice Girls
laoshih	老師	teacher
mei	妹	younger sister
mu	母	mother
meinyu	美女	beautiful woman
nan jhu wai, nyu jhu nei	男主外、女主內	men manage the outdoors while women manage the indoors
nansheng	男生	young man; boy
nyusheng	女生	young woman; girl
po	婆	a feminine lesbian identity
putonghua	普通話	the official language of the People's Republic of China
rujhuei	入贅	for a man to marry into a woman's family
sajiao	撒嬌	to act in a spoiled and childlike way
san	桑; さん	an honorific appellation originating from the Japanese language
shao bu geng shih	少不更事	young and inexperienced
shuangcin	雙親	both parents
shualai	耍賴	to behave in a shameless and sly way
siao nyusheng	小女生	little girl
singyu tejhih	性慾特質	one of the Mandarin translations for 'sexuality'
syuedi	學弟	junior male study colleague
syuejhang	學長	senior male study colleague
syuejie	學姊	senior female study colleague
syuemei	學妹	junior female study colleague
T		tomboy; a 'masculine' lesbian identity
tai niao le	太鳥了	it sucks
tang	唐	a term referring to a type of Chineseness
tongzhi	同志	comrade; a term widely used to refer to LGBTQ communities and identities
thut-tshue	脫箠	to make a non-intentional mistake
wuliao	無聊	boring, mundane and nonsensical
yijie	一姊	top woman; a woman who is good at a specific activity

Index[1]

---

[1] Note: Page numbers followed by 'n' refer to notes.

© The Author(s) 2018
T.-F. Chin, *Everyday Gender at Work in Taiwan*,
Gender, Sexualities and Culture in Asia,
https://doi.org/10.1007/978-981-10-7365-6